Some are Dead & Some are Living

by

Mr. Craig Parker

Cynthia C. Parker

Contents:

Preface

This book "Some are Dead & Some are Living" was handwritten by Mr. Craig Parker over many years. It is an honor that Mr. Craig Parker entrusted me to take his original manuscript and to transcribe his words to prepare for publishing. Mr. Parker has since passed, yet his wishes are being carried out to see this book published. It is important to know that there may be some words that appear misspelled, however, they are taken from his original manuscript and transcribed verbatim to the best of my ability to reflect Mr. Craig Parker's way of thinking. Mr. Parker references in his book "I think I write the way people talk."

In the latter days of writing, Mr. Parker's cancer had returned. He writes "I think I'm probably good for two more chapters and they are important to me and I hope they are important for others." This directly reflects having two Chapter 23's which once again has not been changed in order to reflect his original thoughts, personal experiences and writings. Mr. Parker also used an uppercase Q in many of his words which reflects his writings during his time.

Mr. Parker speaks about a song "In My Life" written by John Lennon. The line "In My Life I Loved Them All" is engraved on his sister Sherri's grave marker. Mr. Craig Parker tributes the Title of this book to John Lennon, Sherri (his sister), and Heather (his daughter).

Bonnie Walton
Transcriber
2015-2016

Photos were taken and provided by Bonnie Walton.

Chapter 1
"Nannie"

Nannie held me tightly and gently pressed my little nose against the cold window pane. She told me it was old Jack Frost Nipping at my nose. The old kerosene heater nearby kept Nannie and me warm as I sat on her lap rocking away as we waited for my grandfather to close his country store across the street and walk home on that cold November night. I was so safe and secure in her arms and knew that my grandmother would always be nearby to protect and love me. I was four years old. Whenever I hear the line in a Christmas Carrol "Jack Frost nipping at your nose," I recall those cold winter nights sitting in the rocking chair with Nannie. I instantly remember the way she looked and how much she cared for me. Myrtle Faye Arthur and Irvin T. Arthur were the parents of Mildred (died as a baby), Cecil T. Virginia (my mother), and Shirley Andrew Arthur. Nannie raised three children while my grandfather toiled countless hours in his general store. She was cheerful, kind, hard working, but always dressed to the max. Grandaddy was strict, hard working, extremely honest, and demanding of his family. Like my parents, the two were opposites, but they managed to become pillars of the community and a couple that many admired. The business like Irvin and the fun- loving Myrtle were a loving, devoted, couple. Nannie took the art of grand mothering to a new level. She spoiled me and pampered me. When Nannie and my mother shopped together, she always bought me new toys. My grandfather would sternly look at me and say "young man you will not leave this table until you eat every mouth ful." Nannie would remain seated at the table and tell my Grandfather that she would make sure I ate every bite. She would allow me to leave the table as soon as Granddaddy left for the store. I have often wondered if the relationship between my grandmother and me had affected the relationship between my mother and grandmother and later the relationship between my mother and me. Nannie did take many child rearing responsibilities away from my mother, unintentionally. My mother was often ill and I spent many nights and days with my grandparents. Perhaps Nannie thought I was better off in the country than in the city with parents that argued and trying to find their way in life. I would understand the situation better as I grew older. Remembering these times is mentally challenging at times, but always rewarding. I always remember another special person of that time. Bertha Woods was an important member of my extended family. Bertha was a small, (about 4'8") widow who had helped my grandmother raise her children and helped my mother take care of me and later my brother and me. Bertha was a caretaker, playmate, and often a liaison between my mother and grandmother and me. The little, energetic, African American lady was close to everyone on my mothers side. Bertha did not have children, but looked upon my uncles my mother and me as her children. We loved her and she loved us in return. I would need Bertha so badly in a few years.

The village of Driver, Virginia is the area my mother was born and raised. A tiny, railroad stop, Driver was a rural land of farms and a few small business. Driver was a place where everyone knew each other and everyone knew each other's businesses. A lot of locals are slightly related. My grandfather depended on white and black business to survive in the grocery business he started in 1925 (during the great depression). Blacks and whites worked the local farms together and depended on each other to survive. They may have not gone to school together, but they grew up together and many were life-long friends. I have heard many white old timers talk about the way life was during the depression. Most people suffered the same consequences and fears. I am not trying to picture Driver as a perfect place or say that everyone got along. I will tell you that most white kids from the depressions days and through out my childhood were taught to respect old people first. Old people included white and black. You were taught to honor anyone older than you and yes sir and no sir and yes mam and no mam were standard replies. Black kids were taught to do likewise. I am sure that many places in the south or many other places were not as social. It does bother me when some individuals (talk shows, some historical shows, religious programs, etc.) picture most southerners (black: white) as a bunch of racist bigots who are lazy and mistreat their children or married their first cousins. I am sure that Oprah Winfrey and Elvis Presley had a lot more in common than most would believe. Both were born in Mississippi. Bertha spent many nights at my grandparent's home and later at my parents' home. She slept in the home bedrooms and ate at the table with us. There were no colored or white bathrooms. These same conditions were common in many Driver homes. Many African American families shared their table and what little food they had with poor white kids. Blacks would stop their vehicles and pick me or other white kids up if we were walking to Little league or school. My grandfather and most whites did the same. It was typical to see black and white kids playing baseball together or working side by side in someone's flower bed. I mention these things because they are important to me. I have been lucky enough to know and be close to many good people throughout my life. Many were black and many were white. John Lennon said it best in his song, "In My Life" "Some are dead and some are Living; In my life, I loved them all." Love brings me back to Bertha. I remember riding in the back seat of my parent's two tone blue (powder blue and dark blue) 1953 Pontiac. My mother would put the radio on a black gospel station. Bertha, my mother and I would listen to Mahalia Jackson, Pearl Bailey, and many other great artists. We also listened to the beloved Louie Armstrong and

Nat King Cole. I imagine Bertha realized my mother and I listened to the same music when she was not in the car with us. I return to thoughts of Nannie. Her death on a November afternoon in 1955 was and still is one of the lowest experiences of my life. I still feel the same pain and hurt as I did when I was six years old. I still get emotional and alone shed the remaining tears. It is a feeling that I have had to bear many times in my life, but Nannie was my first experience with death. My mother (Virginia) and Nannie were shopping at the Leggett's Department Store on High street in downtown Portsmouth, Virginia that day. They were also visiting my mother's best friend, Mae Murray, who worked as a clerk at the clothing store. Mae and Bob Murray rented the upstairs apartment from my other grandparents (John and Addie Parker) who lived next door to us in Portsmouth. Thank God Mae was with my mother on that afternoon. Nannie suffered a blood clot in one of her legs and passed Quickly. In an instant, she was taken from us. I believe she was only fifty seven years old. Bertha was at the house with me when my mother's younger brother, Shirley, came to the house. Uncle Shirley talked with Bertha a few minutes and then lead me to the backyard. I noticed he had something in his hands. My uncle handed me a Davy Crockett comic book. My mother and Mae had taken me to see Davy Crockett-King of the Wild Frontier movie months before this day and the Crockett rage was in full bloom. Uncle Shirley told me something really bad had happened and I would have to be strong like Davy Crockett. He told me we both would have to be strong because Nannie was gone and we would not see her for a long time. My uncle was grieving, but his first thoughts were of his six year old nephew's pain. As the case with many instances, my father was not immediately present during the time of my grandmother's death, like my brother's birth, our birthdays, family functions, school functions, little league and scouts, etc. My father was hunting deer or carousing with the boys. On that dreadful day, someone would have to track him down and give him the news. This is the reason I am glad Mae was with my mother that day. She would need her best friend many times in the future. An incident occurred the following summer after Nannie's passing. My father decided to take the family to Cherokee, North Carolina. It was probably another attempt to smooth things over, but we did travel to Cherokee on many occasions. The Cherokee reservation of 1956 was not the massive tourist mecca it is today. There was no Dolly Wood or any of the other close attractions that exist today. Cherokee had one or two hotels and the So Ho diner. What Cherokee had was real Native Americans. Some scenes of the Davy Crockett movie had been shot earlier in Cherokee and the reservation was more crowded with visitors that summer. My father drove around looking for a place to stay and was told to go to a certain house that might rent rooms. We spent our vacation with a Cherokee family in their home. We returned to the small house and small room each night. I remember many noises coming from the living room through out the nights. Maybe the Cherokees were partying. After a few days, my father needed to get back to his gas station in Portsmouth (and more time with the boys). We said good bye to our new friends. My father reached to the back seat of the car and handed the young Cherokee boy my Davy Crockett book Uncle Shirley had given me. He was ecstatic, but I was crushed. Parents do not always know what things are truly important to children. Children need safety blankets in their childhoods. It can be a priced possession, a close friend, or an object of very little value to others. My first cousin, Cliff Parker carried a white blanket with him every where he went as a child. The blanket was smaller than a handkerchief when he realized he no longer needed it. My father did not understand my feelings. He could have given the young boy any toy I owned and it would not have bothered me. The book was very special; it was a connection to my grandmother. I was angry with my father for a long time and in secret shed many tears over the book. I hope the young Cherokee did enjoy the book and I hope there was some secret medicine passed of that day from me to him with the book. I sincerely hope he has had a good life. One certain picture of Nannie would become important to me. My mother had many pictures of her mother through out our home in Portsmouth, Virginia and late (1957) in our home in Driver. The small, oval picture of my grand mother rested on the counter of my mother's half bath that was adjacent to my parent's bed room in Driver. When something was wrong in my life or I missed Port Norfolk (Portsmouth), I would go to that half bath and look at Nannie's picture. When I looked at the picture, I knew in some way she was still nearby and still watching over me. She may not have seen me play Little League, graduate from high school, or be at my daughter's (Heathers) baptism, but she knew. Nannie never left me completely and she never will. I can live to be 100 years old and she will still be a big part of my life. Maybe one day she will press my nose to a window pane in a safer, more secure world. As time went by, I began to realize something about the small picture of my grandmother. It was small, but that particular picture had a special meaning to her like it did to me. She probably stared at it when she was down and when she also shed tears. Brian Wilson said in his Beach Boy song, "In My Room"; "There's a place I can go and tell my troubles to", "In My Room."

Chapter 2

John and Addie Parker

John Parker was born in Driver, Virginia. His father, my great grandfather, was also from Driver. John's father was a railroad (train) master at the railroad station in Driver. He was responsible for preparing passengers and checking all incoming and outgoing freight. My great grand father also worked on watches in his spare time and loved to work in his garden. I remember my great grandfather Parker with much fondness. He passed about the same time as Nannie did, but I remember visiting him at his house in Driver with my father or sometimes at the Driver Variety Store my great aunt, Margaret, owned. My father, great grand-father and I would often eat a small can of beanie- weenies and crackers together while the two discussed family members. My father would often take my great grandfather, my mother and me to Petersburg, Virginia on Sunday afternoons to watch the many long passenger and freight trains going in and out of Richmond, Virginia. My great grandfathers railroad tenure began back in the late 1800's. Grandaddy John also worked for the railroad. He was hard working, stern, but was very capable at having a good laugh. He never drank and was a dedicated father and Belt line Railroad trainman. John was very muscular and was liked and respected by all who knew him. The Belt Line moved my grandfather and his family from Ahoskie, North Carolina to Driver, Virginia (in the 1920's) to Portsmouth, Virginia. A few elderly Belt Line retirees, who worked with John, have told me stories of how powerful he was and how hard he worked to provide for his family. Workers would often throw off fire wood from the train as the train passed my grandfather's house in Driver. John was proud, but like many others, the Great Depression greatly affected his life. John did not allow his grand children to call him grandaddy or any other name except John. I never understood this but I'm sure he had his reasons. All the grand children called him Grandaddy John when they were not with him and no one ever Questioned his authority. John was never ashamed of being a grand- parent. He would load us grand kids into his old Dodge and head to Rodman's Restaurant or High's Ice Cream parlor. Once there, he would proudly tell the waitress he was our grand father and introduce each of us. He could control half a dozen children by himself better than anyone I knew. The good part was that everyone was happy. I have often heard stories throughout the years about what a great catcher (baseball) my grandfather was. My uncle Jerry was a pitcher in the minor league. (Florida State League) for a time; so he possibly inherited some of John's skills. The last present my grandfather gave me on my birthday was a Green Bay Packer/ Paul Hornung football helmet. He probably envisioned me one day playing for the tough Vince Lombardi. I saw many similarities between my grandfather and Coach Lombardi. Both strived for perfection, both demanded respect, and both were loved by the people they care about and disciplined most. I wish I could have spent many years in the company of grandaddy John. He passed in (1958) when I was 9. He was a year from retirement from the railroad and planned to move from Portsmouth back to Driver and grow a gigantic garden each spring. Grandaddy John would come out to Driver every Christmas morning. I guess he felt like he belonged in Driver on Christmas morning and each visit probably brought back childhood memories. He would stare out the kitchen back window to the field behind our house each Christmas and say "It's going to be a good spring, a good spring for a garden."

My grandmother, Addie Savage Parker, was the very opposite of grandaddy John. Together they raised one daughter (Dorothy-Dot) and four sons, Harold,

Melvin, Gordon (my father) and John Gerald (Jerry). I will refer to my grand mother as "Bye Bye" from this point on. I called her this as a baby and the name stuck. Everyone in the Parker family called her "Bye Bye" for the remainder of her life. My father, aunt and uncles, and cousins would sometimes call her Addie as a joke; but she loved my nickname and knew it was a different but affectionate name. Bye Bye was not the disciplinarian grandaddy John was. When a Parker child or grandchild got into trouble, it was either a mistake or someone lead the Parker child down the wrong path. My father never meant to hang out with the boys till the wee hours of the morning; he happened to run into some fellows he knew during WWII. Bye Bye's approach to discipline would often be a sore point with my mother and the other Parker wives. Bye Bye was predominantly Cherokee Indian and she grew up in an era when people did not boast of their Native American Heritage. Too many people of that era looked down on Native Americans the way they did African Americans. My father and uncles always told me the Parkers were English, Scotch-Irish, and Indian. Our ancestors were not noblemen or plantation owners; they were indentured servants.

My father was an Indian sympathizer long before Dee Brown's 1960's book; "Bury My Heart At Wounded Knee" was published. As a young man he often hunted with Nansemond Indian Chief Earl Bass. Being the son of a Cherokee helped my father to treat people as individuals, not as a member of a race or group. He used to tell me as a child that we were related to the great Sioux Chief Sitting Bull. We weren't, but we did have Cherokee blood running through our veins. Bye Bye was a very important person in my life. Nannie had passed on and I was very lucky to have Bye Bye as a grandmother. She cared for us grandchildren like a mother hen and wanted only the best of life for all of us. She was a protector, care-giver and confidant to many of us through out our lives. She was never financially able to give us the things she wanted to but she gave us the things money could never buy.   No one in the Parker family can think very long about Bye Bye without thinking of food. Like many women of her time, my grandmother spent much of her life slaving over a hot stove. The difference was that my grandmother actually enjoyed all that cooking. Daddy would often remember the depression and recall how hobos and train jumpers (poor people who illegally got on trains seeking destination with food and shelter) were often present at Bye Bye's dinner table. She would tell John and the Parker children to tighten their belts and each person eat a little less. She and John were democrats and they firmly believed Franklin Delano Roosevelt would guide them and their loved ones to better days. I enjoyed watching my grandmother cook and she would often include me in the meal preparation. As a small boy, I could do the lattice work for the top of a big cherry pie or roll out the dough for her famous biscuits. Ambrosia was a Quick easy desert that cannot be duplicated. Bye Bye's cupcakes were more difficult and I think they were the overall favorite of everyone. Like so many others, my grandmother graduated from a wood stove to a gas stove. She and John also graduated from wood and coal stoves to kerosene heaters. Bye Bye never owned a modern washing machine or any dryer. Her long time electric clothes washer was a fixture for many years on the back screened in porch. It was one of those with the giant round, horizontal tub with the big rollers on top. I don't believe Bye Bye ever fixed a hot dog or hamburger in her kitchen. She did not know what fast foods were. Meals were something to be shared and enjoyed, not gulped down out of necessity. Bye Bye could take a jar of plain apple sauce and turn it into a delicious side dish. She could do magic with some brown sugar, nutmeg and cinnamon. She did not use canned goods when fresh fruits and vegetables were available, but when she did they were ten times better when she finished with them.   Betty Crocker could not hold a candle to Bye Bye.

My aunt Dot's son, Vernon Mayberry, spent much of his childhood life at my grand parents' home. Dot's husband, Vernon was in the Navy during WWII and his ship the USS Roching was torpedoed by a German U-Boat. Vernon never got to see his infant son. I never had the opportunity to meet my Uncle Vernon Mayberry, but I know a lot about him. My cousin (Vernon), my grandparents, Uncles, my father, and anyone who knew him praised him and said what a great person he was. I know my cousin's father attended Military School, played the saxophone, pitched in the big leagues for a while, and could eat one dozen of my grandmother's biscuits in one setting. I know most people are remembered more fondly after passing, but this is not the case with Vernon Mayberry. He was a well-rounded and much respected man. My father was so affected by Vernon Mayberry's death he wanted to join the service at age 16. The Marines and Navy turned my father (Red) down because of his age but he lied to the merchant Marines and told them he was 17. He became a Merchant seaman and saw much of the world two times. I remember the night my cousin Vernon brought his father's Purple Heart medal over to show my parents. I looked at the medal and said I would like to have one some day. My father told me to never say that again and my father went into his bedroom and shut the door. He wasn't mad at me. The pain of losing his brother-in-law was too great.

Saturday morning was usually a great time for my cousin Vernon and me. Living next door to my grandmother may have been hard on my mother occasionally, but it was a God send for me. Often Bye Bye would call my mother on the phone on Saturday mornings and ask if I could eat breakfast with them. My grandmother would take vanilla Ice cream, Vanilla extract powdered sugar, milk, and make the best Vanilla shake on the planet. Combine this with her great cinnamon toast and Vernon and I were set. Bye Bye would bring us tall glasses full of the Vanilla shake and set them on the tv trays she had set up for us. We munched away on the cinnamon toast as we watched

17

Tarzan movies, Captain Midnight, or Howdy Doody. For a kid in the fifties, life did not get much better than this. I can truly understand why the food Network on television is watched by so many people. People want new and exciting recipes, but many want the smells, tastes, and surroundings they enjoyed during their early years. I know the older I get, the more I miss the great food my two grandmothers, my mother (Virginia), and my Aunt Mildred prepared. Each specialized in certain recipes and made them their own.

As I said earlier, I think of many great foods when I think of Bye Bye. I think about her great fried chicken, the great biscuits, the ambrosia, the cakes and cupcakes the homemade peach ice cream and much more. I remember the whole home made pickled peaches on Christmas Day. We kids would walk around for an hour after dinner with the large sweet peach seed in our mouths. Although I was very young, I remember Nannies specialty at Christmas. It was home-made pound cake covered with cherry- jello and lime- jello. She smoothed the two jellos with sweet thick custard. My aunt Mildred was famous for many items, but I think she made the best banana pudding I have ever tasted. Like my mother her macaroni and cheese (not what people eat today) and fried chicken were also great. I will probably speak more about my mothers cooking later, but I will say that her chicken salad and tomato pudding were the best I have ever eaten and most people who ever ate them would agree. I'm sure many of her recipes came from Nannie. I guess it is appropriate that I mention all of this while thinking of Bye Bye. Age makes you realize that some things will never be the same and some things can be redone but never really duplicated. How much would I pay for fried chicken exactly like Bye Byes or how much for custard like Nannies'. These things are gone forever, but I was lucky enough to have had them in my life. A teacher once told our sixth grade class that you could only love something that will love you in return. You can love a person, horse, dog, cat etc. because they can love you back.

Maybe food can't do tricks or shake hands but it sure has been pretty important throughout man's time on earth. It is even better when someone added their love to please us or make us happy. Maybe the bee loves us when he is making the honey. Enough of this nonsense about Bees and love. Everyone knows Americans, French, Germans, and most countries, have a love affair with food. Things have changed since sixth grade. My father would smile if he saw Paula Deen on TV showing millions her secret recipes. He would hear that sweet southern voice and say "Son this gal really knows what she's doing in the kitchen; she didn't just fall off the collard truck". Bye Bye would agree. I remember looking out the kitchen window one morning when I was thirteen years old. Bye Bye was staying with us in Driver because my mother was in Maryview Hospital at the time with veracose veins. My parents 1961 Pontiac Catalina had a broken windshield and both sides were dented. My father had obviously been in an accident. As I looked at the car, Bye Bye told me my father had a terrible case of the flu and ran into a ditch. He did run into a ditch, but he had a hangover and not the flu. This was the type of thing that drove my mother crazy. Grandaddy John did not make excuses when his children or grandchildren misbehaved. He probably mellowed with time because the grandchildren only received a stern lecture as a remedy. This was more than enough to make us walk the line. My father and his siblings earned a trip to the woodshed to meet Mr. Strap when they misbehaved. My grandfather could also be very protective parent and grandparent. My father's older brother, Harold, was in the Navy during WWI. His ship was attacked by Japanese planes. Harold was severely injured in the attack. He spent a year in Naval Hospitals in Hawaii and later Boston, MA. Doctors placed a steel plate in his head and he had to be very careful the rest of his life and make sure nothing ever hit him in the head (such as a baseball or even a broom handle). My father (Red) and My Uncle Harold opened an Amoco (American Oil) filling station in Portsmouth after the war. For many years they sold more heating fuel than any business in Tidewater.

One Saturday night, four marines pulled up to the gas pumps at the service station. After filling their car, the driver told the attendant they did not mean for him to fill the tank and they were not going to pay for their gas. The four marines got out of the car. The attendant called for Uncle Harold and he came over to see what the problem was. Grandaddy John realized there was a problem and he headed for the pumps. My father was off work that night. The driver verbally attacked Harold, and he and his three buddies surrounded my uncle. He made the mistake of swinging at Harold's head and the other three jumped my uncle. No one got another punch in because John jumped in and fought the four Marines. Grandaddy John was pushing fifty at that time but he was not afraid of anyone. When John finished, four young Marines were lying on the driveway licking their wounds. This story may seem far- fetched, but too many people have recounted it to me throughout the years. Knowing how big my grand-father's arms were and how he worried about Harold ever being hit in the head; I know the story is true. No telling what would have happened to the four Marines if my father had been working that night. Better for them they faced one powerful Parker instead of two.

Like most families during World War II, my grandparents did their part during WWII. They always had a garden every year and three sons fought in the war and a son-in- law was killed. Uncle Melvin (the second son) steered one of the boats carrying soldiers to the beach at D-Day. Uncle Harold or Uncle Melvin never talked about their heroics in the Navy during the war. They only spoke of Vernon Mayberry.

Chapter 3

Good Bye Larry, Shelton and Port Norfolk

September 1957 brought a much dreaded change to my young life. My parents were moving away from the friendly confines of Port Norfolk, VA to the tiny village of Driver where my mother's father lived and owned the local general store. Although I only moved once as a child, I can truly sympathize with the children who are constantly moved from state to state and town to town. New schools, new teacher's, new friends, etc. are difficult changes for children. I think kids are much like old people. They want stability and do not welcome change. I spent my early years on Chautauqua Ave. in Port Norfolk, which is a section of Portsmouth. Port Norfolk's streets were lined with old two and three story homes with freshly mowed lawns. Cotton's Confectionery , Gleason's Drugstore, Coverts Drug Sore, Frank's Barber shop, Chubby's Bar, Sands Grocery store, the old A&P Tea Company Grocery Store, Port Norfolk Elementary, the Chinese Dry Cleaners, the Port Norfolk Fire Station and other fixtures added to the uniQue flavor of this well knit community. I sometimes think of Port Norfolk when I hear the Beatle's song "Penny Lane". There is a barber showing photographs of every head he's had the pleasure to know of. All the people who come and go and stop and say hello. "Penny Lane is in my ears and in my eyes, there beneath the blue, suburban skies". Port Norfolk was in my ears and in my eyes. Leaving Port Norfolk also meant leaving close friends and family. My grandparents lived next door or to the right of us. Uncle Harold, his wife, Marion and my cousin

Cliff lived directly across the street from my grandparents. Uncle Melvin, his wife, Edith, and my cousin, Carolyn, lived beside us on the other side.

I have been lucky enough to grow up with two life long friends. Larry Graybill is two years older than me and grew up directly across the street. Shelton Hale is one year older than me and also grew up across the street two doors down from Larry. Shelton once dumped a whole gallon of red paint over my six year old head. Larry and Shelton both had great parents. Mr. Graybill worked for Sands Grocery (manager) and Mr. Hale worked for the railroad. Mrs. Hale worked for Leggett's Department Store. Larry had an older brother named Ronnie and Shelton had an older sister named Barbara Ann. Ronnie Graybill has played stand up bass for years. We younger kids always got a kick out of him hauling the bass around in his small car. Ronnie has been a member of the Virginia Symphony Orchestra for many years.

Everyone on our block were not only neighbors, they were friends. They cared about each other and worried about each others children. The Graybills, Hales, Brits, Glenns, the Whiteners, the other set of Parkers, the two Hill sisters, the Birchs, the Hatsels, and Raymond Blowe were families who lived in our vicinity. They were all good people. In my ears, I could hear the bells of the ice cream truck cruising through Port Norfolk on a summer afternoon. I could hear the cannon fired nightly at 8:00 at Norfolk Naval Shipyard Marine's Barracks. I could hear the roar of the crowd at Portsmouth Stadium during a Portsmouth Cub's (minor league affiliate of Chicago Cub's) baseball team or a Wilson High football game.

The most predominant sounds of Port Norfolk were the ships in the nearby Elizabeth River and the trains pulling in and out of Port Norfolk. We were used to the sound of trains in Driver, but no ships. I remember visiting my grandmother one summer (mom was in the hospital) when I was fourteen years old. I could hear the trains pulling in and out and adding or deleting cars.

22

The sweet summer breeze moved the bedroom curtains and I kept hearing a thud sound. I thought I heard someone outside the open window. I woke up my cousin, Vernon who was sleeping in the other single bed. Vernon assured me the thud was only apples dropping from the trees in the next yard where my family used to live.

The men played baseball in an old field every warm Sunday afternoon. Larry Shelton and I eagerly watched and talked of how we would be playing ball with them one day. Sunday morning brought the sound of church bells throughout Port Norfolk, but the afternoon brought the sounds of the crack of a baseball bat and the sweet smell of freshly mowed grass. Port Norfolk was also the home to a small park that had a lighted softball field. Many people would attend the men's and women's softball games there and the kids could climb the monkey bars or swing on the swing set located beyond the out-field. The park was later renamed Freddy Cobb Sports Complex. Freddy was killed in Vietnam and Bobby Cobb (his younger brother) played second base on my little league team. Father Bill Cobb was a tall man who had played first base professionally in the minors, and was one of our coaches. The Cobbs were Port Norfolk boys.

Johnny Britt worked for a cookie company in Portsmouth. He would often pull his truck in front of his mother's (Bye Byes good friend Mamie Britt) house and whistle. He would pass out out of date cookies to the Port Norfolk boys and girls. Needless to say, Johnny Britt was well known and very popular in Port Norfolk. Johnny had also been a very good pitcher in the minor league. One day he was pitching a good game in the minors, but he had the feeling he wanted to do something else in life and Johnny walked off the mound, changed into his street clothes, and walked away from professional baseball. Baseball was very important in Port Norfolk. My Uncle (Jerry Parker), Bill Cobb and Johnny Britt were only a handful of men who went on to play professional baseball. The Sunday games on the old lot lead to bigger things. My father got one of his friends to build a barbecue pit in our back yard. Neighbors and friends would fill our back yard on warm summer nights. The smell of hamburgers and hot dogs would fill the air. Ladies would bring their special concoctions to the cookouts. The children of the couple (Chinese) who operated the laundry World always come to the cook outs. The oldest girl would watch over her younger siblings. The children were very polite and mannerly. Our parents raved about the Chinese kids and told us to act more like them. I have always admired Chinese people. Since childhood, I have noticed how family oriented they are and how hard they will work to be successful. They appreciate the things many people take for granted.

The owner of the Port Norfolk laundry was the brother of Nancy who was a good friend of my parents. Nancy and her brother, Richard, were customers of my father's and they traded at his Amoco Station for years. Nancy and Richard owned the Chinese Restaurant known as the "Chinese Maid". For years, my family ate dinner at the "Chinese Maid". Nancy would pick me up in her arms and carry me to the kitchen to see Richard. It was amazing to watch Richard Quickly slice the fresh vegetables and meat to make chow mien or some other great dish. "Nancy's" (what we called the restaurant) was a busy place, but Nancy and Richard always had time for my family and me. Richard would try to teach me Chinese and Nancy would fill me up with almond cookies. I have eaten chicken chow mein sub gum many times, but none ever came close to Nancy's. My father's Amoco station was across the street from a popular Portsmouth bar known as the White Rabbit. A Chinese fellow named Johnny Chung bought the business in the late fifties and renamed it. "Johnny Rickshaws". Johnny changed the business from a bar to an all American restaurant. He served chops, steaks, burgers and other popular dishes. Johnny did not prepare Chinese food. Johnny was a smart, industrious business man.

He installed a sliding window beside the front door of the restaurant. Long before the arrival of the first McDonalds in Portsmouth, Johnny Chung was selling hamburgers, fries, and shakes through a sliding window. His prices were never higher than McDonald's. I remember one of my parent's anniversaries like yesterday. My father took the family (my mother, my younger brother, Gregory, and me) to the movies to see the movie about New Orleans and the War of 1812. We had missed supper to get to the movies on time my father decided we would eat at Johnny Rickshaws. At the end of the meal, Johnny brought out a bunt cake with a large candle in the center. It was a kind gesture by a good man. I was close to Johnny Chung and I spent many hours in his kitchen watching baseball games on television. We were both Yankee fans and we spent hours talking baseball. I think of him often and the hours spent in his restaurant were some of the best in my childhood. Johnny seemed to know how to bring out the best in both of my parents.

Before my mind leaves, Port Norfolk, I will mention some things I will always miss about that special place. I miss the frozen Baby Ruth candy bars (gigantic for a nickel) at Cotton's Confectionery and I miss the root beers in frosted mugs and the fresh squeezed lime aides at Coverts Drug Store. I miss the funky odor of Gleson's Drug store. The old place is a craft shop today and that old medicine smell still lingers in the building. I miss Susie, Raymond Blow's black and white Boston bull dog, sitting on a stool in Covert's Drug Store. Raymond would place Suzie on a stool an order a scoop of vanilla ice cream. The waitress would bring the ice cream in one of those funnel shaped paper cups that rested in its own stand. Suzie would lap up the ice cream as we kids watched in amazement as Suzie wagged her stumpy tail. I also miss "Champ". "Champ" was a large boxer with a very large choke chain collar. The massive, muscular canine moved the sidewalks of Port Norfolk. Champ was a gentle giant who loved kids, but we all knew when to move over and let Champ have the sidewalk to himself. He was watching over good, old Port Norfolk. I miss Jesse; Jesse was an army lieutenant during WWII who saved some men of his platoon by trying to get rid of a grenade thrown at his men by a German soldier. The grenade exploded near Jesse and he was shell shocked. Jesse would ride his bicycle throughout Portsmouth. With bags of groceries or produce hanging from his handlebar, he would travel through the streets of Port Norfolk each afternoon. Jess would ring his bell on his bike and wave and holler at every kid he encountered on his journey. He was special to all the kids of Port Norfolk and Portsmouth. Jesse was a real hero who knew how to relate to children. Any child who lived in Port Norfolk still remembers Jesse and what a special person he was. Most of us kids never knew Jesse's last name, but we will always remember him.

Chapter 4

Hello Driver

At the age of seven, I began my transformation from city slicker to country boy. I know most city kids referred to country kids as country bumkins. The last thing in the world I wanted to be was a country bumkin. Moving to Driver from Portsmouth was like moving cross country for someone my age. Driver was a small village in Nansemond County. The county was named after the Nansemond Indian tribe who were part of the Powhatan Confederation (Jamestown). Captain John Smith of Jamestown had traveled down the James River in the early 1600's. The James River connected to the smaller Nansemond River and Captain Smith would meet some of the Nansemonds on a small island near Driver. Dumpling Island would serve as a market place for the English settlers. They would trade their iron pots, axes, and other wares for staples such as corn, fish, berries, tobacco, and many other natural products that are still important to Driver and the State of Virginia. Every time a Driver farmer plowed a field, he could walk over the freshly tilled soil and find arrows, part of clay pipes or other artifacts. Most artifacts had been buried in the Driver soil for centuries. My family had moved from Portsmouth, a city named after an English sister city; to Nansemond County, a rural area of Native American names and influence. Chuckatuck, a tiny village six miles west of Driver, is an Indian word. A few days after moving to Driver, my mother enrolled me in Driver Elementary School. The old school built in 1898 had originally been built as an agricultural college. Women teachers lived in the nearby brick cottage near the old 3-story schoolhouse. I started the second grade in Mrs. Richard's class. The classroom was located at the end of the old red tin covered gymnasium. Any child, who misbehaved, would become acQuainted with the tiny storage room located between the gymnasium and the classroom. Mrs. Richards was a well-dressed, caring educator. She was a great improvement over my first grade teacher at Port Norfolk Elementary who most would describe as a "sour-puss" or prude.

I knew one person in my second grade class prior to the school year. William Ellsworth Cattenhead III and I both attended Glebe Episcopal Church. The church was located near the entrance to Driver and was an Anglican Church built in 1752. Parson Agnew sided with the king of England (George) prior to the American Revolution and was banished from the church and parrish. He returned to England. I would spend much time with W.E (William Ellsworth) from second grade through high school. We were accolytes in church, always in the same Sunday school class, played little league baseball together, were in the scouts together, and graduated together. W (Dub) and I might have traveled in different circles, but we both always liked each other and were good friends. W was always well rounded and well-liked. He has never married and has lived in Florida, for several years. He was a ladies' man from the time I first met him, and he still has those charming good looks today. Other guys thought of W the way other Yankee players thought of Mickey Mantle. W.E. was a great student and intelligent guy. He was a good ball player and even played high school football as one of the smallest players on the team. W seemed to glide through life effortlessly. I always envied and admired him. W is currently fighting cancer and as we did as little league teammates, I am rooting and praying for him every day. I was playing shortstop and W was playing third base for Driver (little league). I caught a pop-up for the first out: made a back handed stab to throw the base runner out for out 2, and dove near W to catch a line drive to end the inning. W came over and helped dust me off and say "you just made all three outs." I have never forgotten that moment." I missed Shelton and Larry of Port Norfolk very much during the first few months of school. I was no longer part of "our gang", but was now an outsider. Bertha would often help my mother, and she was the only person I confided in. She always told me not to worry because I would find new friends. The Massengill family lived next door to us in Driver. Mr. Massengill worked for the railroad and the family had moved to Driver from a small place called Rich Square in North Carolina. Mr. Massengill was a huge, jovial man. He had lost one of his eyes in a railroad accident, and he would occasionally remove his glass eye and show it to us kids.

Herbert and Sally Massengill were parents to five children. Carolyn was already married and lived in North Caroline, Jerry was married and working at Newport News shipbuilding, and Lance was working for the Virginia Highway Department. Patsy and Roger were attending school. Sally Massengill and my mother became great friends. Mrs. Massengill was older than my mother and moma often confided in her. My mother would make the coffey and Mrs. Massengill would often bring cakes or deserts. Mrs. Massengill would bake our family a Japanese fruit cake every Christmas. I became friends with Roger who was the youngest Massengill child. Roger was more than a year older than me and was one grade higher than me in school. He would be the person who would help transform me from "city slicker" to country boy." I looked up to Roger as an older brother. Most days after school or Saturdays, we would explore the surrounding fields and woods near Driver. With our pack of family pet dogs, we would travel for miles. Roger's dogs were named George and Mr. Smith. My family owned a white Spitz named Snowball (female), a female boxer named Princess, a black and white collie named Candy Box Delight, and later a blind cocker spaniel named Trixie. The white Spitz (Snowball) was my mother's pet before she was married. My mother always told me how protective of me Snowball was. She watched every movement Dr. Ward would make when he came to our house in Port Norfolk for house calls. Snowball

29

would anxiously await my return from school each day. Snowball would always join the pack in Driver even though she was an old dog by that time. Wherever I went, Snowball followed. It is as hard for me to recall my dogs, as it is to remember my friends, who have passed. Dogs are definitely "man's best friend". I have been with them all my life: and I have never seen more loyal friends. They will love you, trust you and be there for you throughout their lives. I have had many dogs in my life and I loved them all. Each one had its own personality. I was recently having a conversation with a good friend of mine named Bob Charles. Bob is a resident of Driver and is a retired psychologist. He graduated from the University of Wisconsin and did his graduate work at Berkley. He later taught at Wisconsin. Bob and I have been friends for about thirty years. While discussing longtime friendships, Bob brought up a good point about the dogs. He noted that their life span was seven times faster than a human's. Man's best friend only lives 5, 10 or 15 years and accomplishes so much good in that short period of time. I think dogs are like humans in one sense. They accomplish what they were sent here for and are called home.

Princess (the boxer) was one of the smartest dogs I have ever seen. She would jump up pound the front door bell with his paw until someone came to the door for her. Princess jumped out of my father's fuel oil truck one Saturday afternoon and did not return. It was the Saturday before Easter and I guess she decided to explore the wooded area like she did with me. My father returned home later that afternoon and broke the news of her disappearance to us. Moma told everyone to get in the car because we were going to find Princess in Deep Creek which was about twenty miles from home. My mother went to the area where my father had earlier parked the fuel oil truck. Princess ran to the car with her stubby little tail wagging and rejoined the family. She would never wander off alone again and we all had a good Easter.

I am sure my old English teachers and professors would penalize me for straying from the subject matter, but I am writing this as things enter my mind. I don't claim to be Shakespeare and I am sure I will never win a Pulitzer Prize. I always considered Roger Massengill to be like William Rogers, the founder of Roger's Rangers. Like Rogers, Roger was always looking for that next great adventure or that uncharted territory. We were explorers and our Rangers were our dogs. Naturally, one of my favorite movies is Northwest Passage starring Spencer Tracy, Robert Young and Walter Brennan. The scene at the end of the movie where Robert Young and his fiancé watch William Rogers leave to lead a new band of Rangers reminds me of Roger Massengill's life. Leaving a safe place in life to find the new horizon was Roger's calling and destiny.

Winter was our favorite time of year. Winter brought the Thanksgiving and Christmas hollidays and more importantly, days away from school. Looking for deer tracks in the mud or snow, drinking ice cold water from a stream, swinging from monkey vines, crossing frozen ponds, watching a bald eagle fly high in the sky high above the trees, or taking the sweet smell of Pine into your lungs were some of the things you could never experience in a classroom. Watching the sun peep through the forest to shine on hanging ice circles to create a prism of colors or to hear the welcome hoot of the wise old owl near sundown, were things you could not experience in science class. Our area received much more snow during my childhood than it does in present times. School was always cancelled because we lived in a very rural area with many backroads that might not be cleared for days. Snow often meant two or three days vacation and watching television or listening to your favorite radio station for school cancellations was one of my favorite past times. Snow days were days for sledding. A giant mountain of saw dust at Nat Sawyers Saw Mill became a mountain of fresh white snow with each new storm. The mill workers lived in North Carolina and did not cut lumber on cold snowy days. Roger and I would gather a pair of tin cutters and some rope and head for the old red barn behind Driver Elementary school. Workers had torn down part of the barn and old tin lay on the ground for the taking. We transformed the old tin into prized sleds. Dragging our new sleds behind us with our pack of Rangers happily following us, Roger and I headed for the mill for a day of sledding. The dogs were happy and we were happy and our surroundings were white, cold and pure; Nature at its best. My brother, Gregory, would join us at the mill in the coming years, as he grew older. Roger and I had become old hands at the mill and we showed my brother how to bury your hands and feet into the warm sawdust beneath the snow to warm yourself up. Standing on top of that old saw dust Mountain and looking down on the snow covered trees and landscape below was exciting. The speedy trip down the slope into the woods was a great experience. It was an experience that I will always remember and appreciate. The mill is long gone, but it will always remain in my mind. Different kids would come and go in Driver as a few houses were rented. Fellows like Roy Lee Denson, Bobby Cowley, the Munsey brothers, and others would sometimes join our group. We would pool our money together to buy 15¢ Quart bottles of soda at my grandfather's store. We would pour the Quart bottles of black cherry, ginger ale, root beer, grape, and orange into a small-galvanized tub. With a dipper, we would take turns drinking our own concoctions. My father usually took Tuesdays off from work and he would often take Roger, Gregory and me fishing in his boat in the nearby Nansemond and James River. My father loved the water, but he also had complete respect for it. As I stated earlier, he had served in the Merchant Marines during WWII and he had seen what water and nature can do. And old newspaper article still remains in our family photo album. The article reports how my father saved the life of a drowning man who had fallen off his boat while fishing. Still in his teens and on leave from the Merchant Marines; my father dove off a pier and swam to the man's rescue by swimming and towing him to the shore. Roger and I never got sea sick, but we did get sick on my father's boat once. We watched my father fish with his big wad of Peach and Honey chewing tobacco protruding from his cheek. I asked my father if Roger and I could have a small plug of his chew. My father said he thought we were big boys at the time and were ready to try new things. He broke off two pieces of tobacco and handed us each a piece. Soon Roger and I both became ill and being on the water only made things worse. We had swallowed more tobacco than we had chewed, and my father had silently proved a point. He showed little sympathy as we suffered from our experiment. Roger and I learned a lesson that day and my father never mentioned the incident to my mother. Native Americans would often allow their children to do things they should not do to prove a point. If an Indian child touched a hot kettle, he or she suffered the consequences and would not repeat their mistakes. My father's parenting skills were often like those of Native Americans. Sometimes a little pain (nothing major) is like a picture and is worth a thousand words. My father taught all four children (my brother and late two sisters) how to swim at an early age. He showed us how to use our arms and feet and then threw us in shallow water. We would Quickly remember what Daddy had showed us and coupled with natural instinct to enjoy the water and survive it; we all became good swimmers who respected water.

My friend Roger was also a great prankster. We played a prank in early October one year that still ranks high on the Driver scale of practical jokes. Roger thought we could get some pre Halloween laughs if we dressed up a dummy and lay it beside the road and the ditch. We stuffed a pair of old jeans and a hooded sweatshirt with news papers. We next safety pinned work gloves and sneakers to our victim and cut out a picture of someone's face from the cover of Life magazine. Roger placed the picture over the balled up papers under the hood of the sweatshirt. We were in business. Roger and I carried the victim to the spot next to the road and spread it out on the ground. We Quickly ran and hid behind the corner of my parents' house, and watched and waited for the results. Many cars slowed down or even came to as stop, but no one got out of the car to examine the victim. Every car sped Quickly down the road after viewing the scene. We laughed hysterically each time someone slowed down. Roger and I were feeling a little braver after about an hour and we decided to move our "victim" to Roger's yard near a street light. We hid behind the far side of his house. A few cars slowed down, but soon we would witness the biggest catch of the night. Mike Matthews was heading home in his brown and white ford Fairlane. Mike was a teenager and his father, Garland Matthews, was the Driver Volunteer Fire Chief and fire chief at the nearby Navy Transmitter Station. Mike slowed down and looked at the "victim" from his car. He took off squealing tires and headed down the nearby dirt lane to his parent's house. Dirt clouds from the dirt lane filled the chilly night air. Mike returned to the scene in a few minutes. Mr. Matthews came back with Mike and the two huddled over the "victim." Mike put his hands on the "victim" and said the poor "man" was crushed and had already expired. Mr. Matthews bent down and realized the victim was a dummy. Roger and I laughed, but we decided we better head for the field behind his house before we were detected. The Matthews returned home, but Roger and I began to worry about the conseQuences of our prank. We never heard a word about who was responsible for the prank and we decided not to "display" our "victim" again. Roger later told me where he got his idea. A fellow named Tommie Hall had also used a paper filled dummy to play a trick on some Virginia State Troopers who often dined at Traveler's Rest Restaurant which was located in Suffolk which was about 8 miles from Driver. Tommie's mother, Jerry Hall, worked as a waitress at the Traveler's Rest and Tommie spent a lot of time there. Tommie was a little pudgy and the troopers would often tease him about his appetite, Tommie got revenge. Tommie pulled into the restaurant parking lot and parked next to a blue-gray State Trooper car. He opened a back door of his car and yanked the dummy out. Tommie proceeded to hit the dummy and toss him all over the parking lot. The state troopers saw the "fight" from a restaurant window and hurried out to the parking lot. The state troopers yelled to Tommie to let the "man" alone. One of the troopers Quickly rushed to help the "man" and realized he was a dummy. The troopers never teased Tommie again, but his mother reprimanded him. Rog, Lance (Roger's older brother) and I played one more good prank a few years later. Lance hooked up some external speakers to his tape player (the old fashioned kind with the big reels) and placed the two speakers on high limbs of two trees in the Massensgill front yard. He taped some strange noises and some audios from horror flicks. Lance would play the tape every time someone would walk down the road at night. Most people would walk Quickly when they heard noises in the trees and a few ran down the road. One night a wino was walking down the road. He was headed to Boney's, which was a local store that sold wine and beer. Lance turned on the tape player and the wino stopped and looked at the trees. The wino told the tree he would not bother it if the tree would not bother him. He spent several minutes conversing with the tree. The fellow was already under the influence of "Spirits" and did not need any other problems. Roger joined the Air Force when he was seventeen years old and I saw him sporadically in the coming years. Lance and I became good friends and did a lot of things together. We were both lifelong Washington Redskin fans and both loved baseball. We attended many Norfolk Neptune football games in Norfolk. The Neptune's were a minor league team and a member of the Continental League. Lance bought a new blue convertible Firebird (Pontiac) as soon as they were available. We had some great times cruising around in that beautiful car.

Lance met his future wife, Linda while she attended Madison College in Harrisonburg Virginia. Lance has retired from the Virginia Highway Dept. and his son is now a doctor. He and Linda have had a very good marriage. Roger spent tours of duty in Thailand during the Vietnam War. He married a Thai girl but she died at an early age. The couple had a son named Jim and a daughter named (Blank). Roger adapted to life in Southeast Asia. He also did tours in Louisiana, Bangor Maine, and the Philippines, but I think his heart was always in Thailand. The kid who once raised pheasants and Quail and hardly ever left home was more at home in a foreign land. Roger come home to Driver and lived with his mother until he could find a house. Sally Massengill was glad to have her son and his two children living with her. Unfortunately, Mrs. Massengill passed within a few years. Driver had changed during the twenty three years Roger was in the Air Force. The rural farms were being crowded out with new houses and many of the older people we knew had passed. The changes were hard for me, so I can only imagine how things seemed to Roger. I have not seen or heard from Roger for several years. Years ago, I received a phone call from a company doing work in Saudi Arabia. Roger had listed me as a reference for the job and I assured the company that he was a great guy who loved the Air Force and his job, and was a dedicated worker. Roger told me often about a young Air Force Pilot who was shot down on Christmas Eve in the 60's. He was the plane's crew chief and he recalled how the crew loaded bombs on another plane on Christmas Day. He said everyone had an empty feeling but everyone loaded each bomb for the young officer. I hope Roger is happy and well. I hope he has had a good life and I appreciate what he did for me and especially what he did for our Country. The Massengills were great neighbors and friends and I will always remember them.

T.K.

Roger and I were very close, but we were not in the same grade in school and it seemed to be an unwritten law that one did not associate with under classman at school. Peer pressure even existed in the country. I met a boy in second grade who (like Larry: Shelton) would take me under his wing and show me the ropes. He was a poor country boy with a North Carolina accent who was not impressed with money or social status. The only thing that impressed Tommy Knowles was baseball and those that played the game. I guess Tommy felt sorry for a new "city slicker" that was not good at playing marbles, Kick ball, or baseball. Tommy was an impressive figure to a second grader. He was respected by the best students and by the new "wise guys" moving from the city to the country. Tommy worked hard after school and on weekends at the dairy where his father worked. The money he spent was money he earned. Tommy taught me to not worry what others thought of you. He may not have had fine clothes to wear, but he had a ton of confidence. He taught me to be confidant when playing marbles or sports. Tommy told me to not be discouraged but to keep practicing to get better. Tommy and his older brother, Cecil, spent their free time concentrating on baseball. The brothers would take turns rolling gumballs off the roof to the batter waiting on the ground. Tommy or Cecil would hit the gumballs with a broom handle. The practice was great for hand to eye coordination. Cecil became a very good pitcher and scouts were looking at him when he was sixteen. I never saw a pitch Tommy could not hit if he had a little time to watch the pitcher throw. Tommy was the only batter to get hits off a college stand out at a Mets tryout in 1970. It is a real shame the two brothers never played professional baseball. The Knowles brothers were the modern day Dizzy and Daffy Dean. The brothers lost their mother when Tommy was 13 and they helped their father who was often ill after his wife's death. The two would have been celebrities if things had gone right for them. Johnny Carson would have loved them. Tommy started his first year in little league. He said I would be a starter the following year and he was right. Early on in the next season, I was put into a game and played centerfield. I made a shoestring catch in center and was a starter from that point on. The coaches discovered I could also field grounders and I was moved to shortstop. I remember the first year our team got new uniforms. We had always worn tee shirts with blue caps with a D (for Driver) on them. The coaches lay the new uniforms on the ground and told us to sort through them to find ones that would fit us. Players Quickly rummaged through the uniforms trying to find a number 7 jersey (Mickey Mantle's Number), a number 8 (Yogi Berra), a number 10 (Tony Kubek) or whatever number their favorite big leaguer wore that would fit. I wound up with number 3. I was a little down when I realized the Yankees did not have a player who wore number 3. When Tommy saw my new shirt had a 3 on it, he told me "I was lucky." "Only the greatest player who ever lived wore number 3; "You got the Babe's number". Tommy said. Tommy pointed out that the Yankees had retired the number in honor of Babe Ruth. Little league was the best time of life for Tommy and me. We played in the County League (Nansemond County) and our team (Driver) played other villages in the county. We played Chuckatuck (six miles from Driver), Whaleyville, Holland, Wilroy, Kings Fork, Bethleham, and Cypress. We played one Saturday on the road and played at home the following Saturday. Each village had a Little League team and a Pony League team. Little League was made up of boys 8 to 13, and Pony Leaguers were 14 to 18 years old. Tommy started when he was eight, but I played short at nine and the rest of our infield were 12 and 13 years old. Tommy was a star pitcher and outfielder. Mike Reed was our tall first baseman. He always yelled at me to throw the ball higher when I threw out base runners. I looked up to the older guys in the infield and they helped me. Our third baseman (Dennis Breart) played professional baseball in the coming years, and he went as far as Triple A. Tommy Joyner was our catcher. He was short, but he was a very good ball player and everybody liked him. Tommy was also very popular in school. Tommy took his own life several years ago. I really miss him. Baseball is a great game. It brings people together and players can be rich or poor, players can speak different languages, players can have different religious beliefs, or they can have any number of differences. Players must work together to be successful and the team is the most important thing. The World Baseball Championship is a great thing and countries should look at baseball and see the good that has come out of the American pastime. Ball players may play hard for their team or country and they may occasionally fight, but they always appreciate other players' talents. A good coach can take 12 young baseball players and he can mold them into a team that is cohesive and selfless. Many kids that play ball will carry the good habits they learned on the field and incorporate them into their personal lives. Tommy Knowles and I were lucky enough to grow up in an era when many small cities had professional baseball teams. Our entire Little League team went to the South Atlantic League (SALLY) LEAGUE) All Star Game during July of 1960.

Portsmouth, VA (about 10 miles from Driver) was to become a member of the Double A league in the spring of 1961. The team was the class AA club or affiliate of the Kansas City Athletics. The team was named the Tidewater Tides and the team played its games in Portsmouth Stadium, which was built during the depression by the WPA. Granny Hamner was the first Tides Manager. Granny had been the short stop on the famous Philadelphia Phillies of 1951 called the "Whiz Kids". He was a versatile player and spent many years with the Phils. Granny Hamner played in many of the Tides games in 1961. He played short stop, catcher, and pitched. Granny learned to throw a "knuckle ball" with the Tides, and he spent the next two seasons with the big leagues Athletics as a relief pitcher. Baseball has changed a great deal since the 1960's.

Tommy and I would enter the stadium after school and we saw Tides uniforms spread on the screen behind home plate. I imagined the team had a dryer, but the club personel took advantage of the home plate screen on sunny days. Money was tight for minor league teams. Tommy and I were members of the Tides "Knot Hole" club. Kids could find the round badge in a loaf of "Mary Jane" bread. Kids could enter the ballpark for 25¢ when they wore their "Knot Hole" badges. My mom would drive Tommy and me to Portsmouth after school when the Tides were playing at home. She would let us off at the ballpark and she would visit Mae and Bob Murray who lived nearby. I would call my mother on the phone in the latter innings and she would pick us up after the games. As with baseball, things were very different in the early 60's. Portsmouth was a city that was home to Norfolk Naval Shipyard and the streets of the city were filled with sailors on weekends and nights. Sailors and civilians rode ferries from Portsmouth to Norfolk to shop or visit the bigger city. I clearly remember the old orange and black ferries that shuffled people across the Elizabeth River in the 1950's.

The end of High Street (near the ferries) was home to famous local taverns such as the "White Horse Tavern." This area of High Street was often filled with sailors. Downtown Portsmouth was home to four movie theaters, which were often crowded with seas of sailors. We kids went to the 25¢ movies often, and all of the sailors were nice to kids. Like the Tides, the sailors were mostly young men who were far away from home. Tommy and I would grab a snack or supper at the old A&P grocery store, which was located near the ball park. The old store housed a bowling alley on the second floor. The Pin boys set up the pins because the old bowling alley was not automated. Tommy and I would go inside Portsmouth Stadium as soon as the ticket locations were opened. We rushed to see which ball players were on the field. Would we be able to talk to pitcher John Wyatt (spent many years in the majors), third base man and local favorite Sal Bentancourt, Centerfielder Chuck Shoemaker, pitcher Ken Sanders (opened several years in majors), or manager Granny Hamner or the other Tides. Tommy and I had many conversations with the young pitcher, Ken Sanders. Ken was probably 19 or 20 years old and he cursed a little, but I think he appreciated kids looking up to him. He gave us pointers and naturally he was our favorite Tide. Kids never forget a ball player who makes a little time for them. Years ago, I came across one of my old baseball cards from the early 70's. The card was a Ken Sanders card and the back of the card noted that Ken had been "Fireman of the Year" the previous year with the Boston Red Sox. Ken Sanders had been the best relief pitcher in the American League the previous year. I am glad Ken had a good career. The Tides became the Single A affiliate of the Chicago White Sox in 1962. The Tides were now a member of the Carolina League. Don Buford (famous Baltimore Oriole), Ed (the Streak Stroud), Rudy May (famous Angel and later Yankee pitcher), and other faces made up the "New Tides". The Tides would become the Carolina League team (A-Ball) for the Philadelphia Phillies in the next few years. Ron Allen (outfielder and Dick Allen's brother), short stop Terry Harmon, second baseman Denny Doyle, outfielder Larry Hisle (from Portsmouth Ohio and a great major Leaguer) infielder Joe Lis and pitcher Lee Meyer, were some of the Phillie prospects. The Tides starting infield would later become the Philadelphia Phillies infield for stretches of time in the coming years. Lee Meyer was a big League prospect, but his wife was much more famous. Lee was married to the famous actress, Mamie Van Doren. Mamie had previously been married to the L.A. Angels pitcher, Bo Belinsky. We would often spot Mamie in a seat behind home plate during games Lee pitched. As a kid in Port Norfolk and later Driver, my pals and I often discussed Marilyn Monroe, Jayne Mansfield, and Elizabeth Taylor. I guess Larry, Shelton, Tommy, and I picked this habit up from our fathers. I still can recall Mr. Hale saying, "just look at those legs" as he watched the June

41

Taylor dancers or "The Rockettes" on television. Mamie Van Doren will always be remembered for the Aqua Velva shaving commercials and her famous line "There's something about an Qua Velva man." Tommy and I also saw many great ball players who were members of the opposing teams. We saw Pete Rose who played for the Macon (GA) Peach during the Tides' first season. Pete ran on a walk to first base as he later did with the Cincinnati Reds/The Big Red Machine. Years later we would see more future members of the powerful Reds. Newport News (twenty miles from Portsmouth) fielded a team called the Peninsula Pilots who were the Carolina League (A-Ball) affiliate of the Reds.

Johnny Bench was a seventeen year old catcher for the Pilots. He once threw out 3 base runners in one inning. Tommy and I knew Johnny would be called up to the Reds at an early age. We saw many great baseball players over several years at the old Portsmouth Stadium and later in Norfolk at Metropolitan Park where the Tides relocated in 1970. Bobby Murcer (Yankees), Cesar Cedeno (Reds), Gene Michael (Yankees), Bobby Grich (Orioles), Doug DeCinces (Orioles), Terry Crowley (Orioles), Fred Lynn (Red Sox), Jim Rice (Red Sox), Dwight Gooden (Mets), Len Dykstra (Mets), Wally Backman (Mets) and Derek Jeter (Yankees) are just a small group of players we were lucky enough to see. The years 1961 and 1976 are two memorable baseball years. The home run duel between Mickey Mantle and Roger Maris of the New York Yankees will never be forgotten. I was twelve years old and a die-hard Yankee fan. After losing to the Pittsburgh Pirates in 1960, the Yanks rebounded to win the World Series with the Cincianciti Reds in 1961. It seems like every one in America got caught up in the home run derby between the "M and M" boys. People Quit worrying about the Cold War with Russia and either rooted for the long time Yankee hero Mantle or the second year Yankee Roger Maris. I knew the "M: M Boys" were great friends and pulled for each other. As "Mick" would want it, he and Maris are remembered as great teammates as well as great base ball

42

players.   1976 was also a classic year in baseball. A tall, lean, frizzy headed pitcher called "The Bird" brought a sensation to the Bicentennial Year that had not been witnessed since the arrival of the Beatles in 1964. Mark Fidrych brought a much needed breath of fresh air to baseball and the American League Detroit Tigers. Talking to the baseball on the mound and putting the mound were rituals when Fydrich pitched. Fans thought he was crazy at first, but they soon realized that "the Bird" had done this for years and he was not acting but was the "real deal." Mark Fydrich was a sincere individual who loved life and baseball. He often commented that he was lucky to play the game and money was not an issue. The Bird told reporters he could easily have wound up pumping gas in his hometown at the local filling station. "The Bird" won 19 games in 1976 and he was the starting American League pitcher in the All Star Game. Fans loved the way Fidrych shook hands with his teammates after they made a good play and they loved the "Birds" attitude and respect for the game. I was a Yankee fan, but I could not root against "The Bird" when he pitched against the Yanks. He is probably the only player in history of major league baseball who home town fans rooted against their own team to cheer on Mark Fidrych. Anyone who loved baseball had to pull for the Bird. "The Bird" was like a rock star and he did for baseball what the Beatles did for "rock n' roll." Many people believe birds are messengers from God. They are sent here to sing and brighten our days. Mark Fidrych was aptly named "The Bird" because he only pitched a short time but he brought inoncence back to a country and back to baseball. I saw "The Bird" when he was in Triple A with the Toledo Mud Hens (Tiger Triple A teams) and later with Pawtucket (Red Sox Triple A) team. Mark was attempting a comeback to the big Leagues. His recent passing takes me back years ago to his games against the Tides. He was not pitching, but the smiling "Bird" laughed and encouraged his team mates. "The Bird" was much like Ronnie Van Zant of the band "Lynyrd Skynyrd." They both brought a needed message and they brought hope to the world. They were with us for only a short time, but now they are both "Free Birds."

Chapter 5

Goodbye Jimmy

I became good friends with two of Tommy's friends in the second grade. The two boys were named Jimmy Cooper and Kenny DeLong. Kenny would move with is family and leave Driver Elementary, but Jimmy and I would go through grammar school and high school together. The four of us would shoot marbles against other teams, or we would spend our recess or time before class talking about Disney's "Swamp Fox" or "Zorro", or "Cheyenne", "Tales of the Texas Rangers", "Roy Rogers show" or any other westerns on TV. We were a team and we seemed to look at our selves as future Texas Rangers. The good guys always won in those days, and we had plenty of heroes to look up to. Matt Dillon and Pallandin were the kind of men we hoped to become. I always admired Jimmy Cooper. He had 3 brothers and two sisters and he spent a lot of time taking care of and watching over his siblings. Jimmy always made sure his younger brothers got on and off the school bus safely. His family lived in nearby Respass Beach, and the kids from that area had a six mile trip to Driver Elementary. Jimmy was a good looking boy with blond hair and he always had a broad smile on his face. He was so kind and unassuming and everyone liked him. Jimmy would become a member of the Driver Volunteer Fire Department during his high school years. Some of the veteran fire fighters still talk about what a good fire fighter Jimmy was and what a special kid he was. He was always dependable and he always did the right thing. The people who knew Jimmy appreciated his friendship. Jimmy left high school in 1968 and joined the Marines Corp. He went to boot camp in Paris Island, South Carolina. Jimmy came back to visit his friends at John Yeats High School soon after he completed basic training. I remember him walking down the high school halls in his sparkling Marine Corp dress blue uniform. Jimmy shook hands with his friends and everyone wished him good luck. He still had that great smile on his face. Jimmy came from a family whose men had served their country as Marines. Jimmy felt a sense of duty and honor to our country and he made the ultimate sacrifice for all of us. Jimmy was killed in Viet Nam shortly after his last visit to John Yeats High School. Friends and classmates were devastated by the news. High school graduation was approaching on June 8, 1968, but many of us graduated with an empty feeling and much sadness. Jimmy would have wished for us to be happy and carry on, but many of our lives would never be the same. The world was so different.

A friend of mine and I visited The Wall in Washington, DC in the early 1990's. Jack had served in Vietnam and had lost friends he served with. I knew two fellows on the wall (the other was Frank Ashley of Chuckatuck) but I had known Jimmy so many years. Seeing the other visitors searching for their loved ones on the wall was a uniQue experience. My heart ached for those people as it did for the service men and women whose names were listed on the wall. How many fathers, mothers, brothers, sisters, relatives, and friends' lives had been changed by the war? I understand why people leave personal items at the "wall" and I know the feeling one gets when your fingers touch the letters of your loved ones name. I think of Jimmy Cooper almost every day. As I do with other friends and family members, I pray for him every day and repeat the "Hail Marys". I am not Catholic (raised Episcopal) but prayer is one way I can honor and remember loved ones. I end my prayer session with the "Lords Prayer". I will never forget Jimmy Cooper, or his friend ship, or smile. I know the world would have been a better place with him in it, but heaven must have needed that perfect smile.

Bobby Cooper (no relation to Jimmy) is a life- long friend who served as a Marine in Vietnam. Bobby was the second son of George Cooper who was one of my father's best friends. George and Amy Cooper had four sons named Billy, Bobby, Jerry and Gene. My brother Gregory, and I grew up with the Cooper boys and my mother thought the world of Amy Cooper. George was a speed boat racer in previous years and the Cooper home was a shrine to his racing career. George was not a barman, but he and my father hunted together, shot bows and arrows together, and did many other things. He was a true family man and was very active in scouting. George and all four sons were musically talented. Our family spent many evenings listening to Billy on coronet, George and Bobby taking turns on drums, and Jerry playing Keyboards (Gene was very young at that time). My mother would sometimes join them and play piano and the Cooper house overflowed with music. I remember a talent show that was held about 1958 at the Old Chuckatuck High School Auditorium. Billy and Bobby were invited to join the show. Bobby whaled away on the drums and Billy hit the high notes on his coronet. The Cooper boys easily won the talent show and our family and the Coopers headed to Travelers Rest Restaurant for something to eat. Someone at the restaurant mentioned to the owner (Jimmy Ward) that the Cooper Boys had just won the talent show. Mr. Ward told the boys to bring in their instruments and he and others moved tables to give the duo room. Patrons at the restaurant really enjoyed themselves that Friday night. Billy and Bobby thrilled the crowed for a few hours and father George was in his element. When I returned to school the following Monday morning, every girl encountered above the age of 12 was talking about the Cooper brothers. Some were in "love" with Bobby, and some were in "love" with Billy, but Cooper mania had spread throughout Driver Elementary and Chuckatuck High. Billy and Bobby entered the service after high school. Billy trained dogs while serving in the Air Force and Bobby served in the Marine Corp and served in Viet Nam. Bobby was a lot like Jimmy Cooper. He was always looking for adventure. Bobby fought in the Tet Offensive and also fought with other

Marines at Khe Sanh. The marines were greatly outnumbered by the Viet Cong Khe Sanh and Bobby was on the perimeter during the battle. Bobby lost an eye in the battle and his leg was badly injured. I have never heard Bobby complain and he has told me many times he thought the Viet Cong were tough people. A good friend of my father named Billy Powell was visiting relatives in Portsmouth five or six years ago and he stopped by to visit my father. Billy and my father had grown up together in Port Norfolk and the two had kept in touch throughout the years. I told Billy that Bobby had served in the Marines and was involved in the Tet offensive and Khe Sanh. Billy had retired from the Marines Corp as a Colonel, but I did not realize he was at Khe Sanh. Billy was above the battles in a Chopper that was dropping supplies to the marines on the ground. Billy warmly greeted Bobby and told him he too was at Khe Sanh, but he was not in the jam that Bobby or his comrades were. Marines in the air were also in great danger, but they were not about to leave fellow marines overwhelmed on the ground. Billy said all pilots were supposed to get instructions from the Air force at head quarters in Saigon. He said many pilots cut their radios off because they knew the situation first hand and they were going to do whatever was necessary to save their fellow marines. I believe everyone at Khe Sanh was a heroe and I am proud to know two of them. Bobby has often told me that the instincts he gained hunting as a boy with our fathers and their many friends helped survive in Viet Nam. My father's friends were all good hunters and most had served during WWII. Bobby has had his share of up and downs since Viet Nam. His marriage fell apart and his beloved mother passed away at an early age. Bobby loved his mother, Amy, and worshiped the ground she walked on. Amy loved Bobby unconditionally, and he has been a great parent to his daughter who is Bobby's only child.

I don't believe any one deserves a free pass, but we don't always know what others have had to deal with in life. I respect and admire Bobby Cooper and he is one the most honest people I have ever known. My father used to say we cannot judge another man until we have walked in his shoes (moccasins). Like these before him at Gettysburg or Bunker Hill, Bobby has walked on hallowed ground.

By now, I am very sure some former English teacher or professor would like to chastise me about jumping from subject to subject and especially stating that Bobby lost his eye. A teacher would ask me how anyone "loses" an eye, but I would say that people "lose" their eyesight and that would be correct. A soldier might lose his sight due to a blow, an explosion, heat, chemicals, fire, fragmentation, or any number of things. I guess it would have made sense to say he had loss the use of his eye, but now does that sound? I think I write the way people talk. Tommy Knowles served in the army during the Viet Nam war era. He told authorities he would gladly serve, but he did not want to go overseas because he took care of his father physically and financially. Tommy went AWOL from the Army at Fort Benning Georgia and returned to New Port News (20 miles North of Driver) after receiving orders for Viet Nam. He went to work as a heavy duty eQuipment operator. Tommy had many skills and he never had problems getting a job. Tommy began visiting me in Driver and I thought he had completed his military service time. Tommy, some of our friends, and I began playing baseball again. We played ball every chance we had and we were getting good again. I need to explain something that affected my skills playing baseball as a thirteen year old and later on the high school baseball team in the eleventh grade. I did not have a good year my final year in little league baseball. I played short that year, pitched (3 and 1 record) and caught some games and did good in the field. I struggled at the plate the latter half of the season and my father could not understand why I was no longer the good contact hitter I once was. He pitched it to me at practice one day and I was having more trouble than usual. My father became frustrated with me and began to lose patience with me. He hollered at me and I hollered (Southern) back. He showed up to practice with empty beer cans in the back of his Chevy pick-up truck that day. The humiliation of my poor hitting and the beer can incident was more than I could handle. I screamed that he did not know what was wrong because he was out drinking half the night before and he didn't know anything about baseball. I was bearing my soul in front of my team mates and I was ashamed. Bill Cobb (a coach on our team and a former minor league ball player) calmed my father down and told him I was in a slump and to let me work my way out of it. I left the field and sat in the pick-up truck until practice was over. My teammates treated me as though nothing had happened and I think they all understood. I entered the eighth grade at Chuckatuck High School that year and I would soon know what the problem was in baseball. I sat in the back of Algebra class and I could not make anything out on the blackboard. As in baseball, I was falling further behind. I told my mother the Algebra teacher moved me to the front of the class so I could see what was written on the blackboard. My mother called and got me an appointment for an eye exam. A few weeks later I went to the eye doctor. As the doctor rotated the eye machine lenses, a new clear world opened up to me. I needed glasses. A few days later I joined the four eyed world. John Sebastian referred to being called "Four Eyes" in one of his songs with the Loving Spoonful. I could easily go on in life being called "Four Eyes" rather than living in a fuzzy world. My first glasses looked very similar to the pair Buddy Holly wore. Soon the world of rockn' roll would be invaded by "four eyes." John Sebastian, Peter Asher (Peter: Gordon) Chad (Chad: Jeremy), the lead guitar player for Herman's Hermits, Beatle John Lennon, and Doors Keyboard player Ray Manzarak were only a handful of "four eyed" "teen idols." I can't imagine anyone calling Ray Manzarak "four eyes. My second incident with glasses occurred in the eleventh grade as I mentioned earlier. My "Buddy Holly" glasses broke and Rogers's brother Lance (Massengill) gave me a pair of his old glasses. The glasses were not as strong as mine, but they were better than being back in the fuzzy world. Now things were only semi- fuzzy. I did not want to let my mother know I needed a new pair of glasses. My mother worked hard making ceramic to help support us. I worked at my uncle's gas station, but I needed the money for car insurance, gas, school lunches, and clothes. My mother had a set of four year old twins to care for (my sisters Holly: Sherri). My father was still busy carousing six nights a week and he was not a big help to my mother during that time. I was the grandson of a prominent business man, but we were expected to keep our chins up at all times and we were expected to be self- sufficient. I began working at my grandfather's store at age 13 and from that point on I supported myself for the most part. Baseball reQuires good vision not second hand glasses. I was horrible on the baseball team and my confidence was pretty low. I could not see very good and I was struggling in baseball for a second time. The coach once put me behind the plate (with catcher's gear) and I had to catch pitches from a pitching machine. I was humiliated, but lived through this experience.

While attending college I met a former professional baseball player who became a big part of my life. I will speak of him in greater detail later. He was like a big brother to me and he gave me confidence and the desire to be a good ball player once again. He worked with me tirelessly and he taught me a great deal about life. My friend also helped Tommy with baseball. Tommy, Steve Wylie (a close friend of my brother), and I joined a local African American team called the Driver Zippers. There was no local league for players over eighteen so many white players joined the "Black League". Most teams had two or three white players on their rosters. Playing in the "Black League" was great. The old wooden ballparks had character and the stands were always filled with cheering fans. It seemed as though we were playing baseball in the 1920's or

51

1930's. The team rosters were made up of workers from Planters Peanut Co in Suffolk, Norfolk Naval Shipyard in Portsmouth, Newport News Ship building in Newport News and many other local businesses. The players worked all week and played baseball on weekends and evenings because they loved the game. The players had much more zest than college baseball players.

The Zippers were managed by Ernest Lassiter. Ernest owned a tour bus company and he was liked and respected by whites and blacks. Any local politician who wanted to be elected needed the support of Ernest Lassiter. Ernest welcomed Tommy, Steve and me to his team. Steve Wylie had been an all-district shortstop at John Yeats High School and Steve did some relief pitching with the Zippers. Ernest was very impressed with Steve's curve ball. We played the Chuckatuck Trotters, the Suffolk Mets, and teams in North Carolina and the Washington DC area. The Zippers traveled on Ernest Lassiters buses. The team always looked good in the white and green pin-stripe uniforms he furnished. I met some very good ball players while we played with the Zippers. I can still see Ernest smiling and laughing when the team won or someone made a good play. I knew Ernest until his passing about 8 years ago. His passing was a sad time for anyone who knew him. I have only fond memories of Ernest and the Zippers. Tommy and I had a scheduled tryout with a local scout, Harry Postove (New York Mets) in September of 1970. Harry had signed the great shortstop, Luis Aparicio, many years before. Tommy did not attend the tryout and I knew something was wrong. I fielded, hit and ran the bases for Harry Postove, but I would have given anything for Tommy to have been there. Harry told my friend that I had the skills of a Double A player and he wanted me to play the next season with the Zippers and would scout me in live games. I often wonder what Harry would have said if he had seen Tommy hit. Weeks passed before I heard anything from Tommy. I finally received a letter and it explained why Tommy did not show up for the Met tryout.

Tommy had heard word of a super pitching machine located in Columbia South Carolina. He drove down there to hit off the machine and prepared himself for the New York Met tryout. Somehow the F.B.I. heard about Tommy's trip to South Carolina and they picked him up while he was hitting baseballs. I later asked Tommy how he hit the machines fast ball and he replied "no sweat". I began receiving letters regularly from Tommy who was held at Fort Leavenworth, Kansas. He once wrote me that he had witnessed some inmates push a fellow inmate to his death from one of the upper tiers of cells. He said it was like some of the things we saw in the old gangster movies. Tommy asked me to send him a baseball glove and I found a Spalding Bobby Murcer model glove and mailed it to him. He had joined a baseball team at Fort Leavenworth and he wrote me that a young Lieutenant who also loved baseball had befriended him and he was doing fine. Tommy had not given up his dream of playing baseball and I think that helped keep him going. Tommy returned from Leavenworth after serving one year and he went back to work as a heavy eQuipment operator. We continued to play baseball and Tommy rejoined the Driver Zippers team. He still had the skills and love for the game, but we were now twenty-two years old. Tommy and I had a tryout with a Cincinnati Reds scout. The scout marked off sixty yards and timed us in the sixty yard dash. He told us we were not fast enough, and we never got to field or hit. The scout told us the teams were looking for players with speed and they would teach them to hit and throw.

Astro turf had changed the game of baseball. Players like Pete Rose adapted to the new surface, but players like Tommy had never played on the synthetic surface. We were country boys who had never seen astro turf; naturally we had never played on it. We were accustomed to playing ball on rough sand lot fields where bad hops were natural and on fields where long hit balls ended up in corn fields. Tommy and I continued to play catch or even play and pick up games as the years passed by. I could always field a little better than Tommy, but I never could hit like him. I still wonder what he could have done if things had worked out differently. Tommy would join my circle of other friends and he would often eat at my house or watch television with us. He once told a friend of mine (Bobby Harrel) that he thought he was beginning to look more like James Garner who was starring in the "Rockford Files" show. Tommy did resemble James Garner a little, but I told him he looked more like Jethro Bodine on the "Beverly Hillbillies." In 1976, President Jimmy Carter pardoned Tommy and other individuals who went AWOL or left the country during the Viet Nam War. The country had been through "Water Gate" and I think President Carter realized we were all going through a healing process. "Baby Boomers" had been through the "Korean War", "the Cold War", the "Vietnam War", marches, riots and demonstrations. The country had been divided and President Carter (like Lincoln) knew it was time for us to be a "union" again. Tommy had been through a lot during his life, but never lost his natural sense of humor. Most of the time he was not trying to be funny, but the Carolina humorous charm would gush out of him. Tommy and I were watching television in my store one day when an elderly lady walked in. A news report was on TV (we were in the Gulf War at the time) and the lady told us the military was calling lawyers and doctors back into the armed forces. The lady asked Tommy had he been in the service and Tommy replied," Yes Mam, I was in the Army." She next asked Tommy was he worried about being recalled into the service. Tommy said, "Oh no mam, they'll call women and little children into the service before they call me again." The woman looked confused and Tommy added, "I spent a year in Leavenworth, but President Carter pardoned me." Tommy, Thomas Rust, Bobby Harrel and I were once in line at a steak house in Portsmouth. We were in line for a while and Tommy Blurted out to the server, "What am I doing?" "I promised myself I would never stand in line to eat again after the Army and

Levenworth." He said for us to go on and eat and he would see us back in the car. The lady behind the counter at a "Highs Ice Cream" parlor once noticed Tommy's accent and she asked him where in the world he came from. Tommy told her he was from "across the river." The woman asked Tommy "the River?" and Tommy said "you know, the Big River." Tommy finally said, "the big River, the James River." Tommy should have told her he was from Newport News, but he was once again having fun with the English language. Tommy had his own business in the late 1970's. He bought a striping machine and a Chevy van and he began striping parking lots. Tommy was the first person I knew to have a mobile phone in his van, and he was making a very good living. Tommy stopped by my house one night and said the day had been so hot that "his grinds were on fire." He explained to me that he had sweated so much the skin on the inside of his legs was raw. I began to realize that Tommy was talking about his groin. I gave him a wash cloth and he put cold water on his "grinds" and all was well. I watched him throw a brand new stop watch about 100 feet after he ran a 60 yard dash and he was not happy with his time. The unexpected was the norm when you were with Tommy Knowles. I have seen Tommy slow down but not stop at every stoplight between Driver and Norfolk. A Suffolk police officer once stopped him because he rolled through a stop light. Tommy handed me the ticket after the officer left and asked me to put it in the glove compartment. I opened the glove compartment door and the glove compartment was full of tickets. Tommy eventually paid off all his tickets. Tommy was always unselfish and good-hearted. He would often buy me lunch or sodas, and he would have given me the shirt off of his back if I had needed it. I have not seen Tommy for a few years now. I have heard he now has severe diabetes and is not doing well. I have put off getting in touch with him because I might not like what I find out. He has not contacted me and it may be because he wants me to remember him as he was. I can still hear him saying," let the whole world drag; but just let me wag." I have been very fortunate in many ways during my life. There is an old saying that when one door is closed, another will soon open. I don't know if Nannie had anything to do with it or it was always an act of God. Maybe it has always been a combination of both. Ringo Starr sang "I get by with a little help from my friends", in the Beatles song "With a Little Help From My Friends." The song has always applied to me and probably most people. I have had a lot of friends in my life and I hope to have many more. I have been lucky or blessed enough to meet the right people in my life. A door has opened every time one has closed and I'm going to "keep trying "with a little help from my friends."

Chapter 6

Ned Thompsen

William E. Thompsen became the new minister of Glebe Episcopal Church (Driver) and its sister church St. Johns Episcopal Church in Chuckatuck in 1959. Reverend Thompsen and his wife, Jane, settled into the rectory in the village of Driver and the couple was a breath of fresh air for the church and village. Ned Thompsen (Ned was the Reverend's Nickname) soon became a major influence in my life. Reverend Thompsen and Jane were from Baltimore, Maryland and both always said whatever was on their minds. The couple had a son, Bill, who was a hellicopter pilot with the army. I was already an acolyte at Glebe Church when the Thompsen's arrived. W E Cattenhead and George Black were also acolytes and our Sunday school teacher, Claudius J. Riddick, was in charge of acolyte training. Mrs. Riddick had been my third grade teacher at Driver Elementary. The Episcopal Church during that time was very rigid and very formal. Episcopalians spent a lot of time on their knees and long hymns were standard. Acolytes were trained to light and put out the many candles properly, carry the cross at the beginning and end of each service, assist the minister with the offering, and most importantly assist the minister with the Holy Communion once a month and during special services such as Moonlight Service (Christmas Eve) or Easter Sunday. We were a polished and precise group in our black and white vestments.

Glebe did not have air conditioning so we really suffered during the hot summer months and were glad when the service ended. My father did not come home until 1 or 2 A.M. Monday through Saturday nights and Bob Murray and Ned Thompsen became the male role models in my life. Bob, who I mentioned earlier, was my mother's best friend, Mae's husband. He always dressed neatly and was secure in his situation in life. Bob and Mae had one child, Barbara, who was older than me (about four years) and the two were great parents. I will write more about Mae and Bob later. Ned Thompsen was also secure in his place in life. Reverend Thompsen lead by example and never followed the crowd. Ministers often cater to the wealthy of influential members of the congregation, but the reverend was not impressed with the trappings of society. The reverend scolded me a few times when I was younger. I once said something derogatory about a lady in the neighborhood and Reverend Thompsen looked at me sternly and told me his father would have knocked him down if he had said such a thing. Reverend Thompsen had my respect early on and I always realized anything he told me was for my own good. I knew Reverend Thompsen was a man of God whether he was behind the pulpit in the church on Sunday morning or working in the flower beds at the rectory on Saturday morning. Ronnie Cross, a black boy who lived down the road, often worked with the reverend in the flower beds. Periodically, Reverend Thompsen would speak about integration in his sermons. Some church members would SQuirm in their pews but deep down they knew the reverend was right. I honestly believe Ned Thompsen made people take a better look at themselves and try to live a better life and I never heard any one complain about his sermons. An old saying states that you have to know how to talk the talk and walk the walk. Reverend Thompsen did this better than any man I have ever known. My brother and I would play football with other kids in the neighborhood on fall afternoons after school. We played wiffle ball in the spring in our front yard. Ned Thompsen would often stop by and pull into the driveway in his 1959 black and white Ford Station wagon. The reverend would tell me to go into the house and tell my mother I was going with him. I was a little <u>miffed</u> the first time this happened, but I soon realized this was another case of something that was for my own good.

We would go to the church and work in the flower beds. The reverend must have known that working in flower beds was some sort of therapy. Reverend Thompsen realized it was a little bit easier to talk about your problems when you were kneeling on the ground and your hands were dirty. We were also doing something good for the church at the same time. Sometimes the reverend would "summons" other fellows my age to help us in the flower beds and he was probably "talking" to them also. I began to look forward to working at the church and it was something I took pride in doing. There was no arguing, bickering or fighting at the church yard. As with the woods and Roger, there was peace, nature and tranQuility. Reverend Thompsen would often show up at Driver Elementary and the teacher would tell me that Reverend Thompsen would like to talk to me outside the class room. He would "put his hand on my shoulder and say "How would you and your buddies who work in the flower beds like to see the Tides play Friday night?" I had one teacher who resented the "interruptions" and she was young and "self- absorbed." The other teachers liked Reverend Thompsen and welcomed him to the school. I detected this at an early age and later this young teacher suffered a nervous breakdown. It was a pity she did not take the time to get to know Ned Thompsen. My friends and I really enjoyed going to the baseball games with Reverend Thompsen. Often Reverend Pierce (the local Christian Church minister) and his wife would attend the games and the two preachers would talk and watch the game together. The Pierce's would also take some of us back to Driver after the games. I lived near Reverend Thompsen so I was usually the last boy to get home. He would always ask me how things were at home and school and let me know I was free to talk to him anytime I needed to. My mother was an organist at the church so I imagine she had similar

59

conversations with Reverend Thompsen, but she or the reverend never mentioned this. Reverend Thompsen never belittled my father or condemned him. I think he knew that alcoholism is a disease and people like my father needed help. I am sure he tried to help my father because my father did Quit drinking for about a year one time while the Thompsens were here. It was a strange situation during the period my father did not drink. I don't know if you are just waiting for the other shoe to drop or you resent that person because they go from trying to do all the wrong things and begin trying to do all the right things. I will write in greater detail about my father later because we did have a uniQue relationship. My father was like my heroe, Mickey Mantle because he was a <u>heroe</u> to everyone else, but he was a stranger at home. As I pause a minute to catch my breath and gather my thoughts, I am thinking of the great Chicago song"25 or 6 to 4". It is about 4: A M and I can relate to Terry Kath (lead guitarist who accidentally shot himself). The lines of the song seem appropriate "Waiting for the break of day, searching for something to say" Twenty Five or Six to Four, Should I try and do some more" "Wanting just to stay awake, wondering how much more I can take." Thanks Terry

My parents did argue and bicker most nights and there were several nights I did not know what was going to happen or nights I did not sleep much. I too often waited for the "break of day" because I knew my father would be off to work and there would be some sort of normalcy in my life. There were many nights my mother, my brother, and I stayed with Mae and Bob because my mother would be more fearful then usual. I think this had more to do with the times my father came home after he had been in fights and was bloodied rather than what he might do to her. My father would do a lot of talking while he was drunk, but my mother was usually the one who grabbed a frying pan or threw water on my father. She would scream at him and tell him how his mother failed to raise him properly and to look at himself and see what he had

60

become. He would tell her he would leave home and go back into the merchant marines and go overseas. I would be the one who in later years would physically suffer from his drunken stupers. Reverend Thompsen had a very religious impact on me also. I went through a period when I thought I wanted to be a minister if I couldn't be a Yankee Shortstop. I wrote a paper in fourth grade about Reverend Thompsen.

My fourth grade teacher, Mrs. Daisy Sullivan, was very tough on me and she was like the reverend in the fact she really cared about me and wanted me to do the best I could. She too was greatly respected, she is always fair. She was one of the best teachers I ever had and I still think of her. Mrs. Sullivan told the class to write a paper on the person we most admired in life and I chose Ned Thompsen because I did admire him more then anyone I knew. I admired my "Uncle Shirley, my Uncle Cecil, My Grandfathers, etc. but I saw firsthand how many people Ned Thompsen helped. Mrs. Sullivan was thrilled with my paper and showed it to the Thompsens and my mother. I think she suspected I wanted to become a minister, and she really took an interest in me as a student. She gave me confidence and I owe her a great deal. I was confident enough to tell other kids not to cuss because it only showed ignorance. I knew the Ten Commandments and I did not like to hear anyone take the "Lords name in vain." I got on my father every time he did this, but he always told me I was exactly right. As a kid I prayed for other kids and even prayed most of the time before I batted in Little League. I asked only to get a hit if it was the right thing. I continued to pray in later years when the Viet Nam War was going on and I was worried about my friends. My prayers were answered. I was also impressed with Rev. Billy Graham and I watched him on television as I had Bishop Fuller in earlier years as a child. I would often grab the Bible or Episcopal prayer book and read verses or prayers to my father in the wee hours of the morning when he came home. He never seemed to mind and I think he knew I understood him and was only trying to help. I have lived long enough to know that many people seem to be more candid when intoxicated. A sober alcoholic who I greatly admired once told me he truly believed that God loved little children, puppy dogs, and drunks because He tried to watch over all three.

Chapter 7

Goodbye Bill

I t is now day break on Sunday Morning, April 26, 2009. My brother pulled his car over yesterday morning (Saturday) and told me that Bill Soule had died from a heart attack on Friday night. Bill and his crew had spent the last few months working under my brother's house which was built in 1830. I have been in a funk ever since my brother broke the news to me about Bill. Bill had done a lot of work for my wife and me over the past years and I had gotten to know and appreciate him. He was the type of guy you could talk to about anything and he took great pride in his craft (carpentry). I don't think Reverend Thompsen would care if I took sometime to think about Bill. If writing truly is therapeutic, I need to write about Bill Soule. The business of death is never easy for me and I know in time things will get better, but at the present time, I am really hurting and grieving. I know we have to think about the good times and Bill is in a better place and there are things we are not meant to understand, but I am presently feeling the way I felt when I lost Nannie. Losing people will never get any easier for me.

People always say we tend to lionize or glorify other people after they pass, but I can pray for anyone (Good or bad) and do not have the need to lionize everyone. I will lionize the people I care about and the people I respect. Bill Soule is someone I really respected and admired. He did not care about nice cars, nice clothes, new houses, or the social status of the people he worked for. He cared about his old motorcycle, his old worn out car or van, old houses and churches, and especially his crew and his friends.

I am sure that anyone who knew Bill or anyone he had done work for will be saddened when they hear of his passing. Bill was originally from Boston, but he settled in good old Port Norfolk (imagine that!) after he finished his time in the Navy. Bill was a highly intelligent person. He attended M.I.T. after high school, but he and a college classmate decided the school tuition was a financial strain on their families and the pair joined the Navy. He once told me it was also a good way to see other places and cultures.

Bill also told me he never really wanted to be an engineer. He said he knew he always wanted to save old houses, churches and other buildings. Bill had great respect for the carpenters that had come along before him and he greatly appreciated their skills, as he did great architecture. I am sure Bill Soule worked with some very good carpenters when he was young. He always hired young people, (male or female) and I felt he did this because he could relate to them and he was willing to take the time to help them. He had a longtime girlfriend, Kelly, but Bill did not have children of his own. Once, while installing a fence at our house, one of Bills helper's (Chad) had cut the end of a section of the fence too short. Bill told me he would get another section and would take it out of Chad's paycheck. I asked Bill if there was any way the old damaged section could be salvaged. He told me he could remove the end board and level the bottom of the board and flip it 180 degrees. I told Bill that would be fine with me and it was just a simple mistake. Bill called Chad over and told him what we had decided to do and that I had been nice enough to cut him some slack. He told the young carpetenter to be more careful in the future and to be sure of his measurements. The fence was perfect and a young man had learned a lesson. Bill never yelled or belittled his workers. He showed them the benefits of patience. Bill had worked on my store, my house, my brother's house, my brother's store, my sister's house, two other stores and had done other work in Driver. He had been a lifesaver after a hurricane hit about eight years ago. Lately, He had been doing a lot of repair work that resulted from the F-3 tornado that hit Driver on April 28, 2008 one year ago. Bill never lacked work. He was a craftsman and he knew that word of mouth is the best kind of advertisement. Anyone who watched Bill work for a few minutes knew they were watching someone who really knew what he was doing and also enjoyed what he was doing. Bill's back had been hurting him for several months and he had great pain when he walked or bent down. I had a hip replacement recently and I knew something about the pain he was experiencing. He assured me he was letting the young guys do the heavy work. Bill continued to work under my brother's house. It would be the last carpentry work he would do. Bill Soule did his last work on a house that took a direct hit from an F-3 tornado and it was a house constructed with pegs and good lumber in 1830. To the memory and honor of Bill Soule, I hope my grandparents home stands another two hundred years. I will always think of Nannie when I hear the Christmas carol with the line about Jack Frost nipping at your nose. I will always think of Bill Soule too. Bill's crew came out yesterday to give us the news of his passing and to assure us that there was only a little work (we knew the job was near completion) and they would do a good job in honor of Bill. I am sure Kelly and Bill's crew are lost and are all suffering greatly at this time, but things will get better. Bill and his crew had become a fixture in Driver and everyone in the village is saddened by his passing. One only needs to look at my house (1898), my brother's house, and some of the other buildings in Driver to realize Bill Soul left his mark on this tiny Virginia village. I will miss Bill's Boston accent. I will miss his philosophy about life and his many "sea stories." Bill may have been from Boston, but thirty five years Qualifies him to be known as a fellow "Post Norfolk Boy". I failed to relate a few other things about Bill. He was only a few weeks older than me (59). A few months ago Bill rode his old motorcycle down to Florida to visit his elderly mother. It was his last visit. A few years ago, Bill was doing some work at my store and he overheard some of us discussing fried chicken as we sat under the store's huge front porch. One fellow mentioned a place near Lynchburg that served great fried chicken. A few of us mentioned a chicken restaurant in Portsmouth called Moseberth's. Bill and his workers went on their lunch break and returned about an hour later. Bill returned with a huge box of Moseberth's fried chicken and he told us he might be a "Yankee" but he knew good fried chicken and Moseberth's was the best. You do have to think of the good times when you lose friends or family. I have many good things to remember whenever I will think of Bill Soule. As he did when I was in grade school, Ned Thompsen would ask me to sit with him in his station wagon. These "sessions", took place in my grandfather's store parking lot or the family driveway. The reverend was checking to make sure things were not too bad at home and my brother and two sisters were all right. My family attended church most Sundays and we appeared to be an average family. My father was definitely not Ward Cleaver and my life was nothing like Wally Cleaver's. Reverend Thompsen always encouraged me and told me things would get better. He often told me he was proud of the other fellows and me at church because we had remained acolytes and attended church regularly. I think he knew we respected him and never wanted to let him down. He never let us down. The reverend would always stop by our Sunday School class after church and check on "his boys". Our Sunday school classes were held after church because our services began at 10:00 A. M. instead of 11:00 A.M.

As mentioned earlier, Claudius J. Riddick was our Sunday school teacher the entire time we attended Glebe. He was the son of a Suffolk doctor and he was a disciplined person with high standards and morals. Mr. Riddick explained early on to our class that we should all rise and stand when Reverend Thompsen or any minister was in our presence. Mr. Riddick was a meticulous man who was a CPA. He had been the C.P.A. to Amedeo Obici who founded Planters Peanuts. Mr. Riddick ran Sunday School like he did acolyte training.

Each of us knew the words to the Apostles Creed, the Lord's Prayer, The Ten Commandments and any other important doctrine of the Episcopal Church. Confirmation is very important in the Episcopal Church. Active church members are usually confirmed at about 12 years of age. The students go through rigorous study and recitals before their confirmation before the entire congregation. Reverend Thompsen and Claudius Riddick were our instructors. Aunts, Uncles, grandparents, cousins and other family and friends attended my confirmation. Mr. Riddick dressed well but he had one problem he could not control. He experienced freQuent nose bleeds and it was not unusual to see him enter the church with his nostrils stuffed with tissue. I'm sure he felt self-conscious, but he never missed church or Sunday school. Reverend Thompsen, Reverend Hand Castle (the Christian Church Minister), George Cornell, Ben Ames and Mr. Riddick were avid bird watchers. Bird watching was once a favorite past time, but television sports have replaced many outdoor activities. Our region is home to cardinals (VA state bird), blue jays, orioles, finches, thrush, black birds, sparrows, etc. and large birds such as hawks and bald eagles. People used to keep crows as pets and many could talk a little.

Ned Thompsen was with me when I passed my test for a state driver's license and he attended my high school graduation. The reverend brought a half gallon of vanilla ice cream to our house after the exercises. He was a very special person and a positive influence on my life. Reverend Thompsen left Glebe church when I was twenty-one. He was unfairly drug into court during a divorce case involving church members in previous years. Reverend Thompsen would not slander the husband (the attorney tried unsuccessfully to prove the man was gay) and the reverend gave his honest opinion. The trial would alienate many family members and the Reverend no longer had their support.

I admired Ned Thompsen for standing his ground. He did the manly thing as well as the Christian thing. How can anyone condemn a minister for practicing what he preaches? The world needs men of principal and integrity not more "yes men" Who cater to a congregation or constituents. Ned and Jane Thompsen did not want to see factions in the Glebe Church congregation and the couple decided to retire to their native Maryland. I still wonder if many members stop and think about what they lost when Ned Thompsen departed. I would see the Thompsens when they would occasionally visit friends in the area.

Years ago I wrote a letter to Rev. Thompsen thanking him for all he had done for my family and me. I also visited Mr. Riddick one afternoon and thanked him for the things he had done for me and for other Sunday School students. Mr. Riddick was overwhelmed and he had tears in his eyes. I truly believe that most people will mentally recall the good things some special person did for them and they will in turn help someone else who might be down or might be having a hard time. The feelings are similar to an umbrella. The focal point or center of the umbrella extends out to cover or protect a larger area. How many people did Ned Thompsen or Claudius Riddick touch? Ned and Jane Thompsen passed away many years ago, but they live on in the other lives they touched. I am so lucky to have known them.

Chapter 8

Irvin T. Arthur

I feel confident most people have a family member or good friend who is important in their life that they don't think they could carry on or survive without that person. My grandfather, Irvin T. Arthur, was that person in my life. Throughout many years of my life I worried that he would leave or pass like "Nannie" did and I worried what would become of my mother and us kids. I needed structure in my life and I believe my grandfather was the most structured man I have ever known. He had a great deal of self control and he also knew how to control the members of his family. There was only one way to do things in life and that was to do things the way Irvin Arthur would do them. My grand father's father passed away when he was only thirteen years old and he learned early on what it took to survive. My grand father, his three brothers (Jim Arthur, Marion Arthur, and Richard Arthur) lived with my great grandmother on a farm in the Bennett's Creek Area of Suffolk which is about 5 miles north of Driver. Someone on his mother's side handled the affairs when his father died and that person wound up owning the Arthurs property. The family lost their farm and moved to the village of Driver. I live in the house that my grandfather and his three brothers grew up in. The house was built in 1898 and my Uncle Richard took care of my great-grand-mother until her death. I remember visiting my great-grand mother and my great-uncle Richard, with my mother. My great grand mother always kept jars of peppermint candy throughout the house. The house has always had a cozy feel to it and my Uncle Shirley used to tell me his grandmother's house was his favorite place to visit. I had the same feeling and I guess it is appropriate that I live in that house. My

Grandaddy's ancestors came to the United States in the early 1800's. They left Scotland and sought a better life in Virginia. Adversary and the Scottish heritage also drove my grandfather and his brothers to become successful in life no matter what circumstances they encountered. Grandaddy attended Virginia Polytechnic Institute, which is now Virginia Tech. He enrolled on the Blacksburg college in 1916 and like all the students of that era; he was a cadet. I still have his black wool cadet hat, which I found in the attic. I have seen pictures of my grandfather as a cadet in an old V.P. I. Year Book. A good friend of mine named Severn Warrington (from an old Driver family) had the year book because his father also graduated from V.P.I. My grandfather worked for a Mr. Brinkley in his Driver Store during the early and mid 1920's. The grocery store also had a post office and my grandfather began working for the U.S. Postal Service. Severn recently told me that two of his great uncles had passed away while doing business at the post office. "Grandaddy" opened his grocery store directly across the street from "Brinkley's" in 1925. He operated the post office in his store (Arthur's) and he was the post master until the late 1970's. He was the local post master for over fifty years and he enjoyed every minute of his work. My grandfather rarely took vacations or time away from work and he always took paperwork to work on when he did. The postal service had a real bargain while the post office was located in Arthur's General Store. People in the village could check their mail or purchase a stamp from 7:00 A M to10:00 P M Monday thru Saturday. Old mailboxes with combinations lined the left side of the store and my grandfather spent a good portion of his life in the narrow aisle behind those mailboxes. He smoked his pipes and greeted friends and customers with the expression "How goes it?"

I loved playing in the grocery store's back room as a boy. The room was filled with empty boxes of all sizes and shapes and made a perfect hiding place. Cases of motor oil, paper towels, ketchup, flour and numerous other items lined the shelves of the back room. My two uncles Cecil and Shirley, and my mother each began working in the store at an early age. My mother usually made sandwiches, cleaned the store, or waited on customers. Shirley was the youngest child and had a few childhood illnesses that prevented him being as involved in the store. My grandfather placed most of the responsibility on my Uncle Cecil. My mother always said that Cecil never had the childhood most boys had. He was my grandfather's right hand "man" and he worked in the store before and after school, every Saturday, and worked in the store after serving in the army in World War II. My grandfather's life was his store, but he also made that choice for Cecil. Cecil spent time in Europe during World War II and spent some time in France as a jeep driver for General George Patton. He had no problems serving directly under General Patton. Cecil had been "trained" by Irvin T. Arthur so the Army service was easy for him. Cecil was one of the hardest workers I have ever known in my life. He was a butcher, a delivery man, a produce man, a feed and seed specialist, a mailman, a clerk and every other occupation reQuired at my grandfather's store. Long hours and pressure were normal for my uncle and his wife, Mildred. I will speak more about this uniQue couple later. My grandfather operated a bustling business until he was eighty-one years old. He sold groceries, hardware, automobile products, boots, hunting ammunition, and anything else his customers needed. Pigsfeet, chittlings, pigtails, dandoodles, cheese sauce, side meat, slab bacon and other meats were some of the items kept in the old store cooler. The coolers also contained fresh ground homemade sausage, fresh ground hamburger, a variety of steaks and roasts, whole fryers and hens, and chicken wings, legs, thighs, breasts, etc. The store favorite was the old round cheese (rat cheese)that was covered by a thin cloth material and was shipped in a round wooden box. Many people have had a lunch consisting of crackers, cheese and a can of vienna sausage. They washed the lunch down with a Pepsi

Cola, Nu-Grape or Lotta Cola. Old timers in Driver will still agree that Nu-Grape was the best soda ever bottled. I was fortunate to grow up in an era where pre packaged goods were in competition with old fashioned goods. Arthur's store was more famous for its loose cookies like the large round "Johnny Cakes", ginger snaps, sugar cookies, oatmeal cookies, lemon cookies, than it was for bags of chocolate chip cookies or pinwheels. Sodas of all varieties came and went with the times of Coke, Pepsi, Dr. Pepper, and many other flavors still exist, but brands like Lotta Cola, 16 oz Tru-Ade, Nu Grape, High Rock, Juicy Pop, Brownie Chocolate Drink, CheerWine, Bubble-Up, Almond Smash, no longer exist or are hard to find. Candy bars are items that have definitely diminished in size since the 1950s. The old Baby Ruth or Butterfinger bars would be considered giant sized bars today. Candy bars such as the Holly Wood bar, the Milkshake bar, the Powerhouse, the Seven-Up Bar, the Black Cow. Most kids in the village of driver worked at my grandfather's store. Many adults also worked at the store as I can remember times when there were twelve to fifteen employees on the Arthur's Store payroll. It was very typical to see ten or eleven clerks working behind the counter on Saturdays which were always busy days. My grandfather and Uncle Cecil ran a tight ship. I can't recall the number of times grandaddy would sneak up behind me when I was trying to find bolts or nuts for a customer. He would puff on his pipe and tell me he was losing money if it took me more than 5 seconds to find the bolt or nut. My grandfather was always harder on family members than he was on other employees. The old black Ford delivery truck was eQuipped with a governor so no one could ever speed. I found out when I began driving the truck that I should never get stuck in a ditch or snow. I got stuck one time and Uncle Cecil had a fit. From that point on, I would use pieces of wood, bricks, and the help of others to free the truck from mud or snow. My uncle was too busy to spend time dealing with escapades. My grandfather was an astute business man and he took pride in his store and the people who worked for him. After my grandmother died, he spent much more time at the store. The hours were hard on Cecil and Mildred and much of their lives centered around my grandfather's business. I often saw my uncle's feet swollen and red from the long hours at the store. Often, he was physically and emotionally drained. The store became my "granddaddy's" home after "Nannie" passed. He reopened the store after he buried my grandmother and the long hours became his escape. Each afternoon, he would travel to Traveler's Rest Restaurant - in Suffolk to eat his dinner, but the remainder of his time would be spent at the store. Grandaddy would close about 10 or even 11 each night and he would go home, sit in his rocking chair, smoke his pipe and listen to opera on his radio. My grandfather, Cecil and Mildred and my family always attended church each Sunday morning. We would all go to Traveler's Rest for Sunday dinner after the service. My grandfather did not care how much each person's meal would cost (prices were very reasonable) and he always insisted on paying the entire bill. My Aunt Mildred or my mother would occasionally prepare dinner after church and they took turns preparing Holiday meals. My aunt and mother knew my grandfather's favorite foods and they both took great care in fixing these meals. My "grandaddy" enjoyed home-made macaroni and cheese more than any other dish. The macaroni was baked with "Velveeta" cheese and the dish was baked until the cheese was nearly brown. My aunt and mother's recipe was the same and no one could even tell the difference in the taste. Fried Chicken or Beef Roast accompanied by fresh butter beans and corn, macaroni and cheese, tomato pudding, collards, candied yams, and other delights were the normal fare. Grandaddy always stopped by the store and picked up a half gallon of ice cream for dessert. Pet Ice Cream once had a flavor known as "Cherry Nugget" and the company sold it near George Washington's birthday. The company made the ice cream for a few years, but it lived on in our memories for a long time. The dinner table conversation consisted of typical world news or news about my grandfather's many customers (who had passed away or who was having a baby, etc). I remember the conversation about the Kansas murderers that Truman Copote wrote about in his book "In Cold Blood". The horrible act seemed to touch the village of Driver and probably made people realize violence existed everywhere. The world had changed.

Christmas Day was the only day of the year my grandfather would close the store besides Sundays. He brought a Lionel train to our house in Port Norfolk on Christmas of 1955. "Nannie" had saved all of her pennies for few years and she told me I would receive a train when the Mason jar was full. "Grandaddy" knew this and it was important to him to keep her promise. My father, Uncle Cecil, and "Granddaddy" set the train up after Christmas dinner and it was hours before I got to play with my new train. The three would continue the tradition of playing with our toys each Christmas day. The three never had such toys when they were children and one day a year they had a chance to relax and relive their childhoods. A day away from the grocery store, the business world, the gas station and bars (my father) was the happiest day for us all. I always hated to see Christmas Day end. Each fall my grandfather would receive a new Lionel catalog and the two of us would gaze over the new items added to the Lionel inventory. "Grandaddy" would order crossings and other items for me for Christmas each year. I think he anticipated the arrival of each new catalog as much as I did. The relationship between my grandfather and my father was a very unusual one. I know my father truly respected "Grandaddy" and he realized early on he would never have the same type of self-control my grandfather had. The two men were opposites, but both were well liked and both were self-made men. My grandfather wore a white shirt and tie every day of his adult life. He represented the U.S. Postal Service as Postmaster and he wore a suit to the store each day. His shirts were always freshly starched and he even wore a tie and white shirt on vacation and fishing trips. He always wore a dress hat while he was outdoors. My father wore his green Amoco shirts and green pants to his gas station, but he also would often wear his hunting clothes to work. I found a picture of my father and me together that was taken when I was about four years old. My father was dressed in his Amoco uniform and wore a derby hat. He had grown a beard for some type of local jubilee and he had his massive arm on my shoulder. I get a feeling of warmth and security when I see that picture. It seems like he is saying "stick with me kid and everything will be all right." Strange, but one of the last pictures taken of us together was very much like that early picture. My grandfather never interfered with my parent's marriage. He never scolded or ridiculed my father and somehow he tolerated the years of drinking and shannanigans. My father used the old expression, "It takes two to tango" to apply to many situations in life. Perhaps my grandfather realized my mother was headstrong and was carrying on her own form of rebellion. She chose a rebel to spend her life with. The city of Portsmouth took about half of my father's service station property to add a new lane on Airline Blvd during the late 1950. The move drastically hurt my father's business and the business declined each year. My father had reached his "hay day" as a young man, but he continued to hang on and to drink more. My grandfather supported my mother, my brother Gregory, and me for the next few years. I did not know untill years later that the groceries we charged at the store were never paid for. My grandfather never Questioned my father and he tore up the charge tickets. My mother realized early on that divorce was out the Question. My grandfather would support her physically and financially, but there would be no "going home." He meant it when he told her to put a smile on her face and act as though nothing happened. "Grandaddy" eventually paid off our house when my father agreed to sign everything over to my mother. We might be embarrassed or worried at times, but we would never be homeless. The night my mother took my brother and me to my grandfather's house and he told her to go back home reminds me of a situation involving my "Uncle Shirley". He had returned home from the University of Virginia for summer vacation. My grandfather asked to see his grades and he noticed my uncle's grades were not too good. "Granddaddy" pulled a one hundred dollar bill from his wallet and handed it to Shirley and told him he could either see if he could get in summer school at U.VA or he could spend the money on a bus fare and never return to Driver. Shirley was close with one of the professors at Virginia and the professor helped get him into summer school. My uncle made high marks from that point on and he graduated Phi Beta Kappa from Virginia with a degree in psychology. My grandfather was stern and he never told his children or grand children he loved them and he never hugged them. We knew he cared about us, but we also knew he was not able to tell or show us. Possibly losing his father and farm at thirteen made him unable to express himself to his family. My grandfather did one thing throughout the years that bothered my two uncles. Whenever my Uncle Shirley and his wife, Darlene visited us or came down from Fredericksburg, VA, my grandfather would constantly brag to Shirley about his brother Cecil. He would go on about how hard Cecil worked in the store or what Cecil had done for someone in the village, or some wise investments Cecil had made (with Grandaddy's help). My grandfather went through the same routine with my Uncle Cecil. He would talk about how smart Shirley was and how good he was doing in Fredericksburg. Shirley sold church furniture (pews, altars, etc) to churches and desks and tables to schools and colleges. Shirley's degree in psychology paid off because he did a lot of business with the University of Maryland, Washington and Lee University, and many other schools. Customers appreciated his honesty and personality and most of his business was done over the phone. Shirley and Darlene were unable to have children so they adopted two girls. They adopted my cousin Beth in the late fifties and they adopted Cathy (Catherine) a few years later. The blond headed girls were fortunate enough to be adopted by a happy loving couple. Cecil and Mildred never had children and they never considered adoption. Their lives centered around the grocery store and trying to please my grandfather. The two would have been great parents, and my Aunt Mildred treated my brother and sisters and me like her own children. She would have made a fantastic mother. I miss Mildred. My grandfather often told Cecil and Mildred what great parents Shirley and Darlene were. I know Cecil and especially Mildred were happy for them, but the couple did not have children and my grandfather's praises for Shirley were a constant reminder of the life Cecil and Mildred were trapped in.

Uncle Shirley left Driver in the mid 1950's and it devastated me. I was close to him and he would often make wooden guns for me in his workshop in the backyard. I was jealous when he adopted Beth and Beth told me years later that she was jealous over me. Shirley would always spend a few hours at our house each time he visited Driver and he and I would play board games like " The Blue and the Grey", "Battle Cry", and "Battle Stations." The entire family would go to Travelers Rest Restaurant each time Shirley and his family came to Driver. My Uncle Cecil always finished his meal much Quicker than anyone else. He could eat a half fried chicken dinner faster than anyone I have ever seen. This resulted from my uncle always having to eat in a hurry at the grocery store. On hand had to be free to fill grocery orders, write orders for the weeks incoming groceries, or even pumping gas. My uncle and customers might play checkers on the long store counters after 8:00 PM, but the early hours were hectic and my poor Uncle never had time to enjoy his meals at the store. The checker games helped Cecil relax and unwind, but the cycle would resume after a short nights rest. Uncle Cecil favored Andy Griffith's character Matlock when his hair turned white and my uncle grew older. He was to Driver what Andy Taylor was to Mayberry much of Cecil's adult life. He operated the store, was a volunteer firefighter, church treasurer and handled neighborhood problems when necessary. Cecil was the man everybody talked to when they needed advice or solutions. Shirley was the psychology major, but Cecil had all of the on-the-job training. Cecil allowed my grandfather to control his life and this control coupled with the constant praises for Shirley created a wall between the two brothers. The two got along, but they would have been much closer if my grandfather had not made either feel as though he was in competition for my grandfather's approval. My grandfather never hugged his children or grandchildren and he was too controlling to ever tell them he loved them. I am sure my mother and uncles heard the many expressions my grandfather used to make a point or to make one think about their actions. I was the recipient of many of these expressions and I can honestly say they still affect me when I recall them.

"Grandaddy" was a very private person in his business and personal lives. He often told me that if you let other people know your business, the first thing you know you won't have any business. He also told me a good name was more important than all the money in a bank. My grandfather told me to never disrespect someone's job as long as it was honest work. He particularly respected vetenarians because they treated patients that could not talk and doctors treated people who could tell them everything. My grandfather respected doctors, but he used many sayings when describing their profession. He said doctors will tell you they are practicing medicine and that's exactly what they are doing, "practicing". He also said doctors spend eight years of their lives learning their job and they spend the remainder of their lives making up for it. My grandfather would refer to a good man by saying "he's a good egg". He always reminded me that I would be judged by the company I kept and not to use the word "guy" because it sounded like slang. He said the word "fellow" is more appropriate. My grandfather was a mathematical whiz and he helped me with my math in high school and college. I was good in general math, but I was terrible in Algebra. My grandfather enjoyed working on long problems and he always came up with the correct number or eQuation. I eventually grasped Algebra and trigonometry in college. The professor opened a door for me and it seemed like a ton of bricks hit me. I began to make "A's" in Math in college and my grandfather was greatly relieved. Years later I ran into my high school Algebra teacher, Mrs. Ann Johnson. She was a great teacher and I was happy to tell her I finally mastered Algebra in college. My grandfather and my Aunt Mildred had a special relationship. My grandfather was the local post master and Mildred was post mistress. They spent much of their lives working side by side and my grandfather became a father figure to my aunt. Mildred called my grandfather "daddy". I spent many hours with my Aunt Mildred. As a child, I would often do my homework in the post office while sitting on one of the two stools behind the post office counter and window. Mildred was a very patient person and she often helped me with my homework and I think she enjoyed the "lessons." I spent many nights at Cecil and Mildred's home when my family lived in Port Norfolk. Nannie was gone, but Mildred was like a second mother to me. The couple owned a small grey terrier named Tag and I spent many hours playing with him. My aunt and uncle never owned another pet after Tag passed away. He was like a child to them and I think his passing broke both their hearts. Tag would always wait for my uncle to return home from the store each night and he would wag his little tail until Cecil picked him up. I spent many nights watching television with my aunt and uncle and my sidekick, Tag. During the 1960's my aunt and uncle bought a camper and rented a lot at Bell's Island, North Carolina. They would leave the store early Saturday evening and head to their camper for their short vacations.

Cecil would fish and Mildred would relax in the sun or visit other camper wives. The couple longed to be away from Driver and the constant pressures of the grocery store. My Uncle Shirley offered to help my grandfather operate the store during the Christmas Hollidays of 1966. He would work two weeks so the couple could take a trip to Florida. I don't know that I should said Uncle Shirley "worked" because he mostly socialized with people he had known for years or went out to eat with my grandfather. People working at the store did not mind because Shirley was very entertaining and everyone enjoyed his "laid back" attitude. Cecil had the time of his life in Florida and the trip helped change his and Mildred's lives. They started taking a trip to Florida each year and they realized work was not the only thing in life. Work may have been the most important thing in my grandfather's life, but Cecil had had a taste of freedom. Things had changed by the 1970's and Cecil convinced my grandfather to start closing the store at 8:00 PM. Competition from large super-markets and chains affected night business and Cecil was able to talk my grandfather into closing at 6:00 P.M. Cecil eventually went to work at the post office in Suffolk part time (He had been a part time postal worker in the store for years), and he was able to work the night shift in Suffolk and operate the store during the day. The post office work was a change of pace for him and he enjoyed the work. Mildred suffered a major stroke during the Spring of 1970. Our house was located next to my aunt and Uncle's house and from our front yard I saw Mildred fall down onto the car port floor. I ran over and calmed her down and propped her head up. I checked her pulse, listened to her heart beat, and made sure she was not choking and was breathing normally. I told the first person to pass by to go to the store and tell my uncle to call the Rescue Squad. Cecil soon arrived on the scene and the rescue sQuad arrived within minutes and they took over. My aunt would spend some time in the hospital and she would be out of work for a few months, but she lived and I was very glad I had been there when she needed me. I went back to work in the store part time while my aunt was out of work. Mildred had lost some of her speech and she went through physical and speech therapy. She would regain her speech and walk normal again, but she would suffer many strokes in the coming years. My grandfather and Cecil were glad to have me back at the store and I spent as much time there as my college schedule allowed. My uncle and grandfather treated me like an adult and I really enjoyed working there. I wanted Mildred to get well and I knew she needed Cecil more than ever during her recovery.

I am not trying to sound like a hero or some great kid that is willing to sacrifice a little by helping his family out. I was not a paramedic, but I was fortunate enough to learn some first aid in the scouts and later in college. I took an extensive first aid class in college as an elective. My instructor was a great teacher named Mac Eure. Mr. Eure had been a great local basketball player and hurt his leg in college. He walked with a limp, but he was an imposing figure. Mr. Eure was the basketball coach at Craddock High School in Portsmouth. He also taught at Craddock and at Tidewater Community College. Mac Eure taught first aid in a uniQue manner. He stressed the importance of first aid to us and made us realize the course was very important and could be something we might use in everyday life. Mac Eure's immortal words were, "If the face is red, raise the head; if the face is pale, raise the tail." I was glad I had taken his course and I would use some of the things he taught me in the years after Mildred's stroke. The credits I earned in Mac Eures' class may very well be the most important credits I earned. My grandfather operated his store until February, 1988. I was working as a Radiological Control Technician (Rad Con) at Norfolk Naval Shipyard in Portsmouth at that time. I was leaving home about 5:00 A M that cold morning to attend an early morning class in the shipyard. I heard a noise coming from my grandfather's house and I walked over to his yard and soon realized the sound was my grandfather yelling for help. I ran to the side door and naturally it was locked. I yelled to my grandfather who was upstairs in his bedroom. I told him him help would d be on the way. My grandfather never complained about his health so I did not know what to expect. I tried to take a few steps back and ran into the door, but had no luck. I moved back some more and I run into the door with full force. The door swung in this time and I ran upstairs. I found my grandfather lying on the cold floor. "Grandaddy" told me his hip hurt very badly and I suspected he had broken it when he fell out of bed. I placed a pillow under his head and covered his body with the blankets that were on the bed. My wife had noticed my car was still home and she went to my grandfather's house to see if anything was wrong. She knew something was wrong when she saw the door. Janice yelled to me and I yelled to her to wake my parents' up and have them call the Rescue Squad. I told her to tell them "grandaddy" was all right but he needed to go to the hospital. My father rushed over to my grandfather's house and my mother followed after the phone call. My grandfather's upstairs kerosene heater had gone out shortly after he retired to bed. He was trying to get out of bed to relight the heater when he fell onto the cold floor and broke his hip. He lay on that cold floor in the cold room for the entire night. I checked my grandfather's vital signs and made sure he was as comfortable as possible. I knew not to move him because his pain was severe in his hip and it was probably broken. The rescue sQuad arrived soon and handled the situation. The rescue sQuad paramedic talked to me shortly and said I had done All – I could do and they would take my grandfather to the hospital. He said I should go to work if I had an important class. My grandfather would be all right. My grandfather's hip was broken and the doctors operated on him shortly after arriving at Norfolk General Hospital. He would recover, but he would never operate his store again. My grandfather would spend the next eight years with my parents. I walked into my parent's home one evening and found my grandfather choking on a piece of steak. My grandfather was having a difficult time breathing, and my father was beginning to panic. I performed the Heimlich maneuver on my grandfather and he spit out the piece of steak. He suffered a few bruised ribs because he was eighty-eight years old and a little frail. My father was amazed by t the solution and could not believe my grandfather was near death, but was normal so suddenly. I explained to him that the maneuver was a simple act and anyone could learn it. Later that evening I taught him the procedure, but he would continue to tell people I had saved my aunt once and my grandfather twice. All were cases where a little bit of knowledge and being in the right place at the right time paid off. My grandfather's life changed drastically during his eight year stay with my parents. He occasionally watched television at home and he had the same set he and my grandmother purchased in the early 1950's. He would become a tv junkie in my parents home. I remember my grandfather babysitting me on the Sunday night that Elvis Presley appeared on the Ed Sullivan show. My mother left to play the organ at the Port Norfolk Episcopal Church and "Grandaddy" turned the set on right after she left. He had probably watched Ed Sullivan before, but he had never seen anyone like Elvis. My grandfather sat in amazement as Elvis sang. Elvis was blocked out from the waist down, but my grandfather would repeat the word "disgusting" over and over to himself as the king gyrated on the stage. He did not tell my mother about the show or Elvis "lewd" behavior when she returned from church. I was young at this time, but I remember being very impressed with Elvis. Someone who could leave my grandfather so confused and bewildered must have been a very uniQue person. A man who was so controlled and so controlling had witnessed a rebel who would change music and peoples attitudes about life. I think I realized that night that young people needed their own hero; they needed a new voice and that voice was Elvis. I am very sure that my grandfather would have liked Elvis if he had ever met the star. My grandfather may not have liked Elvis' gyrations, but he certainly would have approved of his manner and the respect he showed older people. My grandfather eventually realized that young people can dance and have long hair and still be role models or good citizens. My grandfather and my father became "buddies" the last 8 years of "Grandaddy's" life. The hidden respect or admiration they had for one another evolved into real friendship. The pair went out to eat together, watched television together, and even went to visit my father's friends together. My father had Quit drinking by this time, and my grandfather truly enjoyed being with my father. The pair watched the tv show "Judge Wapner" faithfully. They went to "Lee's Garden" Chinese restaurant for Chow Mein nearly every Saturday night. The two Chinese girls who helped in the family business gave my grandfather and father Christmas gifts each year. I can still hear those nice girls saying "How are you tonight Mr. Arthur," and "How are you tonight Mr. Parker." The Chinese family was so kind to my family and I hope they are doing well in New York. My grandfather had eaten most of his meals alone since my grandmother's death in 1955. He really enjoyed breakfast and dinner every day with my parents. He was just as happy eating a bowl of cornflakes with my father, as he was eating roast beef with all the trimmings. Someone who had spent so many years alone had become an even bigger and more vital part of the family. My grandfather would spend a lot of his daytime hours working on store paper work in his recliner in the living room corner. The chair was located where he had a direct view to his house and the street. My grandfather had certainly improved his relationship with my mother, but he still had the antiquated Idea that a woman's place was in the home and her job was to constantly watch over her husband and children. The woman could shop or even work in the family business, but she had better be a dutiful wife first. My mother had kept her mouth shut most of her life and seldom earned praise from my grandfather. She did not mind caring for my grandfather, but I think she became feisty enough to demand some sort of respect. She reached the boiling point one day and I was glad to witness her actions. My grandfather was looking at his house through the picture window in the living room late one afternoon. He had been at my parents' house for about two years and he told my mother he thought he should be going home soon. He was seeking sympathy and my mother knew it. Moma told my grandfather she would help him pack some things the next morning and my father would begin taking his belongings to his house. My grandfather was speechless and shocked, but he said he better take some time and think about the situation. My mother had finally stood up to her father. No cursing, no tears, no blame; just the kind of remarks my grandfather might have used if the roles were reversed. My grandfather could punish you with words and my mother had learned that lesson well. My mother knew my grandfather was actually very happy and would never think about leaving their home. My grandfather began to appreciate my mother more (as much as someone like him could) and everything was forgiven. He would never mention his home again. My grandfather outlived two of his children. His fist daughter, Mildred, died when she was a baby, and my Uncle Shirley passed away in 1985 after a courageous battle with lung cancer. My mother visited my uncle often in Fredericksburg at home and in the hospital. Shirley suffered greatly, but the pair spent many hours reliving their childhoods before his passing. Shirley was a light hearted, highly intelligent individual. I never saw him get angry and I think he truly touched most of the people he met in life. He was a charismatic Christian and he often told me that God did not put us here to be miserable; but to help each other and to find some humor in life and enjoy life. The day of Shirley's funeral in December of 1985 would be a day of morning, but it would also be a day of humor. The cold, grey day was a day I will never forget. If people truly see their funerals, my uncle had a few good laughs that day. My grandfather was given a small, grey terrier dog named Charlie a few years after he moved in with my parents. The dog would spend his days next to my grandfather's recliner or on my grandfather's lap. My grandfather fussed and worried about the dog more than he did any human. If dogs are really man's best friend; Charlie was certainly I.T. Arthur's best friend. Charlie often needed a bath, but like a child he would often hide or do anything to avoid a bath. My father would have the honors of bathing Charlie and each bath became an adventure. My grandfather would remind my father not to use cold water that might make Charlie catch a cold or not to let the dog get soap in his eyes. If my grandfather and Charlie had had their way, Charlie would never have been bathed. My grandfather owned a yellow 1977 Lincoln Continental that someone had given him as partial payment on their bill at his store. My conservative grandfather had always owned black Fords before the huge Lincoln. He once snuck out of the house and drove the car to church one time after he was told to Quit driving. My mother and sisters, Holly and Sherri, left earlier from my uncle's funeral in Fredericksburg. My grandfather, father, brother- Gregory, and I would drive my Grandfather's Lincoln.

My father told my grandfather it was time for us to leave and my grandfather replied he needed Charlie's leash. My father said Charlie needed a bath and we could not carry him to Shirley's funeral. My grandfather said, "I guess I'll just have to stay here if Charlie can't go." Daddy tried to explain the situation, but my grandfather would have no part of it. As usual, things would be done I.T. Arthur's way and Charlie would ride on the front seat between my grandfather and me. I seem to often run into these sort of predicaments in life and I should not have been surprised when my father asked me to drive the Lincoln. The comedy of errors was only beginning. The four of us, with our suits on and riding in the Lincoln, looked like the Mafia riding along Route 17. My grandfather had his hat on as usual and smoked a cigar. I guess anyone who saw four men in suits with a grey terrier on the front seat would have to wonder what we were up to. During that trip, I noticed smoke in the rear view mirror. I told the others about the smoke and my father had the same kind of reaction he had when my grandfather choked on his steak. I had already began to pull off the road when my father panicked and started to yell for us to get out of the car and the car was on fire. I stopped the car and ran to the back and noticed the tail light was smoking, but it soon stopped. A wire must have caught on fire after some sort of short. We remained stopped long enough to make sure the smoke no longer existed and the car was "safe." People who saw the smoke from the tail light or four men in suits with the grey dog staring at the back of a yellow Lincoln must have had a good laugh. I had to use hand signals all the way to Fredericksburg and my arm nearly froze, but we never got stopped by the police. There would be one more humiliating act before we reached our destination. I guess the tail light was sort of a blessing because the cold air that came in each time I made a signal cut down Charlie's odor. It probably also made him long for the outside and he cocked his let Quickly and urinated on my arm.   I was pretty disgusted by this, but my grandfather Quickly defended Charlie and said he knocked over a cup of water my grandfather had left in the car. I knew better, but what could I say? It wasn't funny then, but the situation became more humorous as the years have gone by. We arrived at the graveside funeral and Charlie remained in the car until the service was completed. I imagine my Grandfather did not want to face the reality of outliving another one of his children and he kept looking back to the car to make sure Charlie was all right. Everyone met my grandfather and Charlie after the service and most of the children petted the gray terrier and asked my grandfather Questions about Charlie. As usual, the pair was on center stage and the weather was so cold that no one got a good whif of Charlie. My father, brother, and I all dreaded the return trip to Driver. Charlie snuck out the house later that summer and was hit by a car. My Uncle Cecil was in his front yard and I heard him say, "We might as well burry "Daddy" too. This will kill him."

My parents got a similar dog named Don Quan for my grandfather. The dog brought comfort to his life, but Charlie was the first dog my grandfather owned since my grandmother passed. The old dog had assumed some of my grandfather's characteristics and hey probably understood each other more than we realized. I miss my grandfather every day of my life. I miss listening to classical music with him and I miss his stories about Carusso, Tchakovsky, Stravinski, Mozart, and many others. I was glad I had taken a year of Music appreciation in college so I could really appreciate his love of music. I recall how he told me about the death of actor Rudolp Valentino. He explained the long lines of women who waited to Valentino's body and the effect he had on his fans. My grandfather assured me that fainting did not start with Elvis or The Beatles. My grandfather lived during a very important time in American History. His life time extended from the Wright Brothers until the Space Shuttle, from Teddy Roosevelt and the Roughriders to the destruction of the Berlin Wall. I was lucky enough to have a grandfather who was happy to share many of his experiences in life with me. I could not emulate my grandfather and I could never hope to be as intelligent and wise as he was. I can only tell him I love him and I was lucky to be his grandson. My grandfather lived a long productive life and he probably accomplished more in life than he ever imagined. He did most things on his own terms and remained a well respected man. The grey December day on which he was buried was cold with daytime temperatures in the teens. My mother looked at his marker after the funeral and remarked that the cold weather kept people from the funeral. My father put things very simply when he said, "No, your Daddy just outlived all his friends."

Chapter 9

Mae and Bob

I mentioned Mae and Bob Murray earlier, but I did not elaborate on their importance to my mother, my brother and sisters, and especially me. The friendship between my mother and the couple would be the measure that I would choose when I made new friends. Mae and Bob were both born in Boone's Mill, Virginia which is located near Roanoke and Blacksburg the home to Virginia Tech University. Mae's family moved to Louisville, Kentucky, when she was young. They lived within a few blocks of Church Hill Downs and Mae often recalled going to the horse track as a child. Bob grew up in an era in Boone's Mill where boot legging was often the only type of employment in the area. Bob and his brothers drove cars carrying boot leg when they were young men, and he told me stories about being out during the night and going to school during the day. I met many local men who retold similar stories and I realized that boot legging had been just as common here as it had been in the mountains. I believe boot legging has pretty much faded away in our society, but it was once a major force in American Culture. It dated back to the first settlers and it became a major concern during this country's first years (The Whiskey Rebellion). Families who had traded their wares to farmers and merchants for their goods to survive did not have currency or cash for taxes. They were descendents of whiskey makers and they were continuing to do business like their ancestors. During prohibition and the Great Depression boot legging was very prevailent. I am sure many men who feared losing their farm, home, or family turned to boot legging to survive. I also think most psychologists will tell us that more people will drink when the economy is bad and people are worried. Bob and Mae once lived in Los Angeles and Bob became friends with a fellow he met while working at the city water department. The fellow was actor Michael Rennie who starred on the famous movie "The Day the Earth Stood Still." Michael was a young actor when Bob knew him and the future star would often eat dinner with Mae and Bob. Bob's mother, Janie, would often visit the couple from Boone's Mill. Janie was an amazing woman and she lived to be more than one-hundred years old. I spent many hours of my childhood listening to the stories she shared with me. Janie was born in Boone's Mill during the beginning of the Civil War and her father fought with the Confederate Army. He fought under Gen. Ewell in the campaigns of Western Virginia. Janie said her father and some of his confederate friends would play cards on Saturday nights after the war and someone would always bring up Union General William Sherman's name. Janie said the old soldiers would become angry when they would recall Sherman's famous saying about Atlanta. Sherman told his men to burn and destroy everything so that even a crow could not find anything to eat. Janie said most of the men only had animosity for Sherman and I am sure the general's statement was more relevant in the years immediately following the Civil War. Janie lost her sight in her final years, but her mind was as sharp as ever. She was a small silver haired lady who dressed neatly and wore her hair pinned up. She was soft spoken and articulate and she brought a world to me that even my grandfather could not recall. The stories of farmers, apple growers, traders, and mountain life in the 1860's and on fascinated me. I was honored to know the gentle lady who lived such a long and fruitful life. Mae was a good daughter-in-law to Janie and she was a good mother to her daughter, Barbara Jean. Barbara Jean was four or five years older than me and she was like a big sister to me. Someone mentioned one Friday night that Driver Elementary was having the annual school Halloween Party. Barbara Jean asked me why I wasn't going and I told her I did not have a costume to wear. The creative wheels in her head began to turn. Barbara Jean found an old sheet and a Sprague of leaves that she spray painted gold. She transformed me into Alexander the Great and the two of us headed for the Halloween party. I won the costume contest and Barbara's creation was the talk of the party. It was the type of thing a big sister would have done for a little brother. Barbara married a sailor name Jim McGrath and the couple moved to Jim's hometown of Wayne, Michigan which is a suburb of Detroit. Jim was good to Barbara Jean and the couple raised a wonderful family and had a good life together. The family would often visit Mae and Bob or the couple would travel to Michigan to visit Barbara Jean. My mother, brother, and two sisters once traveled with Mae and Bob to visit Barbara Jean in Michigan. I was working at my grandfather's store by this time and I missed the trip, but everyone had a good time on the trip and were really impressed with Canada. Jim died from cancer several years ago and his passing left a void in many lives. I still remember him as a young smiling, sailor in his blue uniform. I 'm sure Barbara Jean does too. Perhaps losing Barbara Jean to Jim and Michigan made Mae and Bob even closer to our family. This and the fact that my father was spending less time at home brought an even closer bond between my mother and Mae. Both had many medical problems and I knew each of them always worried about the other one. I remember going to Mae and Bob's house one afternoon with my mother. Bob had just returned home from work and found that Mae had coughed up a lot of blood. He wasn't sure what to do, but my mother called Mae's doctor and the doctor told her he would meet them at nearby Mary View hospital. Mae would spend some time in the hospital, but she would bounce back. I will have to borrow a line from Dickens when I say this was the best of times and this was the worst of times. Mae and Bob helped stabilize our family, but my father was drinking more. I believe alcoholics often need someone else to blame for their problem and often their family or friends can help fuel that fire. I know many mothers have said, "My son wouldn't drink so much if so and so didn't drink around him" or "My boy would not drink if he was happy at home" Excuses. My father often blamed Mae and Bob for his drinking, but my mother would never let the drinking affect her friendship with Mae. My mother, my brother, and I would spend many nights in Portsmouth with the Murrays. We would stay with them when my father left on hunting trips or things were becoming unbearable at home for my mother. Mae and Bob were my god parents and they were at my confirmation service. Mae gave me my first bible one Christmas and they came out to see us Kids (my brother and twin sisters) whenever we had a birthday. They came to my high school graduation and Bob got me a summer job after my first year in college. He gave me his old white 1960 Plymouth that looked like a white bat mobile. The couple helped my mother constantly after my sisters were born on February 24, 1963. My mother still had problems with veracose veins and circulation problems, and she would often be bed ridden. We were lucky to have the Murrays and a black lady named Easter Vaughan to help with the twins. Easter Vaughan had thirteen children of her own, but she helped my mother whenever she was able. She watched over my sisters like they were her own and she called them "my babies." I will speak more about this great woman later. I remember the first time I heard the news that I would soon have twin sisters. My parents took my grandfather to Fredericksburg to visit my Uncle Shirley and his wife Darlene. The trip was probably to tell them about the twins. It was the Sunday in August, 1962 that followed the Saturday night death (or early Sunday) of Marilyn Monroe. The news of her passing was on the radio several times and I guess I felt the way Elton's John's song "The candle in the Wind" later expressed Marilyn's Life. I couldn't believe she was gone. My brother, Gregory, and I were seated on the back seat when my father told my grandfather about

92

the twins. I almost went into shock. My first thought was "Why in the world are they bringing two more kids into this mess?" Is this an attempt to save their marriage or were they what I often thought about myself, A mistake." I know what my grandfather said, but I really would have liked to have known what he thought. My father continued his partying and his ritual of staying away from home. I had a good idea of what the "twins" early life would be like and I was glad Mae and Bob and Easter were there for them and my mother. The three would cook, wash clothes, grocery shop, or do whatever my mother needed. Mae, Bob and my mother would often pass the hours away putting together huge puzzles on the dining room table. The puzzles would become a target for my father's wrath and he would usually flip them over leaving puzzle pieces all over the dining room floor. It was his way of blaming someone else and possibly feeling guilty, about the things he should be doing. My father's tactics for punishing me changed after the twin's birth. He no longer used switches or my early friend the hard hair brush. His hands and fists were now his chosen weapons. My father was a powerful man and he really could have beaten me senseless anytime he wished, but he usually didn't hurt me.

One Christmas Eve morning at the kitchen table I told my father we probably would not see him Christmas Eve night because he would be drunk. He always drank a lot on Christmas Eve and other family friends usually helped my mother set up on Christmas Eve. My Uncle Melvin (father's brother) always had the job of assembling toys when we lived in Port Norfolk. My father reached over and slapped me across the left side of my face with his open hand. I ran to the bathroom to see how bad it was because I had to go to work in my grandfather's store within the hour. I had red finger marks on the side of my face, but the fact that my father would slap me on Christmas Eve morning hurt more than any blow. I went to work and my Uncle Cecil saw my face and asked me what happened. I tried to brush it off, but he figured it out and left the store in a rage. He went to our house looking for my father, but my father had already gone to work. I was glad there was no confrontation, but like every Christmas, my father came home drunk. I can't remember the number of times my father would drag me form the bed at 2:00 A M and tell me to follow him outside so he "could make a man out of you". Sometimes I followed him to the back yard and sometimes I ignored him. My early Christmas gifts included a punching bag and boxing gloves. My father had been an amateur boxer, and I think he was hoping I would become a boxer. The early evenings of my life were spent on the couch with my father watching boxing matches. He didn't drink Quite as much in my early years and I think he enjoyed showing me how to protect my head or how to weave. I spent many evening as a buffer between my mother and father. He would threaten to leave and go back in the Merchant Marines, and she would tell him to go or threaten to hit him with a frying pan. I would plead with them to go to bed and talk the next day, but both usually acted as though nothing happened when the next day came. I guess both really hoped a new day would make things different. I experienced many feelings while growing up. My mother had sent me into ever bar or tavern in Portsmouth, VA to beg my father to come home. He would usually say he would be right home and sometimes he would follow us home. He would often hide his truck behind the building. As I grew older, I realized my father was probably treating me the way he had been treated when he was growing up. It was that "old thing" called "learned behavior" that I would learn about in psychology 101, but had already had much practical application. I realized both parents were products of learned behavior. Not to make an excuse for my father's Christmas Eve behavior, I realized later that Christmas is not a happy time for everyone and many people struggle with the Hollidays. My father often told me the only gift he and his sibling got was a piece of fruit. The only toy he ever received was a toy cap gun his Uncle Ben Parker gave him.

At times, I actually hoped my father would die or just go away. Other times I missed him and wished he wanted to be with me more. I know all verbal and physical abuse is wrong, but I know first hand that words and even intent can hurt as much as physical pain. The fact that my father was willing to hit me always hurt much more than a punch. How could you do this to your own son? My mother could do with her words what my father could do with his fists. Whenever I did something they did not approve of she would say, "You're going to grow up to be just like your father" or "You're just like him." This probably hurt more because it made me feel as if I was a burden or my mother could have gotten out of the marriage if it wasn't for me.

One of my father's favorite sayings was "it takes two to tango". The first half of my parents marriage was rocky because they let learned behavior affect their marriage. It took both to fall in love, and it took both to make their marriage work in the long run. The word "love" was not in my grandfather Arthur's vocabulary and it would take years for my mother to realize what power the word held. A sincere hug would later reinforce that word. Some might say when reading this that this is someone who hated his parents. Kids don't really hate their parents when they are young. A puppy will avoid a master that constantly yells at him or beats him. Kids face social pressure, peer pressure, puberty, adolescence, and everything else adults are faced. Is the problem that kids grow up to be adults or do they grow up to forget what it was like to be a kid. All kids want to be loved and accepted. They did not ask to be brought into this world and we owe it to them to help them anyway we can. Kids also have the memory of an elephant because they will never forget those who were kind to them on this journey. They soon learn that life is not a 100 yard dash but a marathon, and they will never forget the teachers, scout leaders, ministers, coaches, friends and others who helped them along their way. I will speak more about my journey with my parents later, but I need to remember more of the good things about Mae and Bob.   As it was with my two grandmothers, I miss the little things when I think about this special couple. Bob was not only neat, gentlemanly, and smart, but he was also a great cook. I have never had a slice of carrot cake that matched up to Bob's. His cake was three layers filled with schredded carrots, walnuts, and covered with Philadelphia cream cheese. Bob was proud of his cooking accomplishments and carrot cake was his best. Bob also cooked the best stuffed peppers I have ever eaten. He would often prepare a giant metal pan of the peppers and like many foods they were better each time they were reheated. My mother and Mae spent several months of the year making ceramics. My mother supported our Christmases with her sales from the ceramics and she and Mae gave many away as gifts. My mother owned a Kiel which is an oven for firing or baking the ceramics and she and Mae owned many molds. The pair made nativity sets, angels, Santa Claus, cookie jars, Santa's House, the Virgin Mary, large and small lighted Christmas trees, and almost anything pertaining to Christmas. Some nativity sets were solid white and some were painted. The sets included the manger and all of the figures including a donkey, camels, and sheep. My mother and Mae and Bob spent endless hours at our family kitchen table trimming the ceramics, (after they set up in the molds and hardened but were still fragile) and painted the items before the final firing. The Blue Boy, clowns, dogs, pitchers, plates, cups, mugs, and countless other items were prepared on that kitchen table. Making ceramics reQuires much patience and concentration. It is an art and my mother and Mae were well suited for the craft and Bob possessed the patience reQuired to fill the molds with slip and he often helped trim the pieces. Looking at some of their items today makes me recall those hours in the kitchen work shop.   Some of the trio's work are in homes as far away as England. One Nativity Set is now owned by the daughter of a family friend near London.   The ceramics have and will be passed down from generation to generation. I can close my eyes a few seconds and remember the smells of ceramics. I can smell the uniQue smell of the grey slip and I can smell the odor of the Kiel. There is no other smell like the smell of "gold" firing in the kiel and it is a smell I have missed. It may have been an unpleasant smell and one I tolerated while watching Washington Redskin football games on Sunday afternoons in the 1950's and 60's, but I do miss it. Bob and I were alone in the back yard one Saturday afternoon when I was nineteen. I knew words were important and I thanked Bob for he and Mae being there for us all the time. I told him the truth when I said he had been like a father to us kids and we all looked up to him and Mae. I was relieved to finally tell him this and he was nearly overwhelmed. Mae and Bob bought a house in Glouchester County, VA where Mae's sister Libby and her family lived. We would see them occasionally, but the visits became more infreQuent. My father slowed down his drinking and I think Mae and Bob decided to build a new life in Glouchester. My mother would talk with Mae on the phone and my mother, brother Gregory, my sister Holly, and I went to visit Mae and Bob one day in the mid 1990's. It was a great visit and the couple still called my mother "Ginny" (Virginia) and everything was the same. We had lunch with them and Mae's sister Libby and brother-in-law Paul Tilson who we had known from Port Norfolk. Bob's health was not good, but otherwise he had not changed. Mae was talkative as ever and everyone had a great time talking about old times. Bob had bought a cake for our visit, but everyone reminded him it didn't compare to his carrot cake. It was a magical day, but I knew it would be. I lived long enough to know that there is really no good bye or hesitation when people are real friends. They can be miles apart and not see each other for years, but that feeling that made them friends returns and all is well. Bob passed away a few years after our visit and Libbys husband Paul also passed. Mae and Libby still live in Glouchester and I understand Libby's daughter Sheryl has moved in with them. I will always love Mae and Bob and only one word can express that. Thanks!

Eddie Stevens

My father took me to Driver Elementary School one September night in 1957 to join the Cub Scouts. He told me a boy I didn't know would also be there and to speak to him because his father had passed a few weeks before and he was having a hard time dealing with this loss. My father pointed the boy out when we entered the building. The eight year old looked like a junior version of Dan Blocker on the tv show Bonanza. Eddie Stevens was not only tall for his age, he was also very heavy. My father told me later that Eddie's father was a good friend of his and Mr. Stevens hunted with him and his hunting buddies. He told me Mr. Stevens was a huge man and he came from Alaska. I talked to Eddie a lot that night and my father told Mrs. Stevens to bring Eddie by our house sometime to play with the kids. Eddie went to Chuckatuck Elementary School instead of Driver because he and his mom lived in the next burrough. Eddie's house was the second house from the old Kings High-Way Bridge and Eddie did not have neighborhood kids to play with. He was a lonely, but bubly kid. Eddie's mom did bring Eddie over one afternoon and my mother asked her to let Eddie eat supper with us. Eddie became a fixture at our house and ate many meals with us and my mother never complained. My father was hardly ever home, and I think my mother truly sympathized with Mrs. Stevens. My mother was sort of a single parent herself and she understood the pain Eddie was experiencing. I described Eddie as bubly because that was exactly what he was. He did not let his weight and size affect him and my friends like Tommy Knowles became Eddie's friends as well. All the guys liked Eddie a lot. They may have cut him some slack at first because of his father, but they all really liked him. Growing up with Eddie Stevens was like growing up with Babe Ruth.

Eddie would wrestle two or three of us at one time and he would always win. He could hit a baseball farther than anyone I knew, but naturally he did not run very well. Eddie was very strong and he would help his uncle on his North Carolina tobacco farm for a few weeks each summer. One year our little league coach, Jimmie Wilder, made Eddie a starting pitcher. Mr. Wilder grinned when he heard opposing players remark how big and strong Eddie was. I was Eddie's catcher and I knew most players were afraid of his fastball and very few ever "dug in". I was on second base one game and Eddie hit a ball to deep centerfield. I have never seen a guy our age hit a ball that far. I could have walked all the way to home plate and probably could have run the bases two times, but Eddie stopped at second. My father and his friends took Eddie hunting with them in Charles city, Virginia near Williamsburg several times. Once, My father went to Eddie's deer stand but Eddie was not there. He found Eddie in the truck and noticed several empty bags. My father asked Eddie why he was in the truck and Eddie told him he had gotten cold and hungry. He had eaten thirteen lunches and this feat was told over and over by members of the hunt club. Move over Babe! My father took Tommy, Eddie, and me to Port Norfolk to visit my grandmother one afternoon after school. The three of us went to Cotton's Drug Store to buy sodas. Some Port Norfolk guys sized us up and knew we were not locals and we were from the "country." The Port Norfolk guy, followed us out the door and one of them said "let's get them." We ran a short ways and the boys followed until I realized Eddie could not run far and I blurted out "Why are we running"? We stopped and the Port Norfolk guys stopped. We may be on their turf, but we weren't going to run anymore. The boys were shocked and said they just wanted to talk to us because we weren't from Port Norfolk. They were intimidated by Eddie and from that point on all three of us were welcome in Port Norfolk. The fellows in Port Norfolk got to know Eddie and became friends with him. Eddie was about a year older than me and he got his driver's license before I did. We would go to Port Norfolk and pick up some of our "Port Norfolk friends" or go shoot pool in Craddock. Everyone liked Eddie and he was kind of a "ladies man." We had stopped playing whiffle ball in my parents front yard. We used the ditch at the end of the yard as a home run wall and I never beat Eddie in homerun derby. I was glad he had girls on his mind instead of whiffle ball because I was sick of being beaten. Eddie lost interest in school and wanted to go to work. He worked various jobs and worked as a welder in Alaska on the pipeline. Eddie was an outdoor person and he eventually found his calling when he became a waterman. Eddie's mom met a great fellow and got married. Her husband had been my grandfather's bread man at his store and everyone was happy for Mrs. Stevens. The couple saved their money and opened a restaurant in Portsmouth. Eddie was at the Restaurant one afternoon. His stepfather was outside in front of the restaurant when two robbers robbed him and stabbed him. Eddie ran outside to see the robbers run away and watched his beloved stepfather take his final breaths. Mrs. Stevens had finally found peace in life and this had to happen. Eddie and I would remain close friends for the remainder of his life. He became a coach for a local women's softball team and became a fixture in the league. Women would tell me what a great coach and what a special person he was and I would tell them I have known him since we were children. Eddie loved softball, the water and outdoors, and life. I think he must have had a lot of his father in him. He was a man who gave more than he took and he was a real friend. I saw Eddie fairly often. He would drop into my store whenever he needed hardware or had a project going. He always had that same laugh and smile he had as a boy. You never put restrictions or limits on friendships. The people who really got to know Eddie Stevens never thought about his size or his education. They soon learned they had met someone who really cared about nature and his fellow man. Eddie's life was never a bed of roses, but he always did the best he could. He lost his father as a child and his daughter drowned when she was a baby. His stepfather suffered a brutal death, but Eddie never gave up on the world or life. Eddie passed away several years ago from pneumonia. People from all walks of life attended the funeral. Many women that played softball for him over the years attended his funeral as did many young people.

I bumped into Mrs. Stevens in a grocery store a few months after Eddie passed. She called me "son" and hugged me. We talked about Eddie and remembered the good times. I felt very sorrow for Eddie's mom after I left. I remembered all her heart aches and losing her only child so young. She passed away in the coming months. I remembered many happy times with my friend Eddie. I remember riding down High Street in Portsmouth with all the colorful lights at night and the old missile with the waterfall at the end of the street. I remember the pool halls and the burger joints. Most of all I remember my friend, a big guy with a very big heart. Big Bill Stevens would have been very proud of his son.

Chapter 10

Gordon and Virginia (Red and Goo)

I stated earlier that my parents were opposites and they were definitely not Ward and June Cleaver from the old "Leave It To Beaver" television show. They were two products of the Great Depression and they were two people from very different environments. Gordon Culberth Parker was born on March 21, 1925 in Ahoskie, North Carolina. Virginia Myrtle Arthur was born in the village of Driver, Virginia on February 4, 1927. The pair would cross paths many times throughout their childhoods and would marry on February 8, 1948. A major snow storm blasted the area on their wedding day. Gordon Parker was born with bright red hair and he naturally acQuired the nickname "Red." My grandmother and Aunt Dot are the only two people who ever called him Gordon. The name "Red" fit because he was everything you expected a kid with bright red hair to be. My father grew up in Driver and Port Norfolk and he always worked part time jobs as a kid. He worked for a company (Kershaw) in Driver that grew orchids and shipped them all over the country. He picked flowers in the fields. He worked for Mr. Gleason at Gleason's Drug Store in Port Norfolk when the family left Driver for Port Norfolk. He delivered prescriptions and cleaned the store. Throughout his life he referred to Mr. Gleason as "Shinny face Gleason". My father worked other jobs in Port Norfolk such as a livery stable attendant, Culpepper's Boat Rentals, shoe shine boy, paper boy, and various other jobs. He was not lazy and he was always looking for a "hustle." Red Parker got into his share of mischief as a boy, and he truly loved to fight. His idols were professional boxers because many of them had fought their way out of misery or poverty. He spent his hard earned money at the movie theaters on Saturdays watching Lash La Rue and other cowboys, and he marveled at the sports shorts with fighters like Jack Dempsey. My father was a very outgoing person his entire life and he became a "ladies man" early on. He was not shy and he never worried about "status" or money when women were involved. He was very interested in having a good time, and he could easily turn on the charm when necessary. Red Parker was just as popular with the men as he was the ladies. Other boys (and later men) saw him as someone who was always willing to take a chance and as someone who was self made. He was loyal to his friends and was with them when they needed him. He was ready to lead and had that never Quit attitude. I can truthfully say that my father had many close friends throughout his life. Since his childhood, others wanted to be his friend and follow him and to especially "know" him. I am not exaggerating when I say others followed him like men followed Davy Crockett and I have often heard him referred to as a modern day Davy Crockett. He was real, but he was also part legend. Friends were a very important part of his life and they defined who he was.

Virginia (Ginny) Arthur was a very popular girl in Driver. She was pretty, intelligent, hard working, did well in school, and was always under the watchful eye of Irvin T. Arthur. Ginny always had a set of rules to live by and standards to maintain. She was expected to attend college and play the piano well. Work and studies left little time for mischief or adventure. Ginny Arthur was every bit as popular with the boys as "Red" Parker was with the girls. She dated fellow that became engineers, successful businessmen, educators, and others who had high goals in life. Ginny also had close friends, but she was too busy to lead an "army'. Virginia graduated from Chuckatuck High School and went off to Meredith College in Raleigh, N.C. "Red" left school in the tenth grade when his brother-in-law, Vernon Mayberry, was killed when a German U-Boat sank his ship, the U.S.S. Rowan. He joined the Merchant Marines and spent the remainder of the war transporting supplies to our military and allies. I am a "baby boomer" and I am the product of a very uniQue marriage. There were more ups and downs in my parent's marriage than there were at the old roller coaster ride at Ocean View Amusement Part in Norfolk, Virginia. I guess their marriage was a lot like that ride because there was great difficulty in destroying that old roller coaster. A movie titled "The Death of Ocean View Park" was made in the 1970's in Norfolk. David Jansen starred in the film and the crew had a very difficult time "blowing up" the old coaster for the end of movie. There were countless difficulties and explosions in my parents marriage, but everyone survived. I have already recounted many instances and feelings I had growing up, and I admitted there were many times I hated my father and did not care what happened to him. I did not always understand the things my mother did either and I spent many hours wondering if one party was totally guilty or was it a joint venture. I realized later in life that things were much deeper than I thought as a child and both parties were responsible. As my father always said," It takes two to tango." I will recount a painful incident between my father and me that defined the influence of alcohol on my father. First, I will list a few things that culminated on that night. I was accustomed to hearing stories of my father's episodes or behavior and it sometimes affected me directly. My final year in little league when my hitting fell off because I needed glasses was one case. Our team had practice Tuesday morning and as usual my father had spent the previous night partying with his buddies. The back of his pickup was littered with beer cans and many of my teammates were joking about the cans. My father was pitching batting practice and he started yelling at me when I missed the balls he threw. Our other coach, Bill Cobb, told my father something was wrong and not to be so hard on me. My father yelled at me again and I yelled back that he was a drunk and did not know anything about baseball and I dropped the bat and ran home. I needed glasses, but I needed encouragement not criticism.

Once in high school, a fellow approached our table in the cafeteria and told me and my friends that he had seen my father at a local store. He said my father was drunk and was trying to tell them what to do. The boy said I better speak to my father before he would be forced to kick his but. Sure: Dream on: The sad thing is that this fellow is a full blown alcoholic and sits in front of grocery stores begging for money.

Another instance involved a girl I had known since the second grade. I had called her the previous night and asked her out. She said yes and everything seemed fine. We talked a good while and we were both excited. The next morning the girl came to my locker and said, "I can't go out with you." She looked like she wanted to cry and turned and walked away. I did not understand and I felt terrible. One of my friends overheard some of our classmates talking and they said the girl's father would not let her date me because of my father. I had forgotten that my father had painted their house a few years earlier and he probably knew about my father's "partying." I still hurt and felt bad because I was not being judged on my own merits. There were countless occasions like the ones mentioned. I had had a young life time of broken promises and let downs. I grew to not expect anything different and thought neither parent cared what happened to me. I had clothed myself and bought my lunch at school with my money I earned at my grandfather's store. I had done this since I was thirteen and I felt like I didn't need my parents, I needed my friends. All of my hidden anger came out one night when I was about twenty-one years old. My mother had befriended the single Methodist Minister who lived in the parsonage across the street. The minister had been raised by his grandmother because his mother was in an institution and he looked on my mother as a mother-figure. We kids all liked the minister and he became a close family friend. Mae and Bob did not visit much at that time and my mother needed a new friend. My father turned his anger and blame to the minister since Mae and Bob were no longer around to blame.

The minister was at our house one night when my father came home early. My father told the minister he was going to beat him and I stepped in. I told my father he would have to beat me first. The preacher was only about 3 years older than me, but he was no match for my father. My mother told the minister to go home and he did. My father told me I had made a terrible mistake siding with the preacher and he pushed me. He said he wanted me to go in the yard with him and he would make a man out of me. I told him I was ready. All of my feelings exploded that night and I told him to swing at me first and he did. I had never hyperventilated before, but I guess I did that night because I found strength that night I had never had. My breathing was heavy, but I felt powerful and I knocked him to the ground. I beat him in the face as I sat on his chest. I told my father I would kill him if he ever came home and laid a hand on anyone again. He promised he would stop and I let him up. It seemed like an hour before I was normal again and I had mixed feelings about the fight. I was no longer afraid of my father, but I did not want to be fighting him all the time either. I never had to fight my father again. He never laid a hand on me again and a few weeks later he told me the same thing had happened to him and his father. That old monster I spoke of earlier. Learned Behavior. When I talk about my relationship with my mother, I need to take in consideration the fact that I was thirteen years older than my twin sisters (Holly and Sherri). I was four years older than my brother, Gregory, and I was working at my grandfather's store when the twins were babies. Gregory was nine and he was a big help with my sisters. Due to many circumstances, my mother had a much different relationship with my brother than she did with me and as I mentioned earlier, I think most of it involved her mother (Nanie). Gregory was very young when our grandmother passed and my mother had the early years raising him alone without Nanie's help or "interference." I was not home as much because I was either going to school or working. I was very competitive when I was young and I liked sports. My brother had to deal with my passion for winning and I was tough on him in baseball and football. I felt guilty for a long time, but I guess competition is always present between brother and sisters. He was like my mother and he is a natural on keyboards and other musical instruments. Being compared to my father every time I did something wrong was bad enough, but my mother had another saying that stung just as bad. Every time she did something nice for my brother she would tell me, "I know you always think Gregory is my favorite, but that's not true." Moma, this is not the Smother's Brothers act and a big joke, but why do you need to bring this up. I was old enough to know parents have favorites, but bringing it up only makes it worse. My father may not have gone to Meredith College, but he never said things like that. I knew I was my father's favorite, but he and I never had to discuss it or make comments about it. He never told Gregory, "I know you think Craig's my favorite, but that's not true." Actually my Sister Sherri was my father's second favorite and I always knew it. The thing that hurt was when friends or aQuaintances would tell me, "You sure can tell who's your mother's favorite; it's all she talks about." You begin to suck it up and say "so what" to yourself and go on. I know many parents have favorites, but please don't let the kids know this. Maybe it's because it was the first child, the child looks and acts like one parent, the child has more initiative or drive, or the child seems to not be so attached to the grandparents, or any other reason. Kids are a lot like dogs in the sense they can often intuitively know things. I know my mother loved all four kids and I never Questioned that fact. Her relationship with my sisters was different. Sherri was always headstrong and my mother and her argued constantly. Holly was very needy and followed My mother everywhere she went. Holly was definitely my mother's second favorite. My sister Sherri

107

was killed in a hit and run accident several years ago and I will discuss this later. My mother would often bring up the fact that everybody thought Gregory and Holly were her favorites, but it was really Sherri. I wanted to tell my mother this was not true and Sherri was headstrong and argued with her the night before she was killed. This was guilt talking and it was not fair to Holly. Parents don't have to say things like this to kids. I said earlier that kids did not ask for this so don't make family life a competition for affection. Kids will eventually see things for themselves in due time and it probably won't bother them. Parents should not be partial or make partiality. They need to put themselves in the child's place and wonder how they would feel if it was them. Everyone is affected by learned behavior. My mother was like my grandfather Arthur in the fact she always needed to be in control. She wanted to control her children much the same way my grandfather had controlled her and my two uncles. My brother, two sisters and I never considered moving to another part of the country. We were all accustomed to controls enforced by my grandfather and our mother. Naturally, my mother had to approve of our friends and she did approve of most of them. She even approved of my father's friends except for a few exceptions. She would often bring up the names of the two fellows and tell my father how the two were bringing him down. To an extent she was doing the same thing my father's mother (Bye Bye) was doing. She was telling my father he would not be the way he was if he were not friends with these fellows. Her nagging did not affect my father because it usually went in one ear and out the other. He was loyal to his friends to a fault. My mother had much less control over Sherri and me than she did Gregory and Holly. I was usually working, playing ball, or simply away from home and Sherri was simply a rebel. Sherri constantly butted heads with my mother and she was the only person who could control my grandfather instead of being controlled by him. She nicknamed him "Spunky" and she was the only person who ever called him that.

I think my grandfather liked my sister Sherri so much for the same reasons he really liked my father. Sherri was a leader and she would not be pushed around by anyone. She would take chances in life and she stood by her friends. Life was an adventure for Sherri and she did more and accomplished more in her thirty year life than many could if they lived to be one-hundred years old. Sherri once pointed one of my father's double barreled shot guns at him one night when he and my mother were arguing during one of his drunken stoopers. I had married and moved out of my parent's house, but Sherri was there to defend the family if necessary. She told my father she would shoot him if he hurt anyone and she meant it. I will divulge an incident with my mother that illustrates her need to control. I was working in the nuclear section of Norfolk Naval Shipyard in 1975 on second shift (4:00 pm till midnight). I called in for leave one Friday night and was granted leave. I had been on second shift for some time and had plenty of leave built up. Anyone who has ever worked second shift knows you have no social life except on weekends. I had run into my old friend Tommy Knowles and another long time friend named Bobby Harrell. I invited my two friends to come over and I called in for leave.   The three of us were each having a beer and were watching television. My mother charged into my house and said "You're not going to do those people that way (the Navy Yard). You should be at work instead of drinking with your friends. You're going to wind up just like your father." Tommy, Bobby, and I just sat there in amazement as my mother slammed the door and stormed out of my house. I was twenty-six years old, had been married for five years, was the father of a three year old daughter, had plenty of leave and never been in any kind of trouble at any job, had been working since I was thirteen years old, paid every bill I owed and owned my own house, and my mother still thinks I will wind up like my father. She jumped to conclusions because she saw Bobby's and Tommy's cars in my yard and never bothered to find out if I had leave. My mother did not even give me the chance to explain the situation. I had been embarrassed many times by my father, but this instance took the cake. No one was drunk and I was an adult. My mother was the only one acting like a child and I was very angry. I guess she was taking her frustrations with my father out on me. There would be other "spells" in the coming years, but the relationship between my mother and me began to change in the coming years. My father stopped drinking in 1979 and that brought great change for our whole family. Holly and Sherri were sixteen at the time and was working a lot of overtime in the Radiological Control Department at Norfolk Naval Shipyard. Red Parker did not Quit drinking without going down swinging and I mean this figuratively as well as literally. The incident took place a few days before Thanksgiving 1979. His final physical battle would attract much attention. My father had left the Driver Variety Store (one of my grandfather's stores that my father and mother were operating) and left for Portsmouth to do some partying. He partied too much and a Portsmouth Police officer spotted his erratic driving and pursued him. The Portsmouth Police Department notified the Chesapeake Police Department that a drunk driver was headed in their direction. A Chesapeake Police officer stopped my father and my father got into an altercation with the officer and hit him and escaped. The Chesapeake Police Department now notified the Suffolk Police Department about the drunk driver and the assault on the police officer. Red Parker now had the Portsmouth, Chesapeake, Suffolk Police and a police hellicopter pursuing him. The "Raging Bull" was finally captured and jailed. Such an incident today would probably be aired live on local television. A long time friend of my father named Howard Satterfield lived near the scene of the "capture" and he hurried to the Driver Variety Store to tell my mother what had happened. Word of the incident spread Quickly and my mother decided the best thing to do was to let the law handle my father. No expensive lawyer was going to get him out of this jam (hitting an officer). None of my uncles or relatives bailed my father out this time and he spent Thanksgiving in jail. We had a Quiet Thanksgiving dinner at my mother's without my father. We all were thankful that no one was seriously hurt, but none of us realized this was the final "episode" for our father. My father attended ASAP, Alcoholics Annonomous, and lost his driver's license. He Quit drinking and did not touch alcohol for the remainder of his life (nearly 30 years). Red Parker became a crusader against alcohol and he would tell anyone who would listen how alcohol had hurt his family and marriage, not to mention all the time and money he had wasted drinking. Anyone who has lived with an alcoholic or been raised by one knows that healing is a slow process. Emotional, Mental, and sometimes physical scars take time to heal. Trust and respect have to be earned, but like with most things in life time can heal a lot of old wounds. My mother had stuck with my father through thick and think or for better or for worse. She came up with her own slogan and used it the remainder of her life. She said, "The first thirty years were his, the next thirty "are mine." The thing that amazes me most about life is how much things begin to even out as you get older. I think more about life in general when I think about my parents. Time allowed things to change and allowed my parents to be in love again. I also realize that everyone is not so fortunate and no amount of time can heal all spouse abuse, child abuse, physical, or mental abuse. Life can be very complicated. Time allows us to run and play as children, but also allows most of us time to remember and reflect on our lives when we are old. Life can be tough enough without someone else making another's life more miserable. Most of us want to reflect on our lives when we are old and remember more good than bad. I grew up in an era where men and women were expected to stick things out, but times are very different. Usually both parents work and that increases pressure at home and work. Many children grow up with absentee parents and have very little direction in their lives. We may work many hours and we may be stressed out, but there is always time to encourage our kids. Tell them you are proud of them, tell them they are smart and can do anything in life they want to, tell them you love them. Like I said kids are smarter than we think. The great John Lennon said, "All I'm saying is give peace a chance." I'm saying give kids a chance and we may have peace one day. Further into this writing you may understand why I ramble. I think part of this is the fact that as a parent I did not want to make some of the mistakes my parents made. I could tell my daughter I loved her and she knew it. My mother and I began to understand each other more as time went on. My grandfather passed in 1988 and she had more free time. I had left Norfolk Naval Shipyard in 1986 and my father and I were operating the Driver Variety Store together. I left a great job after my mother talked to my brother Gregory and me about the stores. I worked for a great guy and good friend named Bill Pruitt who encouraged me to give the store business a try and I thought about switching careers for a month. I failed to make the money I did at Norfolk Naval Shipyard, but I believe many things in life are done for reasons we don't understand at the time. I spent more time with my daughter, my father, my mother, and others than would have been possible if I had remained at the Shipyard. My parents may have had their faults and I am certain many thought we were a dysfunctional family, but through it all we were a family and that's important. We four kids may have sQuabbled at times, but none of us ever truly hated or disliked each other. I have seen brothers and sisters that don't speak or socialize with each other.

I bought my parents a 27" RCA color television in the early 1970's and I did it because I needed to, not because I was a good person. My mother had never had color tv and things were financially tough for my parents and twin sisters at the time. I wanted my two sisters to be able to watch the "Partridge Family" and "The Brady Bunch" in color like other kids. I mentioned before that my mother was a very generous person. Soon after my grandfather's estate was settled, she had a company install a central heating and air system in each child's house. None of us could afford to do that at the time and it was money my mother could have spent on herself. I guess learned behavior is not all bad. My mother stuck by me through two marriages and other hard times. I began to realize even more that parents always suffer each time one of their children suffer. I was hung up on one girl in high school. The girl went to another school and she always confused me. My mother eventually explained to me that the girl's parents did not want her to get serious with me because she was Catholic and I was not. Thank God things have changed. My mother and I would go out for lunch about once a week as time went by. She also called me to take her different places like the grocery store, DMV, Dentist office, shopping, etc. She knew my father could operate the Variety Sore and it gave us time to talk. I am so glad my mother and I began to spend so much time together. It's as though we made up for all the time she was busy raising the family or I was busy working or whatever. We talked more openly than we had my entire life and we really enjoyed being around each other. We understand each other and I found out that it's really never too late to make things better. My mother spent a great deal of time in hospitals her final ten years. She had always had medical problems, but the problems seemed to accelerate after my sister Sherri's death in 1993. Her death devastated my parents and I witnessed the toll it took on my parents physically and emotionally. My daughter died from cancer in 1995 and I will discuss Heather and Sherri later. Heather's passing also took a toll on my parents and she was their first grandchild. The longtime saying that God never puts more on us than we can stand applies to my family because we surely have been tested.

It seems my mother always became severely ill each Christmas day or soon thereafter. It was as though she had to make it untill Christmas the final years, but Sherri's and Heather's passing had a definite effect on Christmas. A time of joy and cheer became a time of worry and fear each year. My mother came close to passing on many Christmas seasons. My mother had bypass surgery, gall bladder surgery, colon cancer surgery, severe kidney problems and other medical problems in the final years. She spent the final five years of her life on Kidney dialysis, but she never Quit. She always said she was going to go as long as she could because a time was coming when she would not be able to go. My parents continued to go out with long-time friends for lunch or dinner like they had in previous years. I know it was hard on my mother, but she wanted to be with friends and enjoy what time she had left. I am fortunate I was close by in my mother's final months. My father would call me at 3:00 A M to help put my mother back in bed or I would have to find someone to watch the store so I could help with my mother. I was lucky to have good friends like Leroy Schmidt or Steven Jones that would help me with the Store. I mention the time I was needed because many people do the same thing and experience the same feelings I did when loved ones pass. You exit a world where someone needs you and depends on you and you enter a world where they are not part of your physical life any longer. I watched my Uncle Cecil take care of my Aunt Mildred for years and I watched my father take care of my mother for years. I experienced this with my own daughter, Heather and I know the loneliness that sets in when you lose someone. You would be glad to be able to continue to help them. My mother would recognize everyone most of the time a few days prior to her passing. She would sometimes slip into spells where she would talk about things and people long past. We had gotten used to these situations during her stays in the hospital. A few nights before my mother passed she looked at my brother and made a reQuest. It seemed like she was talking to my grandfather. She asked my brother to please take care of her children. She knew her time was near, but she wanted to make sure her children (Holly and I) were taken care of. My mother did not live to see her 76th Christmas and she passed on Monday morning, December 1, 2003. She passed away forty years after the birth of Holly and Sherri, thirty years after my daughter, Heather's birth, fifteen years after my grandfather's death, and ten years after Sherri's death. I can't leave my mother without mentioning her love of humming birds and her relationship with the tiny birds. Her love for the beautiful creatures began on the morning of July 28, 1993 which was the morning after the death of my sister Sherri. My mother was looking out the kitchen window when she spotted a hummingbird that fluttered outside window. It seemed to her that the tiny messenger was letting her know that Sherri was all right and she was now at peace. My mother sent my father to Jake's Feed and Seed Store in Driver to purchase a hummingbird feeder and some food. My father installed the feeder on the outside of the window and my mother's new friend showed up every morning to cheer her up. The little bird showed up every day until it was time to fly south, but he showed up every Spring to visit my mother. I think she found more comfort in the hummingbird than any words or other earthly things could. The 1970's song "Humming Bird Don't Fly Away" by Seals and Croft took on more meaning to me. A little bird brought so much peace. Family members and friends gave my mother "Humming Bird" gifts after this instance on her birthday or hollidays. My mother received humming bird necklaces, statues, books, ear rings, blouses, sweatshirts, dishes, and many other items. My daughter Heather passed away on the late afternoon of May 16, 1995. My daughter's passing would bring my mother a new messenger and friend.

My mother was washing dishes on the morning of May 17, 1995 when she spotted her little humming bird outside the window at the feeder. The messenger had brought another humming bird with him.

My mother yelled for us to come to the kitchen window and we all huddled at the window in amazement. My mother took this as a sign that Heather had joined Sherri and both were now at peace. I will divulge more information when I discuss Heather later. The two tiny birds visited my mother her remaining years and they were both a source of comfort for her. Family members have not seen humming birds at the kitchen window since my mother's passing but some of us have seen them at places that were special to my mother and us. I know most people identify with some of the things their loved ones cared about or liked during their time here. My mother also liked snow and Gregory, Holly, and I get excited each time we hear that we might get snow in the area. We see snow as a cleansing, white blanket that purifies the earth and brings hope. We simply think of our mother. My father was a changed man after attending ASAP and AA Meetings, but I did have some good times with him before and after the change. I think I can identify with Mickey Mantle's kids because Mickey spent more time with his team mates and Soldiers than he spent with his own children. I knew how it felt to resent your father, but a lot of times I wanted to be with him. The best times I had with my father were the times when he and I were alone. I remember helping him on the fuel oil truck when I was young and how he taught me to fill the tanks and talk to the customers. He may have gone back to Driver to let me off before he turned the truck in, but I was glad to spend the day with him. Times like that were the times I hoped he and others were safe when he partied those nights. My mother would also make sure I went with my father to retrieve or look for his hunting dogs that wandered off during a hunting trip. I remember riding down old country roads with one lane bridges during the fall and winter

116

months. My father would tell me how old the bridges were or how old the farm houses were. "Daddy" and I both found peace in the Quiet Woods with the multi colored leaves and fresh clean air. The scent of pine or cedar filled the air. My father's pick-up once broke down in "The Great Dismal Swamp." My father, Bobby Cooper, and I were searching for dogs on that beautiful fall Sunday morning. We came upon a couple of fellows that were actually swimming in the canal in the swamp that day. We also saw an abandoned vintage milk truck in the swamp. It was warm on that early fall day so water moccasins were also swimming in the canal. The sights and sounds of that day are things I will never forget and I was never worried because I was with my father and I had never seen him afraid of anything. The birds, deer, rabbits, Eagles, raccoons, foxes, and other animals were our hosts that day. We also saw old cabins, old cars, deer stands, old posters, and other interesting sights. We must have had similar feelings that the great Virginian, George Washington, experienced on his first trip to the swamp. Our first president engineered the digging of the great canal on the Dismal Swamp. The three of us eventually came upon a fellow with a truck in the swamp and he carried us back to my father's truck. The fellow worked on the truck a little and jumped it. The truck started and we were on our way home. Bobby Cooper and I were full of new stories to tell our friends at school the next day. I have had more experience dealing with tragedy and death than I would have ever imagined, but I found out that one old saying is absolutely true. You should always remember the good times you shared with a friend or loved one. I am a lucky mortal because the good has always outweighed the bad and the good memories keep me going. My father was a loving, caring husband the last several years of his life. He spent countless hours and nights at local hospitals with my mother. He would occasionally peep into other rooms to see if someone he knew was in the hospital. Amazingly, he often came across someone he knew and would visit with them for a while. My father and mother were also great with elderly and handicapped people. Mom would prepare enough food for a few Shut-ins and holidays or Sundays. "Daddy" would take the meals to the people when we finished our meal. We always had one or two guests for Thanksgiving or Christmas dinner. They were people who did not have local loved ones or family. My parents welcomed them to our home. I really believed that my father would live at least five or six years after my mother passed. "Daddy" passed away on October 8, 2004. He lived ten months after her passing and he was seventy-nine years old. I spent more time with my father than I ever had before during the last ten months of his life. My wife and I took him out to eat a couple of times a week and he was at the store with me every day. We had breakfast together every Sunday morning. My father would really miss my mother most during the evening hours. He would often call me about 10:00 PM or even later and ask me if I wanted to watch t.v. with him. I would tell him I had to get up at 4:00 AM and had to go to bed, but I would see him in the morning. My father did not show up at the store by 10:00 A.M. that Saturday and I knew something was wrong. I called his house several times, but no one answered the phone. A neighbor came into the store about 11:00 A M and I told him I needed to check on my father and he said he would be glad to watch the store. I entered the house and went from room to room and called out for my father. I felt better when I did not find him in one of the bedrooms and thought he might be out in the back yard. I spotted him in the bathroom from the corner of my eye as I passed by. My heart sunk as my fear became reality. My father was gone. My parents marriage may not have been the traditional love story, but it was a love story none the less. The two did love each other through the good times and bad times and most importantly they became "best" friends again. Things somehow evened out and my father grieved himself to death over my mother. How much more can a spouse or anyone else ask for?

I miss my father every day, but the thing I miss more than anything else is having him around to tell me what to do all the time. I said before that you never grow too old for your parents to stop treating you like you are twelve years old. I always think of my father each time I tighten a screw or bolt and nut. I can hear him saying "don't tighten it too much and strip the threads." I laugh to myself and say to myself "I'm going to do it my way and take my chances." Mickey Mantle is remembered on his marker at Yankee Stadium as "a good team mate." I truly wanted the expression "I'll be right back" added to my father's grave marker, but my sister and brother didn't like the idea. I know any friend or person that knew him would have laughed to themselves if that phrase was on the marker and they saw it. They knew that phrase really applied to him.

Chapter 11
My Sister, Sherri

Today, July 27, 2009/Monday, is a very tough day. My sister, Sherri, was killed in a hit and run accident on this date in 1993. I have been writing and am trying to stay busy. I have learned that staying busy helps on days like today and it's something I have always preached to people who are grieving. A funny thing happened a few minutes ago. Sherri's twin, Holly, called me to find out how I was doing today. Experience has also taught her that things go better on such days if you stay busy or talk to someone. Saturday night, my brother Gregory, friends Ronnie (father) and Jason Gould (son), and Jason's friend Chris attended the Bob Dylan, Willie Nelson, and John Mellencamp concert at Harbor Park (Triple A Baseball Stadium) in Norfolk. My sister Sherri encouraged me to listen to John Mellencamp years ago. Naturally I already liked his music, but I became a big fan after taking my sister's advice. The other four fellows could not get over how great John Mellencamp sounded, even though I have preached this to them for years. Now everyone wants to borrow my Mellencamp CD'S and John now has four new fans. I think of my sister Sherri, every time I hear the song "Cherry Bomb" and Mellencamp did a solo acoustic version Saturday night. It was fitting and maybe even in the stars that he did the song another way. Sunday (the day after the concert) I turned the television on and there was John Mellencamp and his band doing a 2007 concert at Walter Reed Army Hospital. The concert fans were military personnel who had suffered injuries and their families. Mellencamp danced with injured female service women and at times he and band members were emotional during the concert. I know John lifted the Spirits of these service members. After the taped concert, I began searching for one of John's CD's when I accidentally came across a Gino Vanelli CD. I bought the CD a few days after my daughter, Heather, passed and I always think of my sister Holly when I hear two of his songs. Holly had another incoming call and I went to the kitchen to get some soda before she called me back. The Gino Vanelli song "I Just Wanna Stop" was playing on the radio in the kitchen. It is a song that reminds me of Holly and Heather. The song ended and Holly called me back. Sometimes I might be stretching, but death has taught me that just as in life, little things are important during emotional or trying times. Our loved ones may not be able to be with us physically, but they let us know in little ways that they are always near us and think of us. They also have things to do and cannot spend every waning moment with us, but they let us know they are always with us. Tonight I will do the same thing I do the anniversary of Sherri's passing. I will put on a John Mellencamp CD and will listen to "Cherry Bomb." Sherri will know this and she also knows that I appreciate her turning me on to John Mellencamp. Thanks Sherri and Thanks John Mellencamp and Keep on Rocking.

Chapter 12
My Father and His Friends

I return to thoughts of my father. I try to live by his sayings like "one day at a time", "you know two wrongs don't make a right", "someday we'll all be old", "a man has to have good shoes", "nothing in life is really free", "we're never too old to learn new tricks", and "everyday above ground is a good day." My father did not have a PHD, but he could figure most things out and many people have told me that his philosophy really was "one day at a time", and many applied that thought to their own lives. None of us can change what happened yesterday, but we can change today and tomorrow. Old Yankee team mates say that Mickey Mantle became your friend for life when he became your friend. Red Parker was like Mickey in this regard because his friends remained his friends throughout life. It did not matter if these people were people of influence or people struggling through life. My father's friends were very important to him and he really cared about them and their families. I feel fortunate to have known these men and their families, and I understand why my father and each one of them were friends. My father's viewing was a very sobering experience for me. So many of his friends and acQuaintenances attended the viewing that my brother, sister, and I greeted people for an additional hour and a half beyond the alloted time. The lines were long and sad faces gazed on my father's coffin. I'm sure many people had shared my personal thoughts and assumed Red Parker had at least a half dozen years left in his life. I nearly lost control of my emotions during the viewing when Blackie (Walter) Blackburn stood at my father's casket. Blackie and my father were like brothers and they were life-long friends. The two may have been separated from each other during W.W. II, but they spent a lot of time together the remainder of their lives. They worked together, they hunted together, they played cards, they celebrated together and they suffered together. Like a solid elderly couple; they stuck together. For some reason the two men often called each other "hugmire" instead of using Red or Blackie. It must have been an expression they conjured up years ago and each man never explained to other people what the word really meant. Each man would only smile and never let another person enter that world of "hugmire."

I knew the word was very sacred when Blackie extended his feeble right hand to grab my father's right wrist and said "Hugmire, don't worry I'll be with you soon." Blackie was very prophetic that night because he passed away the Saturday after Thanksgiving which was five weeks after my father's passing. They both passed on a Saturday. Blackie had served in the Marine Corps during W.W. II and he was one of the first marines dispatched to Hiroshima shortly after the bombing. He never talked about the horrific sights he witnessed, but he suffered many physical setbacks following the war. My father always thought Blackie's health problems were related to his service in Japan. I will leave the memory of my father with a listing and short description of my father's closest friends. I am sorry if I fail to mention every friend and family member.

Shelton Bright

Bright or "Bones" as my father called him had been my father's close friend since the two met as boys in Port Norfolk during the Depression. The pair would hop freight trains to Utahville, South Carolina to visit some of my father's relatives during the Summer months. Shelton joined the Merchant Marines after high school graduation and served on many ships with my father. He entered the Army and served in Korea during that war. "Bones" was wounded in Korea. He has a daughter and is still very active and stops by to see me and chat fairly often.

Clayton Jensen

Clayton also grew up in Port Norfolk and had been a friend since childhood. Clayton was about nine years older than my father, but he was someone my father always appreciated and looked up to. Clayton was captured by Rommel soldiers during the North African campaign of W.W. II and he spent 3 ½ years as a P.O.W. in Italy and Germany. He met a fellow named Kenneth Harrell at Norfolk Naval Shipyard after the war. Kenneth was a upper turret gunner on a B-17 and his crew flew 27 missions over Germany. The two men (heroes) visit me nearly every Tuesday morning. My mother always told me Clayton was one of the finest men she knew. Clayton has a wife and a son, Clayton, Jr.

Walter (Blackie) Blackburn

I have already talked about Blackie as my father's friend, but I need to mention that he was married to Mary until his passing and the couple had two daughters, Ginger and Robin. Ginger is about one year older than me and we have been life-long friends. The Parker family and Blackburn families were always intertwined. Mary passed away about a year ago and I think of her and my mother often. The two always enjoyed being together.

Bud Yost (Basil Otto Yost)

Bud and my father were also lifelong friends. He was born in West Virginia and the two became friends after his family moved to Portsmouth. Bud was tall (6 feet 5 inches) and was a very good basketball player. He was a very Quiet but articulate man and was a fine gentleman. Bud was a dentist and served on the Virginia Dental Association in Richmond during his final career years. My

124

mother and many of the other wives would talk about how handsome Dr. Yost was and what a gentleman he was. Bud's wife, June, was highly intelligent and she actually returned to college after raising four children. I was in one class with June and she maintained a 4.0 GPA in college. The happy couple had four children: Sharon, Buddy, Betsy, and Sussy. Bud was a Purple Heart recipient. The Yost children are all very intelligent and have all done well in life. Bud passed away several years ago and he is missed by everyone who knew him.

George Cooper

I wrote about George earlier and I mentioned his four sons, Billy, Bobby, Jerry, and Gene. George's wife, Amy, passed several years ago and she too is greatly missed by everyone who knew her. Amy was one of the kindest and sincere people I ever met. My father and George's friendship began in 1945 when the two young men sat next to each other on a bus leaving New Orleans at the end of W.W. II. The two were headed home from the war and began talking about home. George had been stationed in New Orleans with the Navy and he mentioned that he was returning to Suffolk, Va. where his wife was staying with relatives. My father told George that he knew all about Suffolk because he once lived in nearby Driver but his family was now living in Portsmouth. George told me years ago that the two were broke and hungry, but a lady on a seat in front of them passed them a basket of fried chicken. The two happily ate their chicken on the bus and formed a friendship that lasted the remainder of my father's life. George retired as a magistrate for the City of Portsmouth and I see him and some of the boys occasionally. George always tells me about some of his and my father's hunting trips or other experiences.

Norman Jenkins

I believe my father met Norman after W.W. II. Norman was a character and he always reminded me of Dizzy Dean. Many hunting stories involved Norman Jenkins and he worked part time with my father and he often helped my father with painting jobs and other side jobs. He was married to Katherine and the couple had one daughter named Chrissie. Norman passed several years ago and Katherine passed a few years ago.

Charlie Crafford

Charlie was a boyhood friend of my father and both men served in the Merchant Marines. Charlie retired from the Merchant Marines. He is married to (blank) whom he met in Germany. The couple has one son and one daughter. Charlie loved to play cards and gamble and he, my father, Shelton Bright, and Walter Butterton made many trips to Atlantic City together. The four men served in the Merchant Marines together. Charlie is still living and I see him Quite often.

Walter Butterton

Walter was also a boyhood friend and he and my father remained close friends. Walter was a good businessman and he owned several properties. He and his wife, Jackie, had three children, Cynthia (my wife), Theressa, and Grey. Walter battled cancer and suffered greatly but never Quit visiting my father and other friends. He was neat and always dressed well. Walter passed several years ago.

Buddy Creekmore

My father befriended Buddy when he was a young boy who hung around my father's gas station in Portsmouth. Buddy looked up to my father and my father took him on hunting trips. Both of Buddy's parents passed when he was young and Buddy was responsible for raising his brothers and sisters. My father greatly admired Buddy and the young man always lived up to his expectations. Buddy married Sharon and the two are a rock-solid couple. They have children of their own, but they have also raised many foster children. Buddy has been very successful with his gyro company, but more importantly he and Sharon have been great role models.

Willie Harris

My father got to know Willie when he and Willie worked together at Diversified Electronics in the mid 1960's. Willie worked his way through Old Dominion University and later worked for a tax firm. Willie met Buddy Creekmore on some of those early hunting trips and the two have remained life-long friends. Willie was the CPA for my parents, my brother, my sister, myself, and Buddy Creekmore. Naturally, I always see Willie each year at tax time.

Don Sumner

I know Don and my father probably go back to the 1950's as friends. Don also worked at Diversified Electronics and he eventually moved to Jacksonville, Fla and started their own company. The pair would visit my parents each time they were in our area and they still reside in Florida.

Ed Lewis

My father and Bright went to work for Ed in the mid 1960's. Ed was originally from Alabama and was a former naval officer. He founded Diversified Electronics and was a very innovative and motivated individual. I worked for Ed some while in high school and college. I admired him greatly because he always stood up for what he believed was right and he adored his wife Nell and their two children. Ed would argue with naval officers or politicians if he knew (which he normally did) what was best for the tax payer. Ed took Nell's passing very hard and he seemed to lose some of his passion for life. He too passed and I miss him terribly. With Ed, all things were possible with creative thinking and hard work. I considered him a genious.

Jimmy Carraway

My father met Jimmy at the end of the war and the two were very close. Jimmy was a great carpenter and he built my parents house in Driver in 1957. He was a little older than my father and my father always looked up to him. Jimmy, like my father, was a man's man and he worked hard when he worked and he played hard when he played. My mother thought a lot of Jimmy and his wife. The couple passed years ago.

Johnny Cruise

Johnny and my father also met after the war. Johnny was a handsome, dark-haired man with a great personality and he was always in great shape. He was a skilled brick mason and he bricked in our house in Driver and he later built a beautiful fireplace in our den. Johnny was a dare-devil, and he played football with my brother and me in our front yard during the time he built the fireplace. I heard years ago that Johnny had moved out west and he was a sheriff in a small town.

Mickey Villa

"Goldie" and my father met prior to the war. He hung out at my father's filling station for years and he still remembers many exciting times on that old corner.

My father once suffered food poisoning during the 1950's and Mick visited my gravely ill father many times. He told my mother to check under a lamp while leaving the hospital one night. He told my mother to use the gift for groceries, bills, or for whatever she needed it for. My mother found $500 under the lamp and she later returned it to Mickey. Mickey shaves his head and he could pass for Kojac. His parents were Serbians and he still talks about the "old country." He and his wife had two daughters and Mick is single and still grieving his wifes' passing.

Philmore Joyner and Harry Land

I mention these two men as a pair because their lives were inner-twined and they usually worked and socialized together. My father knew Philmore when the two were boys. Philmore was a local legend and star football player on the state champion teams of Wilson High School during the late 1930's. He was sought after by many college football powers, but the war broke out and Phil entered the Navy. He and Harry both worked for local beer distributors and knew each other for years. Philmore was close friends with Shotgun Brown, Ace Parker, and many other former football stars and coaches. Ace Parker played professional baseball and football during the same years and he is a member of the NFL Hall of Fame. Ace is considered the greatest athlete of all time from this area (Tidewater). Phil passed away about a year and a half ago and is still considered to be one of the State of Virginia's eleven greatest high school football players of all time. Philmore always carried an old autographed baseball card of the great "Dizzy" Dean in his wallet. Phil was responsible for the beer set up at the hotel that was sponsoring the Dizzy Dean gathering. He asked Dizzy if he would like a beer and Philmore told him he only had Miller products because he worked for the Miller distributor, and Old Diz declined the offer. Diz said he only drank Falstaff because the company sponsored his Saturday television ball games. Philmore left the hotel and went to a local bar down the street. He borrowed the Falstaff lever from a keg behind the bar and went back to the hotel. He Quickly removed the Miller lever and replaced it with the Falstaff lever. Phil found Dizzy Dean and told him he had ordered some Falstaff for him. Dizzy was greatly impressed with Philmore's actions and praised him for being so dedicated. Philmore showed Dizzy the Falstaff lever and proceeded to pour him a cold "Falstaff" draft. Old Diz took a big gulp and told Philmore how much he appreciated him ordering his Falstaff. Phil had made a new friend.

Harry Land

Naturally my father would become good friends with Harry because Harry worked for a beer distributor. Harry worked during the off season because he was a professional baseball player. He played in the Chicago Cubs organization and his future was very bright before the war. Harry played with the Los Angeles Angels at the old "Little Wrigley Field" for the Cubs and spent some time with the Cubs. Harry was a very good defensive catcher and he was also a good hitter. He served in the Army during the war and returned to baseball after the war. He later played with the local Portsmouth Cubs and was hit in the head with a pitch. Harry suffered vision problems, but he remained a very good player. He would later manage the Portsmouth Cubs and other minor league baseball clubs, Harry's son, Butch, also played professional baseball and played Triple A for the Pittsburgh Pirates. Harry played with and against many good ball players during his career. Joe DiMaggio, Chuck Connors (the RifleMan tv shows), Ryne Duren, Chuck Stobbs (from Norfolk, VA.), Gil Hodges, Yogi Berra, Gus Triandos, Vince and Dominic DiMaggio, Vern Stephens, Mel Parnell, Joe Black, Whitney Ford and Phil Rizzuto were some of the players Harry knew.

Dave Laughlin

Dave Laughlin worked with Harry and Philmore in the beer business for several years. Dave grew up in Chicago and got to know George (Papa Bear) Halas when Dave was playing youth football. The Bear's owner and coach would lend Dave and the other kids footballs and eQuipment for their games. He later became good friends with Dave Robinson who had been one of the great Green Bay Packer players under the great Vince Lombardi. Harry splits time between Florida and Portsmouth and he and Dave visit me almost weekly between the months of June and December. I think a lot of Harry and Dave and both of them have enlightened me with their stories about people and events from the past. I will talk more about other friends of my father in later pages, but I am very fortunate that many of my dad's friends became my friends as well. Like my father used to tell me "Son, you can never have too many friends." I have reached a point where my thoughts begin to run together. Do I recall close family members that have passed or do I recall close friends, some living and some deceased? I will recount some close friendships because without them, I doubt I could have faced some of the hardships I have had to deal with. Real friendships are much like strong marriages. The good times and good things are twice as good and the hard or sad times may be half as bad.

Chapter 13

"You Gotta Have Friends"

Thomas Rust

I met Thomas when we were second grade students at Driver Elementary School. Thomas had an older brother name Leftridge and an older sister named Patricia (Patsy). Parents, Jimmy and Myrtle Rust, rented a house from my grandfather. Jimmy and Myrtle were loving and protective parents. Mrs. Rust would walk the three children to school each morning. The family had moved to Driver from the city and Mrs. Rust wanted to make sure her children were always safe. I know the three children took some grief from other kids because of this, but I understood because my mother was also very protective. I must have heard the expression "Never take candy from a stranger" a million times during my childhood.

I recall an instance that made me respect Thomas even as a second grader. He was always very Quiet and respectful in the class room and never whispered or tried to draw attention to himself. He always sat up very straight in his desk and listened to the teacher. Thomas became nauseated one day in class and he vomited on his desk and floor. Mrs. Richards immediately rushed to his desk and poor Thomas assured her he would be all right. Mrs. Richards cleaned the desk and floor and told Thomas to sit in a vacant desk while she went to notify the principal, Mr. Phillips. She told the class to read while she was gone. Many classmates began to laugh shortly after the teacher left. I noticed Thomas had hung his head and was terribly embarrassed. The situation wasn't funny to me because it was easy for me to put myself in Thomas' place. I was not only the new kid in school; I was the son of a heavy drinker. I knew how it felt when kids laughed at you or called you names. I could have been the one who became nauseated and had to sit helplessly by as the teacher cleaned up the mess. My "city slicker" friends in good old Port Norfolk may have teased me later, but they would not have ridiculed me in such a situation. Mrs. Richards soon returned to the class room and told Thomas his mother would come soon to take him home. Mrs. Rust arrived and took Thomas home and naturally some kids said he was a moma's boy during our next break. Thomas returned to class a few days later and he proceeded as if nothing had ever happened. He let the "country bumkins" have their fun and he continued to be himself. I never have told him this, but his sickness was an important step for me in the second grade. I told myself if Thomas could handle such humiliation, - so could I. I wasn't the "Lone Ranger." Thomas and I were always cordial to each other, but we really solidified our friendship in the last two years of grammar school. Mrs. Rust eased up on Thomas a little and she allowed Thomas and his older brother Leftridge to come over one Saturday afternoon and shoot some basketball in our car port. My brother, Gregory, was four years younger than me and besides he had a close friend named Wayne Matthews that was closer to his age. I liked the Rust boys and my mother liked them too because they were so well behaved and polite. It was great to finally have some close friends in our tiny village. Roger Massengill had dropped out of school by this time and he was working a lot of hours in his new construction job. Thomas and I would become inseparable. We were like Jerry Lewis and Dean Martin or the Smothers Brothers the way we complimented each other. We were a team and whoever became a new friend became a friend to Thomas and me both. Thomas and I were like Buzz and Todd of the Old Route 66 tv show. Thomas was dark headed and I had light hair and adventure was dead ahead each time we got behind the wheel of a car. Thomas's brother, Leftridge, was drafted into the Army after high school and he was sent to Germany. He had bought a new 1966 green Chevy II before being drafter and he left Thomas in charge of the new car. He told Thomas to drive the car and keep it up. Thomas did what he was told and he spent two years driving the Chevy II. My first car was a green 1961 Pontiac Tempest. The little four cylinder was great on gas and we often bought gas for 19.9 cents a gallon during "gas wars." One could travel a lot on $1.00 worth of gas (5 gallons) during the 1960's. I still managed to occasionally run out of gas. If Thomas and I weren't cruising in the Chevy II, we were playing follow the leader. If one of us drove one front and back wheel on the curb, the other had to do the same. Sometimes we would also drive on the mediums. We grew up in a rural area and there never was an abundance of police officers to patrol the entire county. Thomas, Leftridge, Patsy, and I were all part time workers at my grandfather's general store (Arthur's General Store). Leftridge drove the delivery truck until he graduated from high school, and Thomas and I became the delivery men when he left. We worked afternoons after school and all day every Saturday. We worked a regular 40 hour week during the summer.   We could work late hours on Saturday and during the summer and we might not finish work until 10:00 PM or 11:00 PM. We could not exceed 40 hours, but my grandfather stayed open at night as long as customers came in. Thomas and I would often get bored being off during the middle of the day when one of us worked later on Saturdays and we would help each other on the truck. He always helped me a lot and the job was much easier with two of us working the truck. A normal winter truck load would consist of 25 bags of coal, 6 – 5 gal. cans of kerosene, and many boxes of groceries.   We would deliver a load and return to the store for another load. Once in a while, we would have to step over someone sprawled out on the living room floor. The men had drunk too much on Friday night and had passed out on the floor. We always had envelopes with grocery payment money or customers change. Thomas and I can still remember most of our old customers and where they once lived. Addie Griggs was a stoop shouldered, frail, black

134

lady who would shake her cane at my Uncle Cecil and threaten to come behind the counter after him. Cecil loved to joke and carry on with Addie and he looked forward to the Saturday ritual. Farmer Roy Jones' wife was a Quaker and she was one of the kindest people I have ever known. She would use expressions like "How art thou" and we really enjoyed delivering to her. Gracie Mills was an elderly African American lady who shopped at my grandfather's store for most of her life. Gracie and her husband, Percy Mills, were kind, caring people. "Miss Gracie" always smelled real nice and I really miss her wisdom. I think of Gracie's neighbor, Carrie Jackson, and one sentence comes to mind. Carrie always said, "Thank You Jesus" every time you did something for her or gave her something. If Gracie Mills and Carrie Jackson are not in heaven, Lord help the rest of us.

B.D. (George) Fenner was a longtime customer of my grandfather and the rotound black fellow was a longtime customer and friend of mine. B.D. once told me that he was very ill one night and something told him to visit Carrie Jackson. Carrie met B.D. at the front door of her house and handed him a bottle of medicine. B.D. had no idea how Carrie knew he was coming or that he was sick. She told him the medicine would cure him and it did. I remember hot summer days and cold winter days delivering groceries with Addie Griggs, Martha Bailey, and Pearl Broadaxe riding with me on the front seat. Martha and Addie were thin, but Pearl was a very heavy Lady. Somehow, we always made it and the cramped conditions seem curious now. Thomas and I met a lot of good people while working at the store, and most of them remained our friends. Working for my uncle could be tough at times and I resented having to leave a football game when a coal shipment arrived. Thomas always got a kick out of my uncle's and my work relationship, but I always knew my uncle expected a lot from me and I know it helped me in the long run. The funky feel of cheese sauce, the sharp cutting bones of neck bones, the coal dust in your nose, the smell of a opened can of sardines, the aroma from a freshly opened whole round cheddar cheese or opened 5 lb can of luncheon meat, the feel of kerosene that has soaked through your work pants onto your skin, the distinctive smell of a 50 lb bag of potatoes or onions that have perished produce in the bottom of the bag, and the smell of kerosene recently mopped onto the old wood floor on Saturday night (signaling closing time is near) are some of the things Thomas and I will always remember. I know baseball players can always remember the smell of grass and the smells of a ball park, but store clerks have their memories also. Leftridge, Patsy, Thomas and I spent many of our free hours of the summer at Lake Ahoy which was located about 8 miles from Driver. The giant man-made lake attracted many young people and the high diving boards were in constant use. The men rode the cable ride from the high platform to the lake's water as girls watched. Thomas and I are both fair skinned and our first season trips to the lake resulted in sunburns. My mother would rub my back, chest, and face in vinegar at night to take away the sting of the sunburn. I smelled like a giant pickle. Thomas and I may have been "country" boys, but we knew that rock n' roll music made the beach, cruising, and everything else more special. We would sometimes go to Virginia Beach and swim or visit the local clubs (the Peppermint Beach Club was special). California Girls by the Beach Boys, Satisfaction by the Rolling Stones, I'm a Girl Watcher by the Occasions, Groovin by the Rascals, and countless other tunes filled the airways. City Park in nearby Portsmouth was also one of our favorite hang outs. The park had a golf course, a small train that carried children and adults through the park, several gardens, and most importantly; tennis courts. The tennis courts attracted girls, so naturally we were attracted to the tennis courts. Thoughts of the tennis courts evoke memories of girls in white shorts with nice tans. Girls would sometimes ask us to join them in a game. The old tennis court became an important element of our dating lives because we would sometimes date the girls we met at the Court and they would have friends that they would later introduce to some of our friends. Thomas and our mutual friend, Lee Carr, met their future wives on one of these trips to City Park. Thomas met and later married Mary Lovelace and Lee met and later married Mary's best friend, Beverly Smith. Both girls attended Woodrow Wilson High School in Portsmouth. We dated more girls who attended Wilson High than we did our own school, John Yeates High School. Thomas and I met two girls playing tennis one summer afternoon named Barbara McCormick and her friend Mary. I won't use Mary's last name because more people will know what a fool I made of myself after meeting Mary. Thomas and I had finished our junior years at Yeates and would be entering our Senior year in September. I had had crushes on girls before, but nothing would compare to the way I felt the moment I met Mary. I have discussed this period of time with my retired psychologist friend, Bob Charles (Berkley), and he assured me he had such experiences. These were times I wasn't sure I was normal. How could this happen the instant you meet someone? I could not help myself. I thought about her constantly and I can't recall the number of times I made a fool of myself. I really don't know if I really loved Mary or if I was in love with love. I don't know if it was her dark hair, her brown eyes, her smile, her laugh, or anything or everything; but I was love sick. I had to meet Mary's parents before our double-date with Thomas and Barbara and I don't believe the CIA could have done a better job interrogating me. Mary's younger sister even asked me Questions. I told them I was an Episcopalian and an acolyte, but I don't think that mattered. I knew I wanted to go to college, but I did not have a clue what I would do for the rest of my life. I was not Catholic (like Mary's family) and I was not career driven, so I guess I started out with two strikes on me. I had been through a case of puppy love when I was fourteen. One Saturday in February of 1964, my brother and I attended a birthday party for my first cousin, Cliff Parker. The party was held at Miracle Lanes Bowling Alley in Portsmouth. My Uncle Harold and his wife Marion were close friends of Bucky and Bunny Hambleton of Portsmouth. The couple had a daughter named Pam who was a friend of my cousin. Pam and I began talking while we waited our turn to bowl. I asked her which school she attended and she said Harry Hunt Jr. High. She asked me the same Question, and I said Chuckatuck High School. Pam followed up with the two words "Oh Really" and somehow her voice and mannerisms sleighed me. It didn't hurt that she was also a very pretty dark haired girl with olive skin. Pam spent the night with her grandmother who lived two doors down from my Uncle Harold and Aunt Marion. Pam, my brother, Gregory, Cliff, and I spent Saturday afternoon going back and forth to the local Confectionary to buy Beatle cards. That Saturday was the day before the Sunday of the Beatle's first appearance on the Ed Sullivan Show. Pam combed each boy's hair straight down similar to the Beatle's haircuts. I will probably talk more about the Beatle influence later, but there was great anticipation among boys and girls during that special weekend. The death of President John Kennedy and the Cold War had affected young and old and these facts have been well documented. Young people especially needed some magic and it came from John, Paul, George, and Ringo. I spent a sleepless night at my cousin's house that Saturday night. I couldn't wait to see Pam on Sunday and I didn't care about seeing my Port Norfolk buddies. Pam seemed so different than the girls I knew in school. She was so bright eyed and down to earth. She was like the girls the Beatles were singing about. I called Pam the Monday night following the Sunday night Ed Sullivan show and we talked about the Beatles and other things like school and friends. She was very easy to talk to and we spent a lot of time on the phone. Pam's mother brought her to Driver on some Saturdays and we would sing Beatle songs together or walk around the village. I would also see her sometimes when we were both visiting our grandmothers in Port Norfolk. We stayed in touch during the coming years and I dropped by her house a few times. Pam was a cheerleader at Wilson High School and she also sang in a rock band. This did not surprise me because she had a great voice. I mention all of this because my friendship with Pam seemed so magical and innocent during this time. Like so many young people; we grew up with the Beatles and we felt like they belonged to us. I still think of the cute thirteen year old brunette when I hear many of the Beatle's first hits. Innocent songs like "I Want To Hold Your Hand" and "I SAW HER STANDING THERE" bring back memories of long ago and Lennon's "This Boy" applied to this boy. I saw Pam in a mall store years ago and she was gorgeous. She looked much younger than her actual age and she talked about her daughter. I'm sure her daughter grew up to be a lot like her mother; pretty but not conceited. Her mother is a very special person. I remember these times of my life while writing about Thomas because he was and always will be a true friend. Your true friends are with you during the good times and bad times. Having friends like Thomas Rust, Lee Carr, Dale Holland, and Bobby Harrell helped me through some awkward and difficult times in life. Like Ringo sang, "I get by with a little help from my friends." I spent too much time in school daydreaming about Mary. I was a good student in economics, but I missed a simple Question from our teacher, Mr. Henderson, because my mind was in the clouds. I would even sit in church and wonder how it would be to attend church with Mary on Sunday mornings. I would have done anything for Mary. I would have switched to Catholicism for her. I would have worked day and night and I probably would have done other insane things. One night I went to Roses Department Store where Mary worked as a clerk. She told me she got of f at 9:00 P.M. and I told her I would walk her to her car when she got off. I would spend the next hour looking in some of the other shopping center stores. I went to a record shop and I got the bright idea that I might get through to Mary if I gave her a couple of 45's that expressed my feelings. I picked out The Rascal's "A Girl Like You" and The Monkee's "Words". I was sure she would like both of these popular songs.   I met Mary outside the store and walked her to her 1964 blue Falcon. I opened the car door for her after she unlocked it. I handed her the two 45's and suggested she might want to listen to them when she got home. Mary told me I should keep the two 45's because she didn't listen to a lot of music at home and I would probably like them more than she would. I was devastated, but I hid my feelings pretty well. I was beginning to realize that any attempts I made to impress her would be futile. I would continue to bore my friends with my love sick blues for the next several months and I would continue to put myself through more self inflicted agony. Finally Father Time took care of everything and I eventually came to my senses. I came to the realization that you can't make someone love you and you can't be something you aren't. I knew I would find the girl of my dreams somewhere down the line. I came out of the fire burned but intact. I'm sure my friends were glad to see me back to my old self and I really began to appreciate what my friends really meant to me. For some reason, I met the majority of the girls I dated when I was with Thomas.   Maybe I wasn't as shy when we were together or perhaps my sense of humor was better. We were best friends, but we still were in competition with each other when girls were involved. I occasionally see the parents of one of the girls that Thomas dated and Dale later dated. The mother still tells me what nice boys we were and how she wished her daughter and her daughter's friends had married us. It is a great compliment and I have to agree with her as far as my friends are concerned. My friends always treated women and elders with respect. Thomas and I were inseparable during our high school years. We rode to school together, we worked together, we socialized together, we played Sandlot Sports together, and we laughed at the same things. We also worried about each other.

Thomas' father was a good man and I really miss him, but he would sometimes drink too much and embarrass his children. Jimmy had been in a lot of combat in the Navy during World War II and I think the memories of the war would sometimes cause him to go into depression. Jimmy was never mean or abusive. He only relived the horrors of the war when he was drinking. Thomas and I were grown men when our fathers Quit drinking. Jimmy and my father became close friends and both spent the last several years of their lives as dedicated, sober family men. Because of the war, the heartache, the drinking, the depression, and other facets of life; I believe the two shared a common bond. The Rust family was a second family for me. Jimmy and Myrtle treated me like a son and I probably spent more time with Jimmy than I did my father. I spent many happy hours in the Rust home and I have many special memories of the time spent in that old house. I can recall entering the door to the kitchen which was adjacent to Thomas' bedroom. The smell of sizzling bacon, eggs frying, coffee, southern fried chicken, or a freshly baked cake usually greeted me. It seems like Mrs. Rust was always cooking. Mrs. Rust would tell me it was time for Thomas to get up and eat and send me to his room to wake him. I will never forget how it felt to enter Thomas' bedroom during the winter months. His bedroom was always cold and I could often see my breath in the cold air. I always asked myself the same Question, "How in the world does he stay in this cold room"?

We spent many hours together watching tv shows like Shindig, Hullabaloo, Lloyd Thaxton, The Glen Campbell Show, The Smothers Brothers Show, and several others. I remember Thomas' father could not tolerate Mick Jagger and he was not fond of Mel Torme. I don't think Jimmy liked Jazz. Thomas and I spent many hours in the old movie theaters in downtown Portsmouth. The State, Commodore, and Colony Theaters were our places to escape school, home, and reality for a few hours. We also shot pool a lot at the local bowling alleys, we played putt putt golf sometimes, we hung out at the Churchland and Portsmouth Shoney's (Big Boy) Drive Ins, but we really enjoyed the movies. I can't remember how many Elvis movies we saw, but "Spin Out", "Girls, Girls, Girls", "Girl Happy", "Fun in Acapulco", "Clambake", "Follow Your Dreams", "Roustabout", and Charro were some of the films we enjoyed. Thomas and I both liked Elvis and we liked his music as well as his movies. Many have said that the "Kings" movies were cheesy or were not creative. I believe Elvis was the greatest entertainer ever and that's exactly what he did; he entertained. Thomas and I were entertained by all of his movies and that's what we paid for. Thomas was and is a great dancer and I think he picked his moves up from watching Elvis. I wonder how many other young people became good dancers or even professional dancers because they were influenced by Elvis. Elvis gave youth a freedom they had never had. Thomas and I also saw many motorcycle movies together. "Born Losers" with Tom Laughlin was one of our favorites. Peter Fonda was the screen heroe in "Wild Angels" and the hit "Easy Rider." Fonda, Laughlin, Nicholson, and others helped replace the void left by James Dean and Marlon Brando. I remember seeing "Dr. Zhivago" when it came out. I thought it was a great movie, but Thomas told me he thought it was a boring picture during the intermission. Thomas was not too thrilled with romantic epics, but he lived through them. We both enjoyed movies like "The Dirty Dozen", "Kelly's Heroes", "The Von Ryan Express" and other war movies that I often see today on cable tv. Thomas and I often saw the gruesome "Cult Classic" titled "The Undertaker and His Pals" which was the story of a mad butcher who ground his victims into hamburger.

I met my first wife while I was with Thomas and he was an usher in our wedding and later I was an usher in his wedding. He loaned me his 1970 Chevelle a few times when I had dates and my car was broke down. It seems Thomas has always been there for me whenever I was in a jam. My first wife used to tell me that I cared more about my close friends than I did her. I always knew what to expect from my friends and I was always glad they had passed my way. We might not have seen each other as much as time went by, but each of us still cared and worried about our friends. Most 1960's circles of male friends probably thought their friendships were much like the Beatles. We always thought we would start a business or company as a group and we would all be successful. Lee Carr once looked into a synthetic marble business we could buy and operate, but the timing was not right for all of us. I often wonder how things might have worked out if we had taken that risk. Looking back on life now, I think I now realize how young men in war thought. Many young men had grown up together and shared the good times and bad times wit heir friends. Northern and Southern boys had grown up together on adjacent farms, small towns, and cities during the years prior to the Civil War. Each person thought if his friend or brother could sacrifice so much it was his duty to be like his friend or brother. They were not going to let each other down. Thomas has always worked hard, but he has had his share of setbacks. He began working for the grocery chain Colonial Stores while in high school. He continued to work for Colonial after high school and made a very good salary. Thomas was dedicated and rose from the third man to assistant manager. Colonial Stores sold out and became Big Star and Thomas was forced to take a pay cut. Big Star eventually went out of business and Thomas started over with Food Lion. Like many other Americans, corporate decisions and actions played a big part in his life. Thomas wanted to serve in the Army during the Viet Nam War. I was very worried that I would lose another close friend. I was selfish because Jimmy Cooper had been killed in Viet Nam a year earlier and I had a hard time dealing with his passing. Like Jimmy, Thomas was a very unselfish person and he would go to any lengths to help a friend, or protect someone he cared about. Thomas failed the Army physical in

Richmond and was classified 4 F. He was told he had problems with his spinal column and long rides in military vehicles would cause physical problems. He insisted it would not affect him because he drove a lot, but the doctors still failed him. I know Jimmy (Thomas' father) was relieved because he already had one son serving in the Army (Leftridge). I still had three close friends who would be facing the draft and I desperately wanted them to be safe. Bobby Harrell, Lee Carr, and Dale Holland had each suffered a lot as children and young men and I will discuss each one of my friends, later. I was bonded to these guys and I worried more about them than I did myself. My feelings about war changed during my last two years in high school. Many of my generation were products of World War II heroes. Our fathers and mothers sacrificed so much so the world could be spared and I really appreciate their valor and patriotism. My generation wanted to be more like our parents than they would ever know. We wanted to marry a girl just like "good old mom" and we wanted the world to respect us. My friends and I wanted to be like Sgt. Chip Saunders (Vic Morrow) on the tv show "Combat" or Sgt. Striker (John Wayne) in the movie, "The Sands of Iwo Jima." We believed our country was always right and someone should love our country or leave it. Thomas believed these philosophies and he very well could have been a Sgt. Saunders. I personally began to Question the validity of the war like a lot of people my age. I knew the Ten Commandments and I knew my father and Jimmy Rust had seen many men die and had trouble understanding it all. Perhaps my generation was a result of the horrors our fathers and mothers saw and experienced during World War II. I am sure they hoped the war would be the war to end all wars. I remember one male teacher in school preaching to male students to strongly consider the military if the students were not college bound. I would have liked to ask the teacher why he didn't consider the military. Was it because he had a degree, a teaching job, and a nice looking wife? Maybe he would never have to go to war if he could convince more young men to enlist. I will say that I have the greatest respect for the men and women who defend our country. Today our service people defend our country by personal choice, but many of the service people of previous wars were draftees. Volunteers and draftees both sacrificed a great deal for people like me and I appreciate them. I believe the Viet Nam War affected many Americans: young and old and male and female. Mothers got tired of burying their sons, fathers watched the news and began to realize the war was different, and everyone knew someone who was killed, missing in action, physically or emotionally crippled, or not able to fit back into mainstream American Society. I was not a hippie and I was not a hawk. One thing did happen during the 1960's that makes me proud. Generally it was not popular to be violent. There may have been riots, student unrest and countless demonstrations but was also a time when you could pick up a hitchhiker. People everywhere were giving the peace sign. People were tired of war and most wanted Social Change. Woodstock was an exclamation point to a cultural revolution. The festival showed we could get along and care about each other. I began to have feelings of guilt during the late 1970's and early 1980's. During the 1960's, I often wondered how I would be affected if I had to kill another person. I'm sure a lot of soldiers have wondered the same thing and I would probably have defended myself if I was in their situation. During the late 1970's, I began to think more about the young people who did fight in Viet Nam. I asked myself many times why my close friends and I were fortunate enough to escape much of the pain of the war. I was not any different from the 58,000 service people who were killed. I wasn't someone special and perhaps many of those who had passed might have made more contributions to life than I had. My neighbor and friend, Phil Harper, had graduated from West Point and was paralyzed from the waist down during the war. Phil played pony league baseball while I was playing little league. Phil was athletic and he was also a very good student. Phil was hurt playing intramural football at West Point, but he studied hard and graduated. I remember my father taking my brother, me, Phil, and another West Point student water skiing one summer. The other cadet skied into a nest of water moccasins, but my father Quickly maneuvered the boat out of the area to safety. Phil always looked great in his West Point dress uniform. I had often watched the old television show, "Men of West Point", but now someone I knew and respected was one of the "long gray line." Phil did not give up after he was paralyzed. He entered the law school at the University of Miami and became a lawyer. Phil saved some others' lives when a wall collapsed on him, but there was plenty of fight left in him. He would learn to drive a handicap car with only his hands and he would take on any obstacle life dealt him. Phil dedicated his life to other veteran's and he fought legal battles for veteran's rights and care. He once addressed the United States Congress on behalf of Veterans. Phil was always a special person and he is very much an American heroe. Phil's organs began to fail after years of being paralyzed and he passed away as a young, caring man. He was married and was always a great son and friend. I know few people who packed as much life into such a short time period as Phil Harper did. I will always remember Phil. Like so many others, I remember him as "forever young." Fred Callis was a teammate of Phil's on the Driver Pony League Team. Fred was the catcher on that team and he was strong and fearless. A hard working farmer's son, Fred considered baseball a picnic compared to back-breaking work on the Callis farm. Fred joined the Army and was sent to Germany where he met his longtime wife, Eva. After Germany, Fred was assigned to Viet Nam. Fred was a veteran of the motor pool and the Army needed his experience and ability in Viet Nam. Like so many other young men, Fred's life was changed forever in Viet Nam. The Viet Cong fired on the Camp Fred was at and Fred was wounded. The doctors were worried Fred might have some metal fragments in his kidney and decided he should be medevacd to a hospital. The camp came under fire again as two soldiers carried Fred on a stretcher to a chopper. The two stretcher carriers were killed and Fred was badly wounded. The injured were eventually taken to a hospital and Fred's (blank) leg was amputated. Fred was awarded two purple hearts and spent many months in a hospital in the Philippines. Doctors thought Fred might not recover and the military flew Eva to the Philippines to be with her husband. Fred made a full recovery, but he has never been able to wear a (blank). He enrolled in college and studied drafting and architecture. He an Eva raised two sons and the family is a vital member of the community. Fred served on the Driver Volunteer Fire Department for years and even drew up the set of plans for the new fire house built in (blank). Fred's son, Buck, is the current chief of the fire department.

Jimmy Cooper and Frank Ashley (both killed in Viet Nam), Bobby Cooper (wounded), Fred Callis (wounded), Phil Harper (wounded), Arthur Powell (wounded), Leroy Schmidt (tumor from Agent Orange), J.T. Savage (died from cancer caused by Agent Orange) and numerous other veterans are friends who sacrificed so much for us all. The special thing about these guys is the fact they have never been bitter towards their peers who did not have to fight in Viet Nam. Thomas and I will be friends until one of us passes. Then again, we may be reunited in the sweet bye and bye as my father might say. Real Friendship does not have to have limits or boundaries.

Chapter 14
Dale Holland

I met Dale Holland during early September of 1963 in <u>Miss</u> Minton's 8th grade Math class. We talked briefly before and after each class, but I had no idea that Melvin Dale Holland and I would become close, life-long friends. I played football with a group of boys from a neighborhood known as Wilroy. We were a bunch of 8th graders and I was pretty decent and the coach, Mr. Turner, put me at Quarterback. I had known the coach's son, Roger, since second grade at Driver Elementary. Driver class mates like Fletcher Beedles, Mike Riddick, Rodney Nelson, and a few others were members of the Wilroy team. Our team traveled to an area known as Elephants Fork one Saturday afternoon to play our first regular game. Every time I broke through the defensive line, a defensive back would tackle me with a hard hit. I began to ask myself "Who is this guy and why can't I get around him." Both teams played hard and we lost the game 8 to 6 on a safety. Monday it dawned on me who the fellow was who kept tackling me on Saturday. It was the guy sitting beside me in Math class. It was Melvin Dale (M. D.) Holland. He was the player who didn't let up. Dale and I talked about the game after math class that Monday, and I realized we had a lot in common. We were both shy and we both were probably starved for attention. We were also the oldest siblings of our families. Dale had a younger brother, Charles, and a young sister named Pat. Dale's mom, Lorraine, worked for an insurance agency to support the family since Dale's father had passed a few years earlier. Lorraine was a great mother and she loved her children. I admired and respected her a lot. A mutual friend of Dale and myself had known Dale since the first grade and he told me the story behind Dale's father's death. Dale's dad and his dad's brother were fresh water fishing in one of Suffolk's many lakes. One brother fell overboard and the second brother tried to save the other. Both men drowned. After my friend told me of the fishing incident, I knew in my heart why Dale and I were friends. The answer was simple: I needed Dale and Dale needed me. Neither of our lives was a pattern for Wally Cleaver. We were both just trying to get through the best we could. Maybe it was Nannie at work or perhaps it was the highest power imaginable, but someone put us next to each other in math class and someone made sure we became friends. I think I already knew something very important by this time in my life. I knew that when one door closes, another door will be opened. I also knew that everyone says you are lucky to be able to count the number of your true friends on one hand. I don't think one can categorize friends in terms of numbers. You know in your heart and in your mind when someone is truly your friend. I will be bonded with Dale Holland, Thomas Rust, Lee Carr, and Bobby Harrell until I take my last breath on earth. I have several other friends, but the friendships with those four guys are uniQue and will always be a part of me. When I see them or talk to them it's always like I saw them yesterday. We may not see each other for five years or more but we always pick up where we left off. Maybe it's because we were comfortable with each other, knew we could always count on each other, or completely trusted each other. Dale Holland was the friend you could count on to be unpredictable or adventurous. He could carry on the thought provoking conversations and debate the deepest topics, but he was at his best when he was daring and carefree. I enjoyed many of the best times of my life when I was with Dale Holland. He was like Peter Fonda (Captain America) and I was like Billy in the 1969 movie "Easy Rider." Dale was an excellent student in high school. He was a member of the Beta Club which was made up of outstanding and gifted students. Dale was also very good in mechanical drawing and all the various math classes such as Algebra, Geometry, and Trigonometry. Dale and I did the typical things boys our age did. We went to movies, shot pool, played put put golf (miniature) and chased girls. We double-dated Quite often and during those years I dated two girls and Dale dated their best friends. The four of us always seemed to have a good time.

I dated a girl our senior year name Connie and Dale dated her best friend, Barbara. Connie's parents were very family oriented and the girls took us conoing a couple of times with Connie's folks. Dale and I had never been conoing, but all of us had a great time. The four of us went to movies, drive-in movies and coffee houses. Folk music was still in at the time and Connie and I were both into all kinds of music. Connie and I would spend hours listening to Beatle albums and singing along with the Fab Four. Connie had a great voice and she eventually became a professional singer. I occasionally see one of the old movies we all saw together and my mind is flooded with memories. I remember the four of us going to Norfolk one freezing Sunday afternoon in February 1968 to see "The Valley of the Dolls." We also saw the movie "The Taming of the Shrew" with Richard Burton and Elizabeth Taylor on Thanksgiving Day 1967. Dale and I would see whatever the girls wanted to see because we knew we could see the action and gore flicks with our buddies. Connie snuck some booze from her father's bar one Saturday night before we went to the drive-in. I think it was a very small amount because it had no affect on Dale or me when we mixed the liQuor with our Cokes. I remember it was raining "cats and dogs" that night. The four of us also went to a dance at the Virginia Armory in Portsmouth on New Year's Eve, 1967. Songs like "My Girl", "Louie, Louie", "Tax Man", "She Shot a Hole in My Soul", "39-21-46" (The Measurement Song), and other 60 Hits brought in the New Year. Dale and I weren't great dancers, but we tried. Connie's parents invited Dale and Me to their house the Saturday night before Christmas. Barbara and Dale exchanged gifts and so did Connie and I that night. Connie gave me the Grass Roots Album "Live for Today" which I still have. I remember stopping at Weatherly's Store after I got off work from my Uncle Jerry's gas station on Christmas Eve about 5:30 p.m. I called Connie from the old stores outside pay phone and we talked for Quite a while. The phone booth was extremely cold, but I was happy talking to Connie about the things we would do during the remainder of Christmas vacation. She told me she would have the family take some pictures of her Christmas Day and give them to me later since we would not be together that day. A few months later, things would change drastically for Connie and me. She and Barbara's School was closed one day and they decided to visit Dale and me during lunch hour at John Yeates High School. Naturally Dale and I were surprised, but it made us feel good to think the girls cared enough about us to track us down at school. My jubilation soon disappeared. I had told Connie a few weeks earlier a fellow in my class looked like Paul McCartney of the Beatles. As luck would have it, Phil walked by us and Connie told Barbara to look because he did look like McCartney. Connie and Barbara followed Phil around the school hall for a short distance. I didn't let on to Connie that her actions bothered me, but the incident was all I could think about during my next few classes. At the end of the day I was seething. I asked myself all kinds of ridiculous Questions. How could Connie often ask me if I really loved her and then embarrass me in front of class mates and friends? Was she just trying to make me jealous and test me to see how much I cared about her? Perhaps it was just an innocent reaction and I was being too hard on her. I had already been hurt by a few girls in the past so I naturally took my hasty, hard-headed position. I waited until night to call Connie and Question her about the incident. She told me there was nothing out of the way and I shouldn't worry about anything. I guess I wanted to hear something like "I'm sorry and I'll never make you jealous again" or "please don't be mad at me; you should know I really love you." Before I knew it, I blurted out "maybe we should breakup." To my surprise, Connie agreed. I regretted my actions instantly. I thought about calling Connie back and apologizing. I knew I had made a mistake, but my foolish pride took over. I hurt Connie and I hurt myself. Days later I received a small box in the mail. It was my senior ring that I had given to Connie. I wasn't happy and thinking about the freedom I would now have. I was miserable and realized I had blown it. I even tried to convince myself that she would be better off without me. Once again I would have to "get by with a little help from my friends." Dale and Barbara would soon stop dating. Barbara and Connie came to see me in Driver a few years ago and both girls looked great. I was really glad to see them and we three talked a long time. It was strange in a way, because it was kind of like talking to Dale, Thomas, or Lee. I was talking to old friends. They are people I really care about. Dale, Bobby Harrell, Lee Carr, and I graduated together on Friday, June 8, 1968. Lee received a scholarship from Chowan College in Murfreesboro, N.C. and Bobby got a job at the G.E. television plant. Dale and I both wound up at Old Dominion University. We would still be together. I had been accepted to Frederick College and Dale had planned to attend Virginia Tech in Blacksburg, VA. The philanthropist (Fred Beasley) who owned Frederick College donated the college to the state and it would change from a four year college into a two year community college. Our high school guidance counselor got me into Old Dominion and Dale decided to go there also. Our graduation was marred by a national tragedy. I remember turning on the car radio while backing the car out to leave for John Yeates to take my final exam. I heard the news that Bobby Kennedy had been shot in Los Angeles. I cut the car off and sat in the driveway for several minutes. I sunk down in the seat and thought to myself "Why and here we go again". The sickening feeling took me back to the Chuckatuck High School Auditorium where study hall was my final class of that Friday November afternoon. The same feeling flooded my senses. It was

November, 1963 again. All the hopes and dreams were once again snuffed out in a matter of seconds. The Youth of America would be cheated again. After the disbelief and despair we would be back in the world of war and escalation, not jubilation. The hopes of peace died with Bobby Kennedy and young Americans lost a voice in their government. Whether people are Republicans, Democrats, or Independents; I think the majority of Americans would have to admit that J F K and R F K both knew how to relate to the youth and both men projected hope and promise for the future. The song, "He Was a Friend of Mine" by the Byrds symbolized what the brothers meant to the young people. The song line "Though I never met him; I knew him just the same" described how many felt about J F K and R F K. The Beatles had brought us out of the darkness of John Kennedy's death. They gave the youth a voice and sang about hope, peace, and love. Times were different in 1968 and the Viet Nam War, riots, and racial tension plagued the country. Who would save us this time? Thomas, Dale, Bobby, Lee, and I went to my parents' house after our graduation. Rev. Thompsen had brought some ice cream and we all had cake and ice cream and talked to the many well wishers. We were free at last and we were entering new chapters of our lives. We all talked about going to Nags Head, N.C. to celebrate our graduation, but Thomas had to work and Bobby had to help his folks on the farm. One of our classmates, Beth Williams, was throwing a party at her family's club house. Lee, Dale, and I decided to attend the party before heading to Nags Head. Beth and her parents had held several class parties at the end of school years while we were in grammar school. I had been through school with Beth since the second grade, but I haven't seen her since graduation night. I know she lives in Milwaukee and I hope she is doing well. Beth was a great girl and she was always available when someone needed a friend. We stayed at the party until 11:00 P.M. and decided we had better leave since it would take us about an hour and a half to drive to Nags Head. My brother's band was playing that night and I remember the last song the band played before we left was the Beatles' song, "I Get By with a Little Help From My Friends." Dale drove his stepfather's powerful Oldsmobile Starfire 88. We figured we were heading for three days of sun, fun, and gorgeous beaches. We were heading to a mosQuito festival instead. Everything was closed when we arrived in Nags Head about 1:00 A.M. The motels were either closed or had "no vacancy" on the signs. There were no McDonald's, Burger Kings, or Wendy's in Nags Head in those years. The only option was to park the car near the beach and try to get some sleep before morning when we could get a room. The guys in the "American Pie" movies had nothing on Dale, Lee, and me. We were three fair skinned lads all of European descent. We were prime targets for mosQuitoes at night and the blazing sun during the day. We took turns sleeping inside the car and on the car hood the entire night. We could not get comfortable and our new winged friends were about to carry us away. I kept thinking about something my father had always told me about "The Lost Colony" which was only about ten miles from where we were parked. He said the settlers were not killed by disease or Indians, but were carried away by the mosQuitoes. My father may have been right. We somehow made it through the night and found a motel (The Cavalier) that had vacancies and was located fairly near the beach. After checking in; Lee, Dale, and I checked out the room. Someone cut the tv on and an event that would air throughout the weekend was being televised. All the stations covered the train carrying Bobby Kennedy from New York back to Washington. We watched in silence and I think each of us realized we were now in the real world; sometimes very violent and cold. The three of us tried to sleep, but I don't think we did. We shared three beds and one of us would try to sleep on the floor or chair in the room. We rested a few hours and then we decided to find a place to eat. We left the motel and headed south down the old beach road. People were beginning to fish and swim and Dale often stopped the car to allow people to cross the road. The air was salty and fresh and there were no mosQuitoes. Tanned girls in bikinis were everywhere. We saw a Kentucky Fried Chicken Restaurant and decided we were ready for some fried chicken. The "Colonel" had not set up shop back home yet and none of us had ever eaten the chicken with all those herbs and spices. The "Colonel" was the only chain at Nags Head at that time. We devoured our chicken dinners and we agreed the chicken was great. No offence to K F C, but the chicken was a lot better in 1968. I guess the reason it was is because Colonel Sanders was so involved with the company in those days. Whoever thought the Colonel would become the most recognizable man in the world during the 1970's? We next went to a place near the beach that was an open pavilion with pool tables and pin ball machines. We shot a few games of pool and played the machines for a short time. We played so much pool back home that we Quickly got bored with the pavilion and thought we should get ready to hit the beach. Dale ran into one of our high school classmates named Steve Arnold when he went to the parking lot. Steve graduated with us and he owned a beautiful light gold colored 1966 Plymouth Barracuda. He was a fun-loving, friendly city boy who grew up in Portsmouth during his early years. I knew Steve fairly well in high school. We both had that combination of city-slicker/country boy. Steve knew many of my old Port Norfolk buddies and went to junior high (Harry Hunt) with my friend, Pam. Steve decided he and his friends should join us on the beach. We followed him to the cottage he and his buddies were staying at and left there for the Cavalier Motel so Dale, Lee, and I could pick up our swimming trunks. One of Steve's friends was a guy named Cliff Nobles. Cliff had just graduated from Woodrow Wilson High in Portsmouth and he also knew many of my old friends. He owned a candy-apple red 1966 Chevrolet Super Sport with a very powerful engine (437 Cu In. I believe). Dale and Lee were very impressed with Cliff's car.

We all went down to the beach and I remember I was very impressed with cliff. He could drink more beer than any person I had ever seen. He told me he could easily drink a case of beer and I asked myself "How in the world does an eighteen year old drink a case of beer?" I knew big time beer drinkers like my father and some of his friends, but they were all seasoned veterans. My friends and I were not big league drinkers when we graduated. There were a few times we had drank a six pack together or even a bottle of champagne or wine, but we were not that much into alcohol. We had more fun discussing "deep subjects" or going to movies. As a group; we were "thinkers" not "drinkers". That Saturday on the Nags Head beach was great. The Sun was bright and hot, the ocean water was cold, and the scenery was very hot. The sounds of the rushing waves and the music from a transistor radio made Nags Head seem like paradise. Music seemed to make places special in the 1960's and the beach was no exception. Songs such as "Tighten Up" by Archie Bell and the Drells, "The Horse" by Cliff Nobles and Co., "You Send Me" by Aretha Franklin, and "MacArthur's Park" by actor Richard Harris were some of the top 40 hits we heard on the beach. My mind always takes me back to Nags Head and the summer of 1968 whenever I hear these great songs today.

Dale, Lee, and I were very tired by the end of the day, but we did cruise up and down the beach road a few times. We came across a small cinder block drive in named the "Snow Bird" and decided to eat burgers and fries for dinner. The old drive in is still standing today among all the chain drive ins. Sunday, June 10, 1968 would be a day the three of us would never forget. We headed to the "Snow Bird" to grab some lunch and decided we would climb the gigantic sand dune known as "Jockey's Ridge." We would also visit the Orville and Wilbur Wright Memorial. We decided to visit the flight memorial first and we decided to buy some beer after leaving the national memorial. In those days, you could buy beer at the age of eighteen in North Carolina and we had one major problem. Dale would not turn eighteen until August. I believe Lee bought the beer which was named "Champale" and came in a green and gold can. I can safely say that I will never forget what the "Champale" can looked like. The three of us took the beer back to our motel room and began to drink it in the room. We finished the six-pack and decided to pick up more beer, ice, and a cheap cooler before heading to "Jockey's Ridge." I had been "getting by with a little help from my friends" but that Sunday I was "getting high with a little help from my friends."

I remember we sat on some chairs outside our motel room and noticed a group of girls who were also staying at the motel. We probably should have spent some time getting to know the girls instead of guzzling beer before we climbed "Jockey's Ridge." We were not experienced drinkers so we did not realize that the hot summer sun, hot sand, cold beer, and physical exertion was not a good combination. One of us grabbed the cooler and we headed for our assault on "Jockey's Ridge." Lee was already sun burned badly from his time on the beach the day before. He was pinkish red on his face and front and he was pale white on his back and back of his legs. Dale and I wanted to laugh but we knew we would soon be in the same condition. The three of us would wind up being "two tone." It wasn't funny at the time, but our "two tone" skin amused us all for years. We drank a few more "Champales" and began to trudget up the great sand dune. The burning sun and cutting sand in the wind made the three of us feel like we were in the Movie "Lawrence of Arabia." The hot sand began to burn our feet and ankles and we began to Question our sanity. We finally made it to the top of "Jockey's Ridge" and we stood on the ridge and looked down and saw other people climbing the ridge. We rested for a short while and fooled ourselves into believing the treck down the dune would be a piece of cake. The Champale, hot sun, and sand took their toil on the way down. Our skin burned and we were thirsty and our latest adventure was beginning to rival

Friday night's mosQuito fest as a "good time". Dale, Lee, and I probably looked like three characters from the horror movie "Night of The Living Dead" as we descended the dune with our arms dangling and our heads hanging down. We climbed into Dale's stepfather's OLDS Starfire and he cut the air conditioner on. We did work up an apetite climbing "Jockey's Ridge" and Dale suggested we have a nice steak dinner at a well known Nags Head Restaurant. We traveled back to the motel to relax a little and shower before going out to eat. We arrived at the restaurant and discovered we were not the only ones ready to eat a steak dinner and all the trimmings. We waited in line Quite a while until we reached the counter and hostess who would seat us. The wait was worth it when the waitress arrived with our thick steaks, baked potatoes, tossed salads and piping hot dinner rolls. I looked around the dining area and noticed most of the adults were casually, but nicely dressed. Most men wore sport jackets and slacks and the women wore the latest fashions of the times. We wore our typical school clothes and we probably looked like "Billy" and "Captain America" in the scene where the two bikers ate at an expensive restaurant in the French Quarter of New Orleans. We met up with Steve Arnold and Cliff Nobles again and decided we would meet them later that night at the "The Casino." We decided we should make our last night in Nags Head special. Lee's sunburn was bothering him so much that he decided he would stay inside the air conditioned motel room and read and watch tv. None of us lived in air conditioned houses and John Yeates High School was not air conditioned in those days, so spending time in a cool room was a good alternative. Dale and I headed for "The Casino". The "Casino" was kind of like a night club for young people. The white, wooden building had catered to the youth when my father was a young man and it was truly a beach landmark. It was a place where boys could meet girls and guys could drink beer and boast about their cars. The first floor of the "Casino" was full of pool tables and pin ball machines. The second floor had an old wooden dance floor surrounded by tables and chairs, and a stage for the bands to play. The second floor also had a bar area where people could buy beer. Patrons could reach the second floor by walking up a nice, wide stairway or they could walk up the old set of external stairs attached to the exterior of the building. Dale and I began our night at the "club" by shooting pool and swilling more beer. My grandfather would have said "we were living in high cotton" while we were at the "Casino". We decided to go upstairs and listen to the band and watch the girls. The band playing that Sunday night was a group from Virginia Beach, Va. known as the "Beach Nuts." They were very good and played top 40 hits and rock n' roll standards. They were a good band to dance to. Dale and I found Steve and Cliff and the four of us spent the next few hours drinking and talking. The Nag's Head Sheriff's Department was tough on public intoxication and fighting. We were very careful at the "Casino" because we had all heard that the sheriff's department was even tougher on Virginia and out of state fellows. Everyone knew someone who had the misfortunate of spending time in the Nags Head jail. The four of us decided to be safe and go to Steve's cottage. Dale and I were pretty "looped" after a few more beers at the cottage and we both became "Queery". I remember my head over the toilet and Steve patting me on the back and telling me I would live and the next time would not end up like this. I just wanted to live through that night and I wasn't thinking about a "next time." Dale had the same experience and we stayed at the cottage until we sobered up. We went back to the motel room and discovered a very funny sight. "Two Tone" Lee was sitting up in the bed drinking a beer and looking at a Playboy Magazine. Dale and I could not stop laughing at our friend, "the half lobster." I began watching television and Dale grabbed a pillow and said he was going to sleep on the beach. It must have been his turn to sleep on the floor and the alcohol must have numbed his memory of Friday night and the mosQuitoes on the beach. He returned about half an hour later and decided to sleep on the floor. I remember waking up the next morning and thinking to myself, "I will never do this again and please just let me make it through this day." Dale felt the same way and he and I cringed every time we saw a beer add on a billboard on the way home. I have been to the Outer Banks several times in my life and each trip takes me back to the graduation weekend of 1968. The old "Casino" burned down, but I rode by the building many times before the fire. The "strip" is now filled with stores, chain restaurants, and expensive cottages. I also think of Steve Arnold every time I visit Nag's Head. Steve passed away from cancer several years ago and I miss him. We used to run into each other a lot at Norfolk Naval Shipyard. Steve did very well in the shipyard and he became very religious in his last years. Like the old song says, "Thanks for Being a Friend."

Lee and I got jobs at Planter's Peanuts a few days after returning home. I was lucky enough to get a job in a unit known as the "candy kitchen". It was a part of the plant where the company made chocolate covered peanuts, chocolate covered raisins, a candy bar similar to the "Reeses Cup", and other sweet peanut related items. Planters was a great place to work; especially for those fresh from high school or the ones attending college. I worked with one fellow (Jim) who was a cadet entering his sophomore year at VPI (now Virginia Tech) and another fellow (Denny Lane) who was entering the University of Virginia. The pay at Planters was good (1.87/hr for students) and everyone was nice. Lee worked in the roasted peanut division and we only saw each other on our way to and from work. I still remember the Friday I returned to my car after my shift and found a huge note from Lee on the windshield that read, "Ha! Ha! Our line shut down during the morning and we get a long weekend". I still remember my supervisor (Mr. Oliver) and our floor lady (Stump) after all these years. The company would have to let us go for a week about once a month while the lines were changed to begin making different items. Mr. Oliver always looked sad when he told us we would be laid off and he always promised the company would bring us back and the company did. We really like the break because we had a little money and knew we could go to the beach or whatever. Planters would allow workers to eat anything the plant made free of charge. Management knew that after a couple of days looking at the same product and smelling it; the last thing you wanted to do was eat the product. The plant was very clean, but there is a mental thing about not wanting chocolate covered raisins or peanuts if you look at them for eight hours. Women who worked in the peanut butter section would never eat any brand of peanut butter. Everyone I know who worked at Planters has a fondness for the Old Suffolk Plant. Mr. Obici may have started out selling peanuts on the corner, but Mr. Peanut is recognized throughout the world. The hard working Italian immigrant made Suffolk, the "peanut capital of the world."

A good friend of mine named Charlie Taylor grew up down the street from the Budweiser plant in St. Louis, Missouri. Charlie has a close pilot friend who was shot down and captured by the North Vietnamese and spent years at the "Hanoi Hilton" (p.o.w. camp) with John McCain and other p.o.w.s.

Tom (the pilot) was asked years later what became of the can of Planters Peanuts that he received from home while imprisoned at the camp and he said, "the guards tried them and gave the rest to him." Tom did not know it at the time, but the can had a false bottom with codes and messages in the real bottom of the can.

Dale, Lee, Thomas, Bobby, and I had a good time that summer and dated different girls, but none seriously. We were all at the point where we really had to get serious about the future. Would we each meet the girl of our dreams? Would some or all of us wind up in Viet Nam? Would we do all right in college? How much would we change? The thing I miss most about my friends is the long debates and discussions we had when 3 to five of us were together. I know most young people have many of the same discussions, but we somehow brought the best and deepest thoughts out of each other. I have been in many college classrooms and I have talked to many educated and brilliant people, but it doesn't seem the same. I really believe we made each other better. I think we were the way we were due to many circumstances: First of all, we were not in the social and economic echelon of our high school class. Each of us was also shy and not ready to disclose his deepest thoughts and beliefs to other people. Each of us had also suffered the same heartaches and tragedies of life and we were very comfortable with understanding/like-minded people. We also respected and trusted each other. Lee, Dale, and Bobby could talk about cars all day, but they could also discuss politics and world affairs. I may not have understood everything they may have discussed about 312 cu inch police interceptors, but I really enjoyed the arguments and conversations. I think we all understood the fact we were living in an age of fast cars (muscle cars), ever evolving music, changes in styles and attitudes, changes in social behavior, and all the other changes the 60's brought. We realized we were living in a very different time and it was a period of Renaissance for us. The times, space, social injustice, the human mind, religious beliefs, human behavior and goals, and many other topics made me realize I was lucky to be a part of a group of guys that looked beyond the typical locker room conversations. I learned a great deal from my friends, but I guess the most important thing was that I learned what real friendship is. Dale spent the summer of "68" working and having fun in his off hours. He used to drive cars ready for auction to and from Richmond, VA to earn money. Dale was always conscientious and industrious and never shyed away from work.

Dale and I entered Old Dominion University in the fall and Lee entered Chowan College in Murfreesboro, N.C. We would see Lee on the weekends he was home and we visited him on campus a few times. I think Dale and I both were overwhelmed by the size of Old Dominion. It is a sprawling, rural campus and attained University status in 1969. I really got in good shape walking from one end of campus to the other for classes. We also had to park far away from our classes. Dale and I graduated from John Yeates High in a class of only seventy-five students. We had never been in classes made up of two hundred students. A large class at John Yeates was about twenty-five students. We soon got accustomed to professors speaking in microphones and using screens instead of blackboards. I remember sitting in a balcony in a math of finance class. The professor was Chinese. I have fond memories of Old Dominion and I met many intelligent people there. One of my good friends was a fellow from Los Angeles, Calif named Frank Wyzpolski. His nickname was "Bondo" and he was a very talented writer and musician. We would ride to city park in Norfolk and discuss music and poetry while watching the animals. I met a great guy named Bobby Mars from Charlottesville, VA. Bobby and I shared some classes and both of us liked sports. I heard years later that Bobby was a member of the Mar's candy family, but he never mentioned it. Whether he was or was not; he was a great southern guy and I am glad I knew him. I must also mention a fellow from Newport News, VA, named Danny Oneal. Danny and I sat beside each other in geology class and we became close friends. We even wound up working with each other many years later at Norfolk Naval Shipyard. Danny became a teacher when he graduated from college. I liked most of my professors at O.D.U. and it is still fun to talk to people who had those same professors. Many of them were very sincere about teaching and had the students' best interests at heart. I learned that American History in college was very different than the history one studied in the fourth grade. A student learned that many great people had the same problems and misfortunes most people endure. One professor I really liked at O.D.U. was a physical education instructor named Ron Edwards. He taught a class named physical conditioning and he was in great shape. Mr. Edwards had been the third string Quarterback with Vince Lombardi's Green Bay Packers prior to coming to Old Dominion. He had been a very good Quarterback at the University of Utah, but he looked like Tommy Smothers. Mr. Edwards was a very competitive guy and he could beat any student in any weight lifting contest, push-up contest or any other physical challenge. We had a student in our class who was small and ran very fast. Ron Edwards could never beat the student in the 100 yard dash, but he tried several times. Mr. Edwards played safety for our Continental Football League team known as the Norfolk Neptunes. The league consisted of players who had either played in the N.F.L. or were trying to prove they belonged in the N.F.L. Otis Sistrunk, who starred with the Oakland Raiders played with the Neptunes. I had pleurisy in my lungs a couple of days after returning to college after the Christmas break. I woke up in the middle of the night feeling like I had knives in both lungs. I thought I had broken some ribs until my mother told me what I had the following morning. I had phys ed. The day I returned to school and Mr. Edwards had everyone run up and down all the seats in the Foreman Field Stadium (college:pro football stadium). I was really struggling to complete the activity and I noticed Mr. Edwards was going up and down the stadium backwards. He never broke out in a sweat. Mr. Edwards noticed I was struggling and he ran over to me and said, "What's wrong today Parker, no gas?" I told him I had just gotten over pleurisy and didn't seem to have any wind. He told me I should have informed him and he would have not made me run and I could stop if I wanted to. I told him I wanted to finish and I did. He was a great instructor and I did not want him to think I was a Quitter. Mr. Edwards's final exam was a test which reQuested the students to properly identify all the human bones of the body and to match the bones with their proper locations on skeletal diagrams. The exam was difficult, but I knew it would be and I did all right. Mr. Edwards showed up for the final day of class wearing a white Nehru jacket and matching pants. He also wore a medallion around his neck. Everyone in class knew Mr. Edwards was in great physical shape and no one was going to rib him about his attire. That was the last time I saw Ron Edwards.

Dale and I could have done much better at Old Dominion if we had studied more. I'm not saying we never pulled any "all nighters" studying or we did not care. We had graduated from a high school where you went to the principal's office if your hair went over your ears or touched your shirt collar. We were not used to this much freedom; even when the calendar said the years were 1968 and 1969. Dale and I often visited a college hangout known as "The Kings Head Inn" which was located down the street from the O.D.U. campus on Hampton Blvd. The "Inn" was a lively place with bands, beer, and college girls. I remember sitting with Dale in the "Kings Head" one cold late December night a few days after Christmas. Dale was busy rapping with a good looking Co-ed, but I was in a more pensive mood that night. The Beatle's Song "Hey Jude" was very popular at that time and for some reason the words meant more that night. McCartney's lyrics like: "Take a Sad Song and Make it Better", "Don't you Know that It's the Fool who Plays it Cool", " the Minute You Let Her into Your Heart, then You can Start to Make it Better." The song was another hit the average young person could relate to. The Mary Anne Hopkins song, "Those Were the Days" was another great song that hit home that night. The song, also written by Paul McCartney, seemed very appropriate for "The Kings Head Inn" and those times. I looked around the tavern and realized that these times were very different and one day things would be very different for everyone in the room. I look back with fondness and think "Those Were The Days". The song applied to Dale and I because we sometimes thought those days would never end or we would fight and never lose. The song sounded like a Russian or European drinking song with lyrics like "Those were the days my friend, we thought they'd never end, it is the life we choose, we'll fight and never lose Those were the days, oh yes! Those were the days." Dale, Thomas, Lee, Bobby and I all worked during the summer of 1969, but we managed to get together on weekends and work nights. 1969 was the summer of movies like "Woodstock", "Easy Rider", and "Good Bye Columbus." Young people at Woodstock proved that half a million people could get together and have a good time without violence or destruction. Music was becoming a greater part of society and more and more people were Questioning Viet Nam. Somehow Lee, Dale and I wound up together again at Tidewater Community College in the fall of 1969. I believe each of us was struggling financially and the Tuition at Tidewater was much lower than Old Dominion and Chowan College where Lee spent his first year. I had been accepted to Frederick College my senior year in high school and the campus was much closer for each of us. The beautiful Tidewater Campus was previously Frederick College but was given to the state in 1968. I think the Tidewater Campus was a very good fit for each of us. The classes were smaller, and the professors were excellent. The classes were in buildings that were part of a World War II Munitions depot, but a river flowed beside the old campus. We were also allowed to take the courses we wanted or needed and were not told that we could not take this class or that class because they were already filled.

Dale and Lee were very good in mechanical drawing in high school and both excelled in the drafting classes at Tidewater. I took more basic liberal art courses and subjects I liked like Economics, Music Appreciation, Psychology, and British Literature. Because of a great math professor, I made A's in Math of Finance and finally mastered Algebra and Trigonometry. Thanks to the great professors at Tidewater, I was now making the Dean's List instead of eeking by like I did at Old Dominion. Dale was driving a dark green 1966 Chevy Nova SS by 1969 and we spent many hours in that car. His Chevy had a 283 cu. in.

166

engine and Dale made a gigantic wallnut ball for his shifter. I had a 1964 ½ white Mustang with red pin stripes and red interior. Dale and I will never forget the Sunday night two sailors pulled up beside us on Airline Blvd in Portsmouth. The fellow driving yelled at Dale "What you got kid, daddy's car?" Dale was furious and yelled back, "This isn't Daddy's car, this is my car!" Dale and the sailor began drag racing down the boulevard. We didn't get but a few blocks before we saw red flashing lights behind us. Dale got a ticket and a summons to appear in court. We did not think the incident would be so costly. I went to court with Dale that day and he told me he had not mentioned the race and ticket to his mother. The judge called Dale and the police officer to approach the bench and asked the officer to describe the incident. Dale was asked to give his side of the issue and he said the officer was correct. The judge fined Dale one hundred dollars and suspended his license for 90 days. Dale asked me how much money I had and I think we had a combined total of $25 or $30. He explained the situation to a court clerk and asked if he could call his mother. Dale's mom came to his rescue and I really felt bad for her. I drove on our double dates during the next three months and Dale and I still hung out together, but Dale really missed his Nova. We both learned a valuable lesson. I was dating the girl at that time who would become my future wife. Janice was in nursing school and a girl named Joyce was a close friend of hers at the nursing school. She introduced Joyce to Dale and the two started dating. The four of us went to Nags Head one July fourth and the day was very special. We rode the various rides at the old amusement park and we went swimming and made a camp fire on the beach. The highlight of the day was the fire works on the beach that night. It was a beautiful display with the ocean as a background. The four of us had many great times together, but Dale and Joyce eventually broke up. I know they really did care for each other, but Dale was still hung up on a girl who lived down the street. I knew how he felt and I sympathized with him. I should thank Dale for turning me on to some very good music. He gave me the "Blood Sweat and Tears" album one Christmas and I Quickly became a fan of jazz rock. He gave me a "Guess Who" album the following year, and I have remained a big "Guess Who" fan for all these years. Burton Cummings, Randy Bachman (later Bachman Turner Overdrive) and the other "Guess Who" members did some of the greatest "message music" ever recorded. The Canadian band wrote beautiful, as well as thought provoking music. The band had many great hits like "American Woman", "No Sugar Tonight", "Hand Me Down World", "She's Come Undone", and the great classic, "These Eyes." Other songs like "Talisman" and "Running Back to Saskatoon" are just a few of the band's vast and great catalogue. The "Guess Who" was a very important band of the times.   Dale also got me interested in the band known as "Iron Butterfly". Everyone automatically thinks of "In-a- Gadda- Da- Vida" when they think of "Iron B", but the band was a big influence on many bands that followed them. Songs like "Flowers and Beads" or "Butterfly Bleu" were staples of the Band. Dale and I spent the summer o f 1970 working for my father. The three of us painted houses and restriped parking lots. Dale was a hard worker and my father liked him very much. Dale bought a Honda motorcycle that summer and we would ride when we got off work. We rode to a place known as the "Fat Rabbit" to shoot pool or other places to get something to eat. Two local hangouts of that era were the two local "Shoney's Big Boy" restaurants. One was located in Churchland and one was located in Portsmouth and both spots were very popular with young people. Guys would wash and wax their cars and take them to "Shoney's" and show them off. The restaurants had a nice inside dining area, but young people liked the curb area where pretty waitresses in white tops and tight, black slacks served people in their cars. Guys would circle the curb area several times to show off their cars and check out the other cars waiting for orders. Dale and Thomas both excelled at this activity. Dale and I completed our studies at Tidewater and both of us thought we might continue our education, but I think money was a problem for a lot of students. My father's car broke down during the summer and the Mustang needed a new transmission. I cashed in my remaining savings bonds so my parents could get the Mustang fixed and trade it in on a more dependable car. For years, people have asked me why I didn't finish college and I usually tell them I was tired of being broke. Many probably assume I am a college drop out, but I actually brought my Grade Point Average up to 3.1. Dale, Lee, and I did not continue college because we could not afford it. Tuition had risen greatly in a short period of time and student loans and aid were not prevailant at that time. We figured we had done better than we expected and it was time to get on with life. We would complete our education later. The three of us each received a 1 A classification from the draft board after we failed to register for the next college semester. President Nixon had recently instituted the draft lottery but each of us received numbers that were sure bets for the draft, especially Dale. I believe Dale received a single digit lottery number and we all thought he would soon be drafted. He was on his way home late one afternoon when an elderly lady switched lanes and hit Dale's motorcycle. Dale's knee was injured badly and he and his bike ended up directly in front of Obici Memorial Hospital. I think Dale's mother called me and let me know Dale would be o.k., but his knee was damaged and the doctors were operating on it. I was worried, but I was glad Dale was o.k. I could have easily lost a close friend that afternoon and I was anxious to talk to Dale.

Janice and Joyce witnessed Dale's knee operation and Janice called me after the operation and told me Dale was fine, but the doctors had to insert pins in his knee. She also told me that Dale's knee injury was severe enough to exempt him from military service. Dale would have answered the call if he had been drafted and I now he didn't want to be injured and be exempted that way.

As with Thomas, I realized that many things are out of our control and some things just happen. Perhaps Thomas and Dale weren't meant to go to Viet Nam and perhaps there was a reason both of them were classified 4 F. I was able to speak to Dale the next day on the phone and I ribbed him good. I was not lying when I told him Joyce and Janice witnessed his operation as part of their nursing training. I did lie when I told him he was lying nude on the operating table and Joyce's entire nursing class saw him naked. He said "Aw Nagh" and then he was silent for a time before he spoke some more. I finally told him the truth and he was very relieved. Dale had a limp for a while, but he slowly recovered and was accepted into the Newport News Shipbuilding Apprentice School as an electrician apprentice. He did great in apprentice school and the shipyard placed him in a five year advanced program for exceptional students. The drafting and mechanical drawing background was beginning to pay dividends for Dale. Dale was the first guy in our group to get married and the rest of us were pretty shocked. The "easy rider" or "car guy" was ready to settle down. He married a Suffolk girl named Lynn Graham. I married Janice in October and Dale and Lynn remained our close friends for the next several years. We played cards together and went out to eat Quite often and sometimes Dale and I would play cards with the other guys. Dale was in the Design Department at Newport News Shipbuilding and his department went out on Strike. He waited to go back to work at the shipyard, but the strike lasted longer than he anticipated and he and Lynn decided to move to Florida where Dale found a job in electrical design.

Dale and Lynn eventually split up and Dale remained single for several years. He would come to Tidewater occasionally to do ship checks for electrical work for his company. Dale and I would get together and go out to eat or visit during some of these short trips. Dale worked for New York Yankee baseball team owner, George Steinbrenner, for a time in Tampa, Florida, but he returned to

Jacksonville. He also worked in Biloxi, Mississippi for a short time, but I remember he wasn't too fond of the area.

Dale told me several of the shipyard workers would call him "Yankee" after they found out he was from Virginia. He would reply that they obviously did not know their history because many of the Confederate generals were from Virginia (such as Lee and Jackson) and most of the Civil War was fought in Virginia, not Mississippi. Dale met a girl named Toni and the two married and started a family. He has a son named Ben who is attending Florida State and a daughter named Dawn. Dale and Thomas (he and Mary have a grown daughter named Katie) are great fathers and both have always taken care of their families. I think of Dale often, but I know he is a survivor and he will always make things work out. His mother, Lorraine, moved down to Jacksonville several years ago and she passed away a few years ago. Dale took care of his mom and he was a good son who was always there for his mother as well as his brothers or sister. Dale's sister, Pat, passed away one year ago and he took it pretty hard. One of my sisters was killed in 1993 and I have also lost both parents, so Dale and I have experienced many of the same misfortunes. We both knew we would lose both parents, but big brothers are not supposed to outlive their little sisters. Dale and I have always stayed in touch, but something happened in the early 1980's that was very strange. I was sitting in the living room one evening thinking of Dale and I was missing him more than usual. I kept thinking about the good times we had and how things in the world had changed so much. The doorbell rang and I went to the front door and there stood Dale Holland. We went out to eat and had a great time talking about growing up together. I have often heard about the great friendship that existed between Thomas Jefferson and John Adams. History shows that the two friends died on July 4th about the same time. Having had twin younger sisters, I have always known that identical twins often know when one twin is suffering or in danger. I also think some friends are so close they may share the same experiences twins do. I tried to call Dale during the Christmas holidays, but I had misplaced his cell phone number and could not reach him at home. My wife went online and we tried to track him down, but there are several Dale Holland's in Jacksonville, Fla. I tried to get in touch with this half brother, but I could not reach him either. I came home from work one day and the phone had a message from Dale along with his cell number. Like many other people, Dale had done away with his home phone service and is now using a cell phone. I called Dale that evening and we talked for an hour. We brought each other up to speed on our families and other activities, and Dale mentioned he would like to come back to Virginia in the future to see his old friends. I hope he will come "home" sometime, but I know we will always stay in touch. Our paths were meant to cross and there will always be a strong connection between us.

Bobby Harrell

I can't remember the first time I met Bobby Harrell, but it had to have been in the eighth grade. Bobby is one of those people you feel as though you have known your entire life. I would venture to say it had something to do with humor because that is what I first think of when thinking of Bobby. Bobby was the youngest of three sons and he has one older sister. His father managed to raise four children by farming his forty acres located near a place called Everett's. Every member of the family worked long, hard hours like many local farmers of that time. Bobby has often told me about the times his father would load the truck with produce and water mellons on Saturday mornings. He would take his three sons to nearby Suffolk to help him sell his produce. The routine would extend to six days during the summers when the boys were out of school. Bobby is not only humorous, but he is also very intelligent. His oldest brother, Horace, was valedictorian of his high school class and he and the middle son, Vernon, both graduated from William and Mary College. Bobby also had that intellect, but Mr. Harrell struggled to send his first two sons to William and Mary and the finances were not available to send Bobby to an expensive college when he graduated from high school. Bobby is the kind of person who children like, women like, men like, and especially elderly people. I don't know if it's his calm southern demeanor or his ability to find humor in most things. My two younger sisters thought he was terrific and my daughter felt the same way when she was young. Bobby has that gift of being able to relate to everyone. Like Lee, Bobby was (and still is) tall (6'1") and thin. He still has stringy, dark hair and he still bears a strong resemblance to the actor, David Carradine. I remember when Carradine's hit television show, "Kung Fu", aired. Bobby favored Carradine so much, the rest of our group started calling Bobby "Weed Hopper", because the monk on the show referred to David Carradine as "grasshopper." I had a Fu Manchu moustache and long hair at the time and people would often call me Crosby (for David Crosby) or call Bobby "Kung Fu" when the two of us were together. Bobby's laughter got him into trouble many times during his high school years. Agriculture was one of Bobby's classes where he was asked to leave the class room because he could not stop laughing. The teacher had invited a guest to lecture the class one day. The fellow was some sort of agricultural supply representative and when the teacher introduced the guest, Bobby began to laugh. The fellow's name was Mr. Pump hammer and when Bobby heard his name he could not control himself. The name was so unusual, I know I would have laughed had I been in that class. Bobby and I were in the same senior English class and our teacher was a fellow named August Earl Ernst III. Mr. Ernst was a very hard teacher, but he was fair and he really knew how to prepare his students for college. I made a few corrections on my senior paper on Dylan Thomas and turned the same thesis in during my freshman year in college. I received a higher grade in college than I did from Mr. Ernst. Mr. Ernst enjoyed reading poetry to the class and I'll never forget him reciting the poem "Tam O'Shanter". He recited the poem in an Irish accent and Bobby could not control himself. I looked over at Bobby and it was all I could do to not laugh out loud. Mr. Ernst had a habit of placing his right forefinger against the nose piece of his glasses every time he read out loud. I would slide down in the desk and imitate Mr. Ernst with my glasses. Bobby would watch my imitation and he would begin laughing. Bobby is known to be conscientious and he is also very frugal. I think it had something to do with the way he was brought up. He never has wasted his money on frivolous things and he has always been very practical. He still owns the white 1959 Ford Fairlane he bought when we were in the tenth grade. Years later, Bobby bought a 1962 Ford from a junkyard for fifty dollars. His father once told me that Bobby would somehow make his 1959 Ford outlast gas. I agree with Bobby's philosophy that the time for a guy to have a nice car is when he is young and able to enjoy it. He also used to say young men should not have to go to war at nineteen, but should serve in the military when they were forty because their best years were behind them. Bobby also disliked cover charges at dance halls or clubs. He always figured he would be spending money once inside; why should he have to pay just to get in a place. Many times he sat in the car while some of us went into a place with a cover charge. We never stayed long and we figured out early on that Bobby was very content sitting in the car. He wasn't about to waste his money even if we were. Bobby is extremely intelligent, yet he goes out of his way to come off as an old "country boy." I remember him saying things like "I already et" instead of "already eaten" or using "ain't" whenever he could. He did Quite well in English so I figured he just thought he was free to speak the way he wanted to. I was always amazed by Bobby's intellect whenever our gang got into a lively discussion or debate. I would see what deep thinkers he and Lee were when they were in an environment (unlike a classroom) that they felt comfortable in and would not be shy or worry about their social or economic standing. I remember one instance in high school that involved Bobby. A fellow student walked up to Bobby and said, "I saw your old man at the Drugstore last night, and he was pretty drunk." Another instance where someone should have kept his mouth shut and gone about his own business. Life has taught me that people who do that sort of thing have plenty of problems in their own lives and don't need to embarrass others. Like my father always said, "People who live in glass houses should never throw stones." I knew Mr. Harrell was a good man and so what if he drank. He worked hard to support his family and farming is a tough occupation. Mr. Harrell never deprived his family or took bread from their mouths. He taught his children the values of life and to not be judgmental. I remember one gag Bobby played on a man in my father's and mother's store one afternoon. The fellow went on a verbal rage about gays and what society should do to them. Everyone in the store was tired of listening to him and Bobby decided to make the fellow uneasy. My father had a display of cheap rings on the counter and Bobby removed several of them and placed them on the fingers of both hands. He also unbuttoned the top buttons of his shirt and leaned against the counter. He started smiling at the man and the fellow became very uneasy. Bobby kept inching nearer to the fellow until he became so uneasy he left the store. Bobby received his draft notice in 1969 and left for basic training in the fall. Thomas, bobby, Lee, and I decided to go to old Ocean View Amusement Park in Norfolk one Saturday morning in late August. I can still remember the four of us riding in the car that Saturday morning. We decided to have one last fling together as a group before Bobby left for the Army. I remember the song "Judy in Disguise" by the John Fred and His Playboy Band was playing on the radio. Somehow the song reminded Bobby about a girl in high school that he had a crush on. We were talking about our trips to Ocean View with our families and churches as children as we listened to "Wait a Million Years" by the Grassroots and "Green River" by Creedence Clearwater Revival on the radio. We were young men now and we were out to have a good time. Ocean View would be torn down later and the park was used in the movie "Death of Ocean View Park" before the demolition, but we said our goodbyes that Saturday. It is still sad to remember the old, wooden roller coaster or the ferris wheel with its great view of the Atlantic Ocean. We may have been young men, but the park made each of us feel like a little boy once more. The other thing I remember about that day is the way Lee Carr was that day. Like John Lennon with the "Beatles", Lee's confidence had grown and it was though he was saying to the world, "These are my friends and as a team we are as good and as confidant as any group of guys, and we are just as smart and perhaps a little smarter! We're hell when we are well." Unfortunately, Bobby got into a minor wreck later that afternoon outside of Suffolk. No one was hurt and I think Lee told me he thought the sun blurred Bobby's vision. In a few months, Bobby would spend his time repairing "Uncle Sam's" vehicles. Bobby left for basic training and was sent to school at Aberdeen, Maryland after basic. We kept in touch with each other while Bobby was in Maryland. The two years would fly by, but we all missed Bobby. I was relieved when Bobby wrote me and told me he had been given orders for Germany where he would work in an Army motor pool. I was very glad Bobby did not get sent to Viet Nam, but Lee and I might be sent there when we were drafted. We would have to wait and see what would happen, but our chances looked very good for being drafted and sent to Southeast Asia. Bobby served in Germany with Cheech Marin who was later Cheech of the famous comedy duo, "Cheech and Chong." Bobby would tell me years later that Cheech and another soldier would play music and do comedy routines at local German clubs on weekends. There is a scene in Cheech's movie, "Born in East L.A." where

Cheech speaks German while standing on a street corner. A woman asks Cheech where he learned to speak German and Cheech replied with something like "In Germany, I was over there in the army in the motor pool." Cheech actually did serve in the Army in Germany. This was also an example of "it is a small world", because our good friend and fellow student, Skippy Holland, later toured with Cheech and Chong as the comedian, "The Mad Hatter." Bobby, Skippy, and "Cheech and Chong" gave the world some of the best medicine that exists, laughter. Maybe Bobby could join forces with Cheech and Chong and become the modern day "Three Stooges". Bobby returned home from Germany, and went back to his job at the General Electric Plant. He took advantage of the G.I. Bill and went to college at night and studied electronics. Bobby is still single. He dated a girl before he went in the army and the two continued to date when Bobby finished his military obligation. I know Bobby really cared for the girl and I used to ask him when he was going to ask her to marry him. He would always tell me that he had to save more money and have a nice house before he asked her. I always told Bobby that his girl had already waited for him to come back from the army and she was not going to wait for him to decide when the time was exactly right. She met another fellow and left for Nags Head one weekend and got married. I ran into "Weed Hopper" (Bobby) a few months ago and he is and always will be the same old guy. He still looks the same and he still laughs a lot. We sat in my car and talked about an hour. I have often heard that some people "remain stuck in the 60's", and perhaps that is where Bobby and I are when we get together. It's a good place to be sometimes.

Chapter 15
Sherri and Holly, "The Twins"

I mentioned previously that I had younger twin sisters named Sherri and Holly. One thing that was true at their birth on Feb. 24, 1963 and is still true is that I was and always will be their "big brother". Being the father to a daughter is very similar to being a big brother to a little sister. Men take care of their "little boys", but they know boys will grow into men and boys will be boys. The daughter will always be "daddy's little girl." I believe Holly took after my mother, because like my mom she is talented and has been very successful in the floral business. My mother's niche was ceramics and Holly's is flowers. Holly also has the same kind of demeanor and temperament my mother had. She will think about things for a long time and often brood over things, but she can be a real "spitfire" at times. Holly is also full of energy and likes to see things done right away; no time for delays or for waiting till tomorrow. Sherri was a lot like my father. She was a "free spirit" who could throw caution to the wind. She liked people very much, but she also could put them in their place if necessary. Sherri, like my father, was not artistic but was a "hands on" person. She did not have the patience to be a designer or to work on ceramics, but she could work on a motorcycle or work on a computer. Sherri and Holly did have one thing in common; a love for animals. They both loved horses and dogs, and both girls owned horses while they were growing up. Holly had a black retriever named "Raven" and Sherri had a brown retriever named "Sonny." I stated earlier that Sherri wanted to be a veternarian when she was growing up. Sherri departed this world doing one of the things she truly loved to do. She was riding her motorcycle when she was killed by a hit and run driver on interstate 664 in Newport News, VA. July 27th, 8:07 P.M. 1993 is a date and time deeply etched in the minds of her surviving family members. Sherri and her husband's friend (Larry) were returning from Richmond, VA that day when the accident occurred. The two had gone to Richmond to visit a friend named John that had lost a leg in an accident in Myrtle Beach, S.C. weeks earlier. It was hot that day and evening was settling in when someone crossed lanes and ran Sherri's bike into a tree. I was at the Norfolk Tides baseball game when the accident happened and I did not know about it until I came home. My wife, Norma, had heard about the accident on the late local news and she was waiting for me at the door. I could not grasp what she was telling me. I went to my parent's house in Driver, and people were already gathering at the house. My father and my brother, Gregory, had gone to Newport News to identify the body. It all seemed like a very bad dream and it did not seem like it could be true. Sherri was indestructible and She was a very careful driver (car:bike). She was coming home. We all loved her; she had to come home. My lifelong friend, William Jones, and I went outside and stood in the driveway. William kept repeating the words "I'm so sorry, I'm so sorry." He had known Holly and Sherri their entire lives. William had become such a part of our family that losing Sherri was like losing a little sister for him also. My father and brother pulled into the driveway and my father looked so hurt. He had identified the body and he kept telling me "It didn't look like Sherri, It didn't look like Sherri." I don't know if he was like me and just did not want to believe it or that Sherri had been so full of life and now his "little girl" was lifeless. I felt so sorry for him and I could not find the words to comfort him. As usual, my mother had to be the rock. She was an Arthur and Arthurs can't fully show their emotions. My mother cried, but she was already looking for answers and reasons. She was emotionally crippled, but she was already searching for the truth. My father went to the far end of the house to my parent's bedroom. I talked to him again, but I knew he wanted to be alone for a little while. I had only seen him like this one time before and that was when his father died of a heart attack. This time was much worse. Sherri was only 30 years old. My father needed to be alone, and I feel like he was saying goodbye to Sherri. He had seen a lot of death during World War II, but this was his child. It comes down to that old cliché "Parents Aren't Supposed to outlive their Children." As with all families that lose a family member, the next few days were a blur. Two old black fellows that had known Sherri (and me) all her life came by the store and wanted to know which funeral home Sherri was in. They went to pay their respects to my sister and I went a few hours later, alone. I remember walking in the funeral home and seeing a very large man sitting on a pew near the casket. I spoke to him and he introduced himself. He told me that Sherri had been his friend since she was a girl and that she was a very special person. I knew the fellow was right and anyone who attended the viewing or funeral could see how many lives Sherri had touched. I remember the feeling I experienced after seeing Sherri in the casket and having to leave her. That was the hardest thing of all for me and I would have this feeling a few more times in the not too distant future. I feel the loss the most when I have to leave a loved one at the funeral home. I want so much for them to be able to leave with me and I am not supposed to leave them alone.

Sherri's funeral was one of the largest I have ever seen and it was a real testament to her life. Bikers, Navy Captains and officers, shipyard workers, bankers, clergyman, neighbors, family members, merchants, sales people, and people from all walks of life attended the funeral. Motorcycles of all colors and types (mostly Harley Davidsons) lined Driver Lane near my parents' house. The motorcycle brigade followed the hearse to the cemetery. I had written a poem for Sherri entitled "Forever Young" because to me Sherri will be forever young. My mother showed the poem to the minister and he insisted on reading the poem during the funeral. I guess the poem touched some people because I had several reQuests for copies during the next few days. Like her brothers, Sherri was a big Beatles fan. Having been born in Feb. 1963, I guess it was natural because the Beatle's music is what she heard in our house for the first seven years of her life. One of her favorite Beatle songs was John Lennon's "In My Life." The song lyrics were a synopsis of Sherri's life. My brother, Gregory, brought a small boom box to the funeral and played "In My Life" during the service. The line "In My Life I loved them all" from the song is engraved on Sherri's grave marker. Thanks to John Lennon for writing such a beautiful song and the title to this book is a tribute to John, Sherri, and Heather. They were two people who both made the world a better place and I miss them both. My mother wanted to go back to the cemetery late that afternoon and we all looked closely at the number of flower arrangements people gave in honor of Sherri. We stood near her grave site and reminisced about the good times with Sherri. Janice Gibson, a close friend of Sherri, went to the cemetery with the family members and other people also stopped by and joined us.

Rumors began to circulate a few days after Sherri's burial because the accident had been a hit and run. Everyone in the family, especially my mother, wanted answers concerning my sister's death. It may have happened Quickly, but the family was finding out what it meant to want closure. I think my brother, sister, and I saw firsthand how my sister's death was immediately affecting my parents. It was as if someone had sucked all the life and energy out of their bodies. My mother and father were each consumed with Sherri's loss and the need to know what really happened to her. The loss was beginning to consume our entire family and many of Sherri's friends. I traveled the streets and car dealerships of Newport News looking for a grey or powder blue "V" car that had fender damage from an accident or paint from my sister's motorcycle. Every time someone had a tip or information, our family would do a follow up. My father, brother, and I went to Newport News to the part of Interstate 664 where Sherri was killed. We did this early on the Sunday morning after Sherri's passing. We were looking for car or motorcycle parts and skid marks, or any other indications of the accident. Cars were whizzing by us and I felt very sorry for my father having to go through such an ordeal, but he insisted on being with us. A state trooper named Sergeant Brown pulled to the side of the interstate and got out of his car. Sergeant Brown told us to be careful and stay off the highway. He told us he would remain at the scene while we did our investigation and he would keep an eye on the passing traffic. I believe Sergeant Brown could see pain my father was going through and I think he could relate to our loss. I know we thanked Officer Brown that day, but I would like to thank him again for what he did for us. Our local delegate in the state legislature (Robert Helms) offered to meet with my family to discuss the accident and to see if the Virginia State Police would further investigate the accident. We met with the State Police a few times and the department did put another investigator on the case, but we were unable to find any new leads.

Officer Lister of the State Police was the first officer at the scene. We talked to him a few times and on the phone a few times. An accident occurred on the north bound section of 664 immediately after Sherri's, and Officer Lister had his hands full that evening. Officer Lister was always compassionate and professional and we appreciate his help. The entire family continued to grieve Sherri's passing and we received very little information about the accident during the coming years. Anyone in our family can identify with anyone else who has lost a close family member. We know that birthdays, Christmas, Thanksgiving, other holidays, and any family occasions will never be the same. I needed something to channel my energy into after my sister's death. Lee and I had always sold goods and set up displays at the annual National Hunting and Fishing Show that was held during the month of September at nearby Sleepy

Hole Park. Mrs. Earl Sheppard informed me that the Hunting and Fishing show for 1993 would be cancelled. I asked Lee if he thought we could put a similar show on in Driver. He said he thought we could do it and I should contact Mrs. Sheppard and some of the vendors and re-enactors who had been a part of the hunting and fishing show. I began to think this could be a good thing and Sherri would be proud of her "big brother".

We began holding meetings at the local volunteer fire department and invited anyone to attend who might be interested in such an event. Fire Chief Steve Moody, Mrs. Sheppard, Gregory, Cynthia Cooper of the Civil War Re-enactors, Dale Davis of the Korean War Re-enactors, and a few others attended the meetings. Cynthia and others contacted the Medieval Knights, the Blue Knights (police officers on cycles), Bee Keeper, Food For the Hungry, and other groups. We decided to hold the festival during the final weekend in October. The Saturday of the festival started off a little slow, and I went down to my mother's house to take a little break. Lee called me and told me to look out the window. It was approximately 11:00 A M when I looked out my mother's den window and saw cars lined up and down both sides of Driver Lane. Driver was full of people. Mrs. Sheppard's group, The Chesapeake Anglers, sold out of hamburgers and hot dogs early Saturday afternoon and had to purchase more food. Mrs. Sheppard and the Anglers have been with the festival since the start and all their profits go to the Ronald McDonald House and the Driver Volunteer Fire Department. People had fun watching the Civil War re-enactors drill and fire their muskets. The Korean War re-enactors were also a big hit in the vintage uniforms and old jeeps and other vehicles. Children were excited watching the Knights battle with the swords while wearing their armor and carrying shields. They reminded people of the Viking warriors.

The two day event was a big success and our annual festival known as "Driver Days" was born. The Fire Department, the local merchants, and the public were all happy. The festival has accomplished much and has improved each year. The festival has brought families together, old friends have become reaQuainted, old and young come together, the Fire Department and Humane Society receive financial help they deserve, and everyone can once again be a kid in good old Driver. I know Sherri would like all of these things. "Driver Days" has continued throughout the years and 2010 will be the festival's 17th consecutive year. My sister, Holly, added a huge motorcycle poker run and show as the main Sunday event. The ride and show, which Holly started several years ago, is to honor Sherri. It is a very emotional thing to hear and see hundreds of motorcycles enter Driver and I know Sherri is looking down and smiling. The annual Saturday car show draws many car enthusiasts and people come from everywhere to check out the food, bands, and crafts. Ben Jones, who played "Coster" on the television show "Dukes of Hazzard" lead the parade during the Tenth Driver Days. Ben lived in Driver as a boy and he came "home" to help out Driver and the fire department. He is truly a nice man who never forgot his roots.

I will miss my sister until I take my final breath, but <u>I do know</u> that she accomplished much in her short 30 years. She was my sister and she was also "my buddy": I remember her wearing my father's old Amoco shirt as a ten year old. I remember shooting pool with Sherri. I remember Norfolk Tides baseball games on warm summer nights. I remember Washington Redskin games on beautiful fall Sunday afternoons and cold afternoon games in December: I remember sitting with Sherri in the end zone at RFK and watching the Skins demolish the Los Angeles Rams 55-7 on a New Years Day playoff game. I remember you pulling up next to John Riggins on East Capitol Street in D.C. and following "Riggo" to R.F.K. I think "Riggo" had as much fun as we did. I remember visiting you at the Great Lakes in Chicago and you picking Jerry and me up at the airport and heading straight to Wrigley Field to watch the Cubs. I remember three consecutive days at Wrigley and watching the Brewers and Red Sox in Milwaukee on Monday night. I will never forget you telling me that you were taking Jerry and me to Lou Minoltas in Chicago to eat the best pizza in the world and you were right. I will never forget how sad it was to catch the plane and leave you alone in Chicago. I remember you and I carpooling with Janice to the Navy Yard for a few years. I remember the day Billy Moore, you, and I captured the wolf hybrid (wolf) and how you nursed her back to health and gave her a good home. "Wolf" spent the remainder of her life with Gregory and she had a long, happy life, but I know she always missed you. I remember how much you loved your Cocker Spaniel, Bailey, and how protective she was of you. I will never forget the little hummingbird showing up at Mom's kitchen window the first morning after your passing. I will always miss you and I will always love you. I could probably write an entire book about my sister, Sherri, but she belongs with my mother, father, and so many others in this book. The old cliché is "they are in a better place" and I agree with that. God creates people that make any place they are in a better place, and heaven is a better place with Sherri in it. Like most people that face the loss of loved ones, there is not a day that goes by that I don't think of Sherri. These people could tell you that these thoughts occur at anytime and anyplace. I was with a friend one night at a Triple A baseball game in Norfolk and I spotted a girl that was the spitting image of Sherri. It was sort of eerie and I could not help noticing she had many of Sherri's mannerisms. That night brought back so many memories. There will always be an emptiness in my heart, but I was also very lucky to be Sherri's brother. She left her mark on this world and for thirty years she made the world better. With God's help, I will be with her again. Until that time, I will never forget her.

Chapter 16
Lee Carr

I met Lee Carr at Old Chuckatuck High School about the same time I met Dale Holland and Bobby Harrell. I mentioned before that the three of them had gone through elementary school together and I think I met Lee through Bobby or Dale. I had been in some of the same classes with Lee and I knew he was very intelligent, but he was also very reserved. I got to know Lee much better after John Yeates High School replaced the high school classes at Chuckatuck. The more I was around Lee, the more I wanted to be good friends with him. Early on I knew he was like Thomas, Dale, and Bobby. He might have been reserved at school, but outside the class room he could be funny and was much more confident. The best thing about Lee was when he became your friend; he was always your friend. He was your friend through thick or thin.

Lee grew up on a dairy farm in an area known as Reids Ferry that is located a few miles from Chuckatuck. Lee's father worked at the dairy and drove a milk truck for the dairy to support his family. Mr. Carr and his wife, Mae, were the parents to four boys and one daughter. Lee's brothers were named Charles, Allan, and Harvey and the youngest member of the family was his sister, Cori. The family lived in an old, run-down house on the dairy grounds and the family was considered "poor". The family may have been "poor", but each member was hard working and honest. The boys could work on cars, guns, farm equipment, and many other things. They did not have the money for repairs; so the boys learned to repair everything themselves. They all had "common sense." Lee, like Dale, had a life altering experience when he was young. He was supposed to work with his father on the milk truck one night, but he and his brother, Allan switched nights. Lee's father and Allan were hit by a train that night and both were killed. The only thing Lee ever told me about the incident was that he was supposed to be on that truck that night. Lee, Thomas, and I would sometimes go back in the marsh near the dairy and target practice with some of Lee's pistols. I remember Lee shooting some water moccasins that would swim in the nearby creek. I can't believe we walked in some areas and were not bitten by a snake during warm weather.

Like the day at Ocean View Amusement Park, another day brings back a lot of fond memories. School let out early on the last day before summer break at the end of our junior year in high school. We decided to go to Lake Ahoy and everyone met back at my parents' house after retrieving their swim trunks. We had a good time swimming and listening to music on a transistor radio. Naturally, a few of us got sunburned as usual, but nothing too serious. Thomas was scheduled to work at the A & P that night so we ended the "party" by late afternoon. I had the night off so I asked Lee if he had any plans and he said no. We went to the Giant Open Air Market in Portsmouth to look around. The market sold food from various parts of the world and also sold fishing gear and record albums. I found a rock n' roll flyer among the albums and I read about a California band that was supposed to be the "next" "Beatles". The band was named "Moby Grape" and the Giant was selling the groups first album. I bought the album and became hooked on the group's sound. Songs like "Hey Grand Ma", "Come in the Morning", "Naked If I want To" and a second album of the two album set called "Grape Jam" were new and refreshing. The group even appeared in a rock movie and seemed like they were headed for stardom. By the late 1960's Americans, especially young people were interested in actors, musicians, and other artists that were not part of the "in crowd" or "beautiful people." Actors like Dustin Hoffman and Jack Nicholson were appreciated for their acting ability and not for good looks. Young people were beginning to be targeted as the future consumers from everything like movies, cars, clothes, and music to the fast food industry. I have always felt that "Moby Grape" was harmed by all the advance publicity the band received. It was similar to ball players that were tagged as the "next Mickey Mantle." If my memory is correct, it seems like a band member was related to Doris Day and that probably made some feel as though the band had special connections. I continued collecting "Moby Grape" albums. The group cut several records and always had a loyal group of fans who did not mind searching for their albums. I finally found a two-C D set that contained many of the group's best songs. Lee and I were getting hungry and decided to eat at Shoney's Big Boy so we could watch the cars and the girls. We passed on the fried grasshoppers, chocolate covered ants, and rattle snake meat the Giant Open Air market sold. We hung out at the Shoney's for a while and thought we'd see a movie. We had both heard about the "Graduate" Starring Dustin Hoffman. The movie was the perfect entertainment for a couple of seventeen year olds who had just finished their junior year in high school. Dustin Hoffman was fantastic in the "Graduate" and the "Simon and Garfunkle" sound track was also great. The movie impressed Lee and me so much that we told Thomas, Bobby, and Dale about it and most of us saw the movie several times. I remember Thomas referring to the scene where Benjamin's parents threw a big graduation party for him. The father's friend who talked about "plastics" being a great investment really impressed Thomas and he also thought plastics were the wave of the future. Truthfully, we were all impressed with the acting and sound track, but Mrs. Robinson was the character that got our attention. We thought Ben was the luckiest guy in the world and our minds always drifted when we saw the movie sound track album cover that pictured "Mrs. Robinson." Later when I got "hung up" on the girl I mentioned earlier I could relate to Dustin Hoffman's character even more. I did many of the same silly things "Ben" did and I continued to make a fool of myself. Lee was the steady hand that tried to keep me focused and convince be I would find someone I could feel the same way about.

One particular incident involving Lee Carr occurred in government class in high school during our senior year. The teacher, Mr. Carter, made a Statement that anyone who watched the "Beverly Hillbillys" tv show was a moron. Some of Lee's ancestors and kin were from West Virginia and might have been considered "Hillbillys." The teacher's comment hit a nerve and Lee Quickly raised his hand to speak. Lee told the teacher the ratings for the television show, he told him what percentage of viewers watched the show each week, he named some intelligent people that watched the show regularly, and he said that President Lyndon Johnson watched the show and said it was his favorite comedy. As usual, Lee had the information and facts to back his belief. The teacher was kind of shocked since Lee was usually so Quiet and our classmates looked at Lee as though he was a lot smarter than they thought he was. They were learning what I had known for a long time: Lee was shy, but he had enough confidence to fight for what he believed in. Truth was very important to him and he did not need to impress anyone. Lee and Thomas were riding through the City Park in Portsmouth one afternoon and met two girls. Lee would eventually marry Beverly and Thomas would marry Mary. I wound up marrying Janice, whom I had met when Thomas asked me to go with him to give a lift to one of his sister's friends. I remember the other fellows envying Lee because Beverly owned a nice, yellow Mustang and she would often come out to Driver and pick Lee up and let him drive her car. Beverly and Mary were attractive girls and the guys were not accustomed to seeing girls come to pick up the guy for a date. We would tease Lee and tell him that was a way Beverly could keep an eye on him. Lee and I were cruising around one afternoon when he told me I was the most "average" person he knew. I didn't Quite know how to take Lee's assessment and I thought about a lot before the next day. My insecurity made me think maybe Lee and Dale liked me because they thought their intellect was greater than mine. I asked Lee what he meant when we went somewhere the next night and I was very relieved with his answer. He said he didn't mean to imply that I was not intelligent; he meant that I was the most normal person he had ever known. He saw me as someone like Wally Cleaver on "Leave It To Beaver." I assured Lee that I had plenty of ups and downs and everything was not as it always seemed. I had many tough times growing up, but my Grandfather Arthur had always taught us to have a stiff upper lip and "carry on". My grandfather could have invented the line in the commercial that says "never Let them see you sweat." I don't' think Lee had the opportunity to see any movies when he was young and he really enjoyed the ones we saw. "Bonnie and Clyde", "The Green Berets", "The Graduate", "Bullitt", "Butch Cassidy and the Sundance Kid", "Rooster Cogburn", "True Grit", "Rosemary's Baby" and "The Sing" were some of our favorites. "Butch Cassidy and the Sundance Kid" with Paul Newman, Robert Redford, and Katherine Ross is a movie I always have to watch if I see it on cable. The movie reminds me a lot of the friendship between Lee and me. I certainly was no Paul Newman, but Lee was very similar to the "Sundance" character. Lee had brownish red or blondish red hair and he had some of the same mannerisms of the character. Lee and I were linked together as a pair in our high school annual. The lines written to describe the future for us described Lee and I as the new prototype for the next strong, silent, type of men. I asked Lee about the line and he said he had asked someone involved with the annual and the person said we reminded some of our classmates of Gary Cooper; strong and silent. The "Butch and Sundance" movie takes me back because Lee would often ask me (like Sundance), "Do Yo Always Have to Be Right"? The scene where Butch and Sundance are trapped on the rocky ledge overlooking the rapids also reminds me of Lee.

Like Sundance, if Lee had not been able to swim and would not jump because of it, but would have to be forced or cajold by Butch to admit he could not swim was like our relationship. Like Butch and Bobby Harrell, I would probably have laughed at our predicament and could have stated "not to worry because the fall alone will probably kill us."

Events that occurred years later reminded me very much of Lee and me. If Lee was pinned down and fighting for his life, shouldn't I be there? I will explain this feeling later in more depth. Watching the movie "Bullit" starring Steve McQueen was a real experience. Watching the chase scenes involving the Dodge Charger and McQueen's Mustang on the huge theater screen made us feel like we were involved. I even had the funny feeling your stomach gets when going up and down steep hills or riding a fast roller coaster. As Thomas, Lee, and I stepped outside the theater that night, Lee told me "I will have a car just like that one in the movie". I thought Lee was talking about McQueen's Mustang and I said I thought he wasn't a "Ford Man". Lee told me he was talking about the bad guys' Dodge Charger and he would soon have one. That was my last thought of the conversation.

A few months later, Lee pulled up in my parents' driveway driving a brand new green Dodge Charger. I could not believe my eyes, but Lee assured me the car was really his. He had gotten some sort of settlement from his brother Allan's death and he used the money to purchase the car. That Charger was Lee's pride and joy and he kept the car the remainder of his life. He repainted the car and changed the colors to a silver body with a black top. Lee also redid the upholstery in the 1980's and changed the interior from dark green to black. The old 383 Cu. In. engine was original and the car was very dependable. Lee and I never discussed the reason for him keeping the car so long, but looking back I think it was a tribute to Allan and was Lee's way of remembering his brother. Lee missed a lot of school days during our junior and senior years, and he was usually one bad illness from exceeding the maximum limit for missed days. Doctors later found that Lee had Crohn's Disease and perhaps that caused him to miss so much time. It was remarkable that he made passing grades those two years. Lee got a job making synthetic marble the summer before our last year in college. The marble slip was poured into various molds to produce table tops and other items. Lee enjoyed the work and was impressed with the entire operation. Lee talked to the company's owner one day and found out the owner was considering selling his marble business. Lee approached Thomas and me and said he thought the three of us could run the business properly and do Quite well. He said we could get the business operating at full force and offer Dale and Bobby part of the company.

Thomas and I talked everything over that evening and Thomas felt like he could not leave A & P and I felt like Lee and I should continue college. I have regretted our decisions many times because I somehow believe we would have done good. We all trusted each other and each of us would have worked hard because we did not want to let each other down. I often think what might have been. Lee and I both knew we would probably be drafted when we stopped going to college. Lee received his notice to go to Richmond for an army physical. We really got worried that night because Lee did not return home from Richmond. Thomas, Dale, and I wondered if he had been inducted and sent to boot camp. Lee returned home and told me the doctors had found something wrong with him and wanted him to return to Richmond in a month. The doctors thought Lee might have stomach ulcers and he had not been diagnosed with Crohn's Disease, but he may have had it at that point. Lee went back to Richmond a few more times and the doctors eventually disQualified him from service because his condition was not improving. He was not overjoyed because he knew something might be seriously wrong. I was worried, but I was relieved because I knew he was not going to Viet Nam. My closest friends were safe and I thanked God many times for keeping them safe.

We all married, except Bobby Harrell, and Thomas and I were fathers of little girls and Dale would eventually become a father too. Lee had a good job with The Army Core of Engineers. Lee and I would get together throughout the years and have dinner together or visit Bobby. Lee and Beverly divorced and I did not see him for some time, but I answered the door one night and there stood Lee Carr. Lee told me a popular song had made him think about us guys and he was hoping we could all stay in closer touch. He told me he had had some rough times and he had met some people at work who were very self-serving and were not very trustworthy. The song Lee was referring to was "Wasted On the Way" by "Crosby, Stills, and Nash". Lee was dead on and it could have been written about our friendships. "So Much time to make up; wasted on the way. Let the water come and carry us away." We all felt like the song stated that we all had more than we wanted or expected and maybe some of our friends did get what they deserved. It was time for us to "Look Around You Now"! We did get close again after Lee's visit, and we all did a better job of staying close and keeping up with each others' lives. I mentioned before that our friendships will always be strong no matter how much time, distance, or travel is involved. Friendship is the physics of our lives.

Lee and I would have our opportunity to be business partners. I left my job at the Shipyard and my brother and I operated the two stores my Grandfather Arthur owned in Driver. My parents were busy caring for my grandfather and my mother's health was getting worse. I had worked the Civil Service for thirteen and one-half years and it was hard to leave a good job, but the two stores had been in our family since the beginning of the century. I sold hardware and camping gear in the store known as the "Driver Variety Store." My father would generally come in about noon and he was pretty much on call most of the time due to my mother's many doctor appointments and hospital stays. Lee approached me about he and I teaming up and selling firearms and ammunition in the store. Lee obtained a federal firearms license and he knew the various calibers of guns and the most popular types of ammunition. He only sold guns on weekends and kept them locked up in a walk-in safe at home during the week. This eliminated many of the problems associated with selling firearms. Lee and I worked several gun shows in the area and Lee built up the ammunition and accessory inventory very Quickly. He had a vast knowledge of firearms, ammunitions, and parts and he was very congenial with customers and the general public. Lee liked people and he really liked what he was doing. Our customers were from every walk of life and I remember one fellow who was very impressed with Lee. Lee's first name was actually Charles and the fellow always referred to Lee as "Charlie". The man became a good customer of Lee's and the two would have long conversations about old guns, cannons, and other weapons. The customer stopped in one day when Lee was at his regular job and the two of us had a nice conversation. He told me he had originally worked for the United States National Park Service, but the government switched him over to the Secret Service due to the need for more agents. He told me about some of the training (nothing secretive) and some of the interesting people he met. The fellow had been assigned to President Nixon at one point in his career. Larry, the agent, told me he had been all over the world and met many interesting and knowledgeable people during his stint with the Secret Service. He said he had met many experts on firearms, but he said "Charlie" knew more than anyone he had ever known. I told Larry Lee knew more about many things than many experts. I told Larry to ask Lee about Dodge Chargers sometime. Lee always gave me good advice and I remember he stopped by one afternoon after Janice and I split up. He told me to look at life as you would riding a horse. He said if you fell off the horse you would probably try to get back on and ride again. Lee said, "don't let life throw you, get back up and ride again".

Lee and I were becoming more successful with the ammo business and we were thinking about our options for the future. Lee thought he may be able to take an early out with his job at age fifty. We talked about him working at the store four or five days a week or perhaps opening another business together in another village. Unfortunately, we never got the chance. Lee's health was deteriorating Quickly and he had four major back operations over the years. He would wear an aluminum brace on his back and would be in so much pain at the end of a day he felt like crying. The Crohn's Disease was worse. As usual, Lee was the constant in my life when my sister, Sherri, was killed in a hit and run accident. He attended the funeral and he opened the store afterwards. I felt the need to stay busy and stay focused on business, but Lee told me I should be with the family. Lee's and my aspirations were never fulfilled. Lee was in an accident in August, 1995 and he was paralyzed on his entire right side. The doctors operated on his right hand several times, but they finally had to amputate the hand. I remember the day of the accident as if it was yesterday. Lee called me early that Saturday morning and told me he had some business to take care of. Our local fire chief, Steve Moody, came to the store that afternoon and took me aside. He told me Lee had been in a terrible accident and the doctors were operating on him at that time at Norfolk Sentara Hospital. Lee was in critical condition. All kinds of thoughts raced through my mind, but I kept thinking that at least Lee is still alive. It was not like the situation with Sherri where she was gone in an instant. There was still hope, and I know firsthand that hope may be all you have at times, but hope is better than nothing at all. I can't go into the details concerning Lee's accident. It was one of those situations where few really know what happened and often things are better left alone. Many times things are either freak accidents or a matter of being in the wrong place at the wrong time.

Lee was transferred to Portsmouth General Hospital for physical therapy after several weeks at Norfolk Sentara. I visited him several times at both hospitals and he somehow remained positive. I continued to sell his merchandise at the store and I would take his money to him; so I saw him on a regular basis. The simple things in life became major obstacles for Lee. Orderlies would bring a lift to his room and roll him from side to side while placing a type of gurney under his body. They would work a lever (similar to a car jack) to lift Lee out of bed and swing him into a wheel chair. The procedure was reversed when he was lifted back into bed. I had seen race horses with broken or injured legs maneuvered the way Lee was, but the procedure made me feel sorry for Lee and the physical and mental pain he was suffering. How could this happen to him? Would things have been different if I had been with him that day? Lee's sister-in-law was helping Lee's wife, Debbie, take care of him during December, 1995. She called me and asked if it was anyway I could bring Lee's money to him. She also told me she was having a hard time waking Lee and he had a doctor's appointment that afternoon. The day was December 11: two weeks before Christmas. I got Lee's money together and left to see Lee shortly after my father arrived at the store. When I arrived at Lee's house, his sister-in-law told me she had knocked on Lee's door several times, but he would not wake up. She asked if I could wake him. I knocked on Lee's bedroom door and he did not answer, so I called out his name and said he needed to get up. I entered the room and everything looked normal, but Lee would not answer me. I moved his good arm a little and called his name. When I tried to move Lee's arm, I realized why he couldn't answer me and I did not want to face reality. I hollered and told his sister-in-law to call 911. I talked to the dispatcher and I told him Lee had gone through four major back operations, had Crohn's

Disease, and was paralyzed on one side. I also told the dispatcher about his arm being stiff and he told me not to do anything and help was already on the way. The paramedics arrived in a matter of minutes and one of them looked at me and shook his head when he started checking on Lee. My heart sank and I got a sickening feeling. Lee was gone and so were our plans. No more deep discussions, no more practical jokes, and no more Butch and Sundance.

The Chesapeake Police arrived and checked everything and Lee's sister-in-law was trying to reach her sister, Debbie. The police talked to the sister-in-law and me and Lee's brother (Harvey) and his wife (Debbie) arrived at the house. When I saw Harvey, I immediately thought of Lee's mother, Mae. She had already been through so much. She had already lost one son and two husbands. Mae had suffered so many heartaches in life and Lee was always a rock for her. Now he was gone. The entire day was very emotional and stressful. I had a terrible headache, but I was trying to rationalize everything in my mind. Lee would not have to suffer anymore and I really believe he would have wanted me to be the one to find him. Lee finally had something that eluded him often in life; peace. I returned to the store very late that afternoon and my father was very upset over Lee's passing. He knew Lee and I had been close friends very many years and he really liked Lee. My father was an expert on friendship and he tried to ease my pain. He told me things I had thought of earlier like Lee did not want to be a burden to others and he was finished suffering.

When I left the store that night; I took an old country road where I could drive in peace and Quiet. A shooting star soared across the sky and it seemed as though it was right in front of me. Call this corny, but I suddenly felt peaceful and felt like Lee was now at peace. Like Buddy Holly said one time; The Sky belongs to the Stars. The next few months were very hard and I went through many changes. Sometimes I would be mad and wonder how Lee could have gotten himself in such predicaments. The selfish side of me would surface and I would ask myself "Didn't he know how much I needed him. We had already been through so much, could I go it alone? Did I even want to? The occasional bitter feelings subsided and I went back to basics. I realized that Lee and I were there for each other and there was no blame or anger. I realized that he had always been there for me, and maybe I helped him reach some of the plateaus in life that he needed a little help to reach. We gave each other confidence. I think each "friend" would say that Lee was one of the smartest individuals he ever met and for me he was the "smartest". Like I do with much of life, (maybe it's the Music and Buddy Holly), but I will take a cue from the best Hollie's song, "He Ain't Heavy, He's My Brother". I have had dreams about Lee and I know we will be like Butch and Sundance and we will ride again. In the first dream he told me we will always be friends and we Will. Maybe Nannie put us together and was trying to make up for her absence. I pray to God that I will be reunited with both of them.

Chapter 17

Heather, My Daughter

I remember the afternoon that my wife, Janice, told me she was going to have a baby. I had just gotten home from my job at Newport News Shipbuilding. She told me she had something very important to tell me, but I had no idea what it was. I could not believe what she was telling me. We had decided to wait and have a child after we were more settled and had a place of our own. We were living in an apartment that my Grandfather owned and I liked it a lot, but we both wanted a house before we started a family. I would soon get over the shock and realize this happens to a lot of people. Who is really completely ready to start a family or change their life very Quickly? It is part of life and like life it just happens. I felt guilty for being so nervous at first, but I began to get excited about the prospects of becoming a father. We started out by looking through baby name books. Would it be a boy (a future baseball player) or would it be a girl? I can honestly say that I just wanted our child to be healthy. I found the name Heather in a baby book and I thought it was the perfect name for a baby girl. I knew our daughter would be a special person and Heather was not the most common female name during that time. I wanted our daughter to be happy, and I wanted her to be free to be her own person.

Janice went into labor on Thursday afternoon February 15, 1973. My brother, Gregory, picked me up in front of Newport News Shipbuilding and we headed for Maryview Hospital in Portsmouth. My mother and a good friend of our family, Reverend Fred Lowmiller, were waiting for us at the hospital. It seems like we waited for an eternity, and our Methodist Minister friend, Fred, stayed with us until Heather was born. I looked at Heather and thought how tiny she was and how precious she was. It dawned on me that I was responsible for this beautiful child and I was very lucky to have her. It was now the wee hours of Friday, Feb. 16, 1973; the best day of my life.

Heather had blonde hair and brown eyes and was always tall for age. I used to think she was going to be very tall and she might play basketball for Old Dominion University. Anyone who knew Heather as a baby or child will tell you that she was very unusual because she was always happy and content. I can't take credit for her behavior because I was a spoiled brat as a young boy. John Denver's hit song "Sunshine On My Shoulder" is very important to me. There was a weekly television show about a musician who was raising his little girl and Heather and I would sit on the couch together and watch the show every week. Janice was taking an evening class that same night each week. Heather was about three at that time and she would run around all week singing "Sunshine on my shoulder". The song was used on the show and I think she related the song to she and I watching it together. I related it to Heather being the "Sunshine on My Shoulder" and I do to this day. I realized early on that Heather and I liked the same sort of things. We liked the same television shows, a lot of the same music, and we both liked to laugh. I think she got that from my friend, Bobby Harrell. She loved the old reruns of the old "Monkees" t.v. show and she was crazy over Micky Dolenz. We took Heather to see the "Monkees" at the Norfolk Scope one Sunday night. Gary Puckett of "The Union Gap", "Herman's Hermits", and a few other "oldies groups" performed many of their hits. Gary Puckett introduced actress Morgan Fairchild to the crowd. Heather's favorite place was Busch Gardens Old Country in Williamsburg. She and I would ride the rides while Janice watched. Heather was crazy over the ride known as "The Battering Ram" and we would try to sit in the back so we would go higher in the air. She also liked the "Log Plume", The Octopus", and

"De Vinci's Cradle, but she did not like the roller coaster type rides like "The Big Bad Wolf".

We went to Disney World one August when Heather was about eight. We took Amtrak to Orlando and it was a nice trip going through so many small towns from Virginia to Florida. It was nice sleeping on the train and I liked it because I didn't have to drive. We were riding in a boat and watching the nightly fireworks at Disney World on our second day in the park. Heather looked at me and said, "Daddy, I think I like Busch Gardens a lot more". I had spent Quite a bit of money on the Florida trip, but after that year I always bought season tickets to Busch Gardens Williamsburg each year. We would put Heather's season pass in her Christmas stocking. Like most fathers, I would put together Christmas toys each year until the late hours of Christmas Eve. The toy stoves, refrigerators, Barbie accessories, doll houses, and numerous other toys would try any sane person's patience. Heather received a toy version of a McDonalds Drive In one year, and she was so funny pushing the little toy cars around and ordering chicken McNuggets. Like many young girls, Heather was a big Barbie doll fan and she obtained many of the dolls and the furnishings that went with the doll. She would carry a bag full of Barbies and related toys in a bag each time we went to my parent's house or out to visit friends. Heather collected the Barbie mansion, the Corvette, the travel home, the swimming pool, and many other related toys.

I met a fellow pipefitter apprentice named Kenny Benton in 1973 at Norfolk Naval Shipyard in Portsmouth. We became close friends in 1975 when we went into nuclear training together. Kenny and his wife, Carol, were like us and had one child at the time; a son named Duane. Our wives became good friends and Heather and Duane enjoyed playing together. The couple would become parents to a baby girl named Lena and years later a baby girl named Crystal. Heather grew up with the Benton kids and she was especially close to Lena (probably due to the closeness of their ages).   Our two families would go on picnics together, go to Busch Gardens and Kings Dominion together, go to the Norfolk Zoo together, and vacation together.   There were not many children Heather's age living in Driver, and she really enjoyed being with Kenny's kids. Heather was like most girls her age, but she was also very uniQue. She was my child, but I can honestly say she never gave me any trouble. The worst thing she ever did was play her music too loud, but I did the same thing when I was her age. Heather liked music from the time she was very young.   She liked Cyndi Lauper, Michael Jackson, Madonna, Wham and a lot of the stars from her youth, but she also liked Harry Connick Jr., Phil Collins, Hall and Oates, and especially Billy Joel. I could not get her interested in the Beatles. Heather was a real big fan of the group, "Tears for Fears" and she got me interested in the British band.   She and a friend from high school were supposed to go to William and Mary College to see a "Tears for Fears" in concert, but her friend got the flu. Heather asked me to go to the concert with her and I did. It was raining hard the night of the concert and we had to take our time driving to Williamsburg. We stopped at a Burger-King and ate dinner and continued on to the concert. The night became more miserable, but we got more excited about the concert the closer we got to it. Heather and I enjoyed the concert and the musicians with "Tears for Fears" were great.   Roland Orzabal (lead singer and guitarist) and the band played their hit "Seeds of Love" with a huge screen showing 60's memorabilia behind the band. The song was very similar to Beatle music and the Orzabal sounded like John Lennon. The flowers, peace symbols, Beatles, and other things on the screen took everyone back to the mid 1960's. One older couple at the concert pointed to Heather and I a few times and I think they were thinking the worst and thought they were seeing an older man with a high school girl. The concert hall audience was made up of people of all ages and everyone seemed to enjoy the band. My faith in mankind (after the staring incident) would be restored when we left the concert hall. Heather and I walked past a group of William and Mary College Students and fraternity members and I could see the guys were eyeing Heather, but were very mannerly. The guys talked to us and offered me a beer; which I declined. They knew without asking that Heather was my daughter and I believe they were impressed that my daughter and I were attending a concert together. I am not bragging, but I have always been able to relate to young people. I can identify with them and recall what it feels like to be in their shoes.

I would take Heather to another "Tears for Fears" concert three years later at Chrysler Hall in Norfolk. I was able to get her interested in classical music, the great tenor from the 1950's, Mario Lanza, and many other great musicians and performers. Heather was a big Billy Joel fan and his song "Keeping the Faith" makes me think of her. She would always laugh at the song line that says "a nice cold beer in the shade". Heather liked Joel's "Piano Man", "We Didn't Start the Fire", "Leave A Tender Moment Alone", "Uptown Girl". Heather had a beautiful voice and she sang in the chorus at Nansemond River High School. She made all-state in chorus and she could sing as high as Whitney Houston. She made a recording of Whitney's "The Greatest Love" one time at Busch Gardens. Heather was also a gifted artist and this was definitely something she inherited from her mother's family. Janice was an artist, one of her brothers was an artist, and Janice's uncle in Roanoke, VA. was an artist. The walls in the uncle's house had paintings hung on every square inch. I remember one painting of the Kentucky Derby that was beautiful. The horses, jockeys, and spectators in the stands were so life-like. The uncle painted very much like Grandma Moses. Heather loved to draw or paint cats, beach scenes, and houses. One local professional artist took an interest in Heather and gave her numerous paints, brushes, and other supplies. She took several art courses in college and she was an art major.

Heather began working in the deli at my grandfather's old store when she was old enough to get a work permit. People would come up to me and tell me how polite and nice Heather was. Many told me she was a very special girl. Heather and I would play Atari for hours. We played games like Asteroids, Ms Pac Man, Car races, and many other games Heather collected. I gave her a Saga Genesis game one Christmas and we played on it many hours. I remember several presents I gave Heather over the years that she really cherished. I gave her a double cassette boom box one Christmas so she could dub songs off the radio or duplicate cassettes. Heather kept the old boom box for years. When Heather got older, I bought her a Marantz Stereo System with huge 125 watt speakers, turntable, tuner, and cassette player. She could not believe her eyes that Christmas morning and she couldn't wait for me to connect the big speakers. Thoughts of that stereo bring back memories of my old stereo system. Heather was recording cassettes on my system one time and she swung the glass door too far back and it hit the corner of the console television. The glass door disintegrated into a pile and Heather looked like she wanted to cry. I told her it was an accident and she couldn't help it. I still have my old stereo and I have thought a hundred times about the door disintegrating. I saw an arcade in a department store about two weeks before Christmas and decided Heather would like it as an extra present. It was her favorite present that year and we played the arcade every night for a long time. I think she enjoyed it so much because she could beat me like she did with Atari. A few years later I would see her looking at the arcade like she missed the times we played it regularly. She was growing up.

Heather was a hard worker at school and her jobs. She worked at The Coast Guard Credit Union in Norfolk thirty-eight hours a week and she worked at a computer store at the local mall in Chesapeake. Heater carried a full load at college during the same period. Heather dated a boy for a short while in high school and he stood her up one Friday night. I was furious and I told Heather she was too good for him and she would meet someone who would know how to treat her. I told her not to judge all boys by one inconsiderate joker. Heather soon began dating a classmate named Jesse Burgess. Jesse was a gentleman and he really cared about Heather. I can only say good things about Jesse and I am so thankful he came into Heather's life. Jesse was a very good student and I believe he graduated something like third in his class. He was also very mechanically inclined and he loved working on cars. Jesse owned an old Ford Mustang and he kept the car in good condition. I knew Jesse's Dad, Ronald Burgess, from Norfolk Naval Shipyard. He was an inside machinist and rose to the position of General Foreman in the Nuclear division. Jesse must have inherited his mechanical skill, and he was a boy who had common sense as well as book sense. Jesse and Heather were suited for each other. Both of them loved the outdoors and both of them loved to fish. Heather spent a lot of time fishing and crabbing as a child, so she was tickled to death when she found out how much Jesse enjoyed fishing. Jesse could have gotten into just about any college he liked, but he applied to the apprentice school at the Newport News Shipbuilding. The apprentice school at the Newport News Yard is considered one of the best in the country and Jesse was very interested in learning a trade. Naturally, he did very well in apprentice school and made outstanding grades. The shipyard decided to put Jesse in an accelerated program and place him in the design division. This was the same thing that happened to my good friend, Dale Holland.

Before I completely made up my mind about a legal separation from Janice, I conferred with Heather. Heather told me she knew things were coming to a head and it was something I had to do for the sake of my own sanity. She said she would stay with her mother. Heather was nearly eighteen at this time, but I did not want her to think I was deserting her. My parents lived directly across the street and had converted the old carport into a room. My brother had once lived in the room and my mother insisted I move into the old carport. The situation was perfect for Heather and me both. She could come over anytime she wanted and study, do homework, watch television, or listen to music. I think she really enjoyed the freedom and she also got to see my parents more. Heather had always been close to my mother and she called her "Nan". That tickled my mother. My father would take over for me at the store and I would take Heather shopping or out to eat. We may have spent more time together than when I lived at home. I attended the high school functions she was involved with and she also spent a lot of time with me at the store. Heather liked hanging out at my store. The Driver Variety Store had been in my family since about 1910 and I began operating it in 1987. Heather liked to play the big Ms. Pac Man machine in the back of the store and she liked to drink YooHoo chocolate sodas. I kept some small pizzas in the Pepsi box that were similar to the personal pan pizzas. She liked to stop by and eat one of the "Little Charlie" pizzas after school for a snack. I don't know if every parent thinks the thought I had one spring day when Heather was about three years old. She was playing out in the side yard facing my grandfather's house and I was watching her play. I had this strange feeling and I asked myself what I would do if I didn't have Heather? My mind could not answer my own Question, but I remember telling myself that I do have her and I don't want to ever think about not having her. I thought about seeing the major events of her life like the birthdays, graduation, college, marriage, having her own children, and all the important things of her life. I did not want to be like my father and be absent for many of those events. I already knew the feeling a parent gets when his or her child is sick, upset, disappointed, has hurt feelings or anything big or small. How many times had I seen my daughter have a fever, cold, or be nauseated and wish it could be me instead? I wanted to love and protect my daughter.

Heather began losing weight around late September of 1994. I had remarried and she had moved in with my wife, Norma, and me shortly after we had married about three years earlier. She had lived with her mother for a short period of time, but decided she really wanted to be with us. I thought Heather was losing weight because she was on the go all the time. She was working, carrying a full load in college, dating, and many other things people her age do. Her energy level was high and she seemed to be enjoying life. Jesse and Heather were engaged by this time and Jesse had bought a nice house in Portsmouth. The two of them spent their free time sanding floors, painting, repairing, and getting the house ready to live in after their marriage. I was so happy for Heather and Jesse. They were meant to be together and he made her so happy and their future looked so bright. They would be living nearby and Heather and I could remain close. I had a great daughter, and I would soon have a great son-in-law.

During Thanksgiving of 1994, everyone began noticing that Heather was losing weight at a faster pace. My mother, I and many other family members insisted she go to her doctor. Heather saw different doctors during December 1994 and January 1995. One doctor thought she could have had pneumonia and another thought she may have pulled a stomach muscle. She had bronchitis a few times during her childhood and one doctor thought that might be the problem. A Chesapeake woman doctor checked Heather in January and decided to take x-rays. The doctor discovered a huge tumor in Heather's stomach and told her she needed to see an oncologist. Naturally everyone was worried, but she was yet to see an oncologist and with some luck the tumor would be benign. Heather's mother, Janice, and I went with Heather to see the oncologist. He looked over the x-rays, examined Heather, and set up an appointment for a biopsy. He also took more x-rays. Janice took Heather to have her biopsy and our next step was to see the oncologist when the results were available. A short time later, we were called and asked to meet with the oncologist. Different thoughts were running through my mind by this time, and I'm sure everyone close to Heather were having their own thoughts. Janice and I took Heather to see the oncologist, and he asked to speak to the two of us alone. He told us the tumor was malignant and so large there were numerous complications. The tumor was wrapped around some of Heather's organs and the oncologist told us he could not handle her case. He would contact Boston General or the Mayo Clinic in Minnesota if we wanted him to, but there was nothing else he could do.   I had experienced many lows before in my life and Janice had also. Janice had lost her mother to cancer when she was a teenager. Neither of us knew what to do or who to turn to. We were despondent and we were helpless. We drove to Driver and I went to my parent's house. I had called my mother earlier and had given her the bad news and she and my father were very upset. I guess we all thought that after all the terrible facts concerning Sherri's death, we might be spared any bad news for a while. We were still trying to heal from Sherri's passing. I was in a terrible funk, but things would change for the better later that evening. My first cousin, Donna White, called me and said she wasn't trying to pry into my business, but she had spoken to someone who might be able to help Heather. Donna worked in the emergency rooms and operating rooms at Norfolk Sentara Hospital, and she knows many doctors. She has a position higher than a registered nurse and she really is an expert in her profession. Donna was a God send for us and she will never know how much her phone call meant that night. Donnas' mother, my aunt Doris, was my mother's best friend. She and my uncle Jerry had moved to Driver in the mid 1980's and I believe the move was a blessing for Doris and my mother. My mother and Doris were like sisters and it seems like they did everything together. The two grocery shopped together, they always went Christmas shopping together, they spent nearly every Saturday together, they went out to eat together a lot, and they were there for each other when one of them was sick. Mom and Doris even looked alike. My mother and Aunt Doris each had their share of medical problems and I discussed my mother's problems earlier. Doris' blood would have high levels of iron and she would receive treatments about every two weeks to lower the level. The treatments would be done at Dr. Thomas Alberico's office and he would later become Heather's oncologist. Jerry used to joke that he had read "War and Peace" several times while waiting for Doris to have her treatments. Mom had to go on dialysis, and like most patients, she received three treatments a week. She had also been confined to a motorized scooter because of neuropathy. These setbacks did not stop her and Doris from making their rounds. Donna told me that night she had spoken to Dr. Stephen Wohlgemuth and discussed Heather's biopsy results with him. Dr. Wohlgemuth was (and still is) an outstanding surgeon with Norfolk Surgical Group and Sentara Norfolk. Donna said the doctor would like to see Heather at 10:00 A M the next morning and we had hope once more. We took Heather to see Dr. Wohlgemuth the next morning and we all knew instantly that he was the perfect doctor for Heather. "Dr. Steve" did not pull any punches and told us the tumor was very large and might be wrapped around other organs. He told us things were very serious, but not impossible. They were exactly the words I wanted to hear and I could see my daughter had confidence in "Dr. Steve" and she felt extremely comfortable with him. Dr. Wohlgemuth went on to say that he felt the doctors at Sentara were as good or better than any place in the country and he felt comfortable with Heather being treated in Norfolk. He said he would investigate Heather's type of cancer and confer with other doctors. He would even check with other hospitals about treating Heather if we wanted him to. Dr. Wohlgemuth also told Janice and me not to blame ourselves concerning Heather's cancer. He said he did not know where it came from, but it did not happen because we let her eat at McDonalds or we didn't watch everything she did or did not eat. It was something that just happened and no one was to blame. "Dr. Steve's" words meant a great deal to me. I had already been blaming myself and wondering how this could have happened. I'm sure this is one of the things most parents with seriously ill children go through and it is probably a normal emotion when someone you love so much becomes ill. One can ask one's self "Why" till eternity, but I can tell you there is usually no answer. We left the decisions up to Heather and She told "Dr. Steve" she did not want to go elsewhere. She appreciated his honesty, his kindness, and the hope he gave her. We were all very lucky that Dr. Wohlgemuth was willing to take Heather as a patient. I can't imagine what we would have done without him. Dr. Wohlgemuth did all the things he said he would do. He got all the information he could possibly get and he talked to many other doctors. Dr. Wohlgemuth discussed Heather's case with Dr. Thomas Alberico (oncologist) and Dr. Walker (radiation) and these two great doctors also became Heather's doctors. Dr. Wohlgemuth had taken Heather and us from a point where we did not have a clue who would treat her to where she now had three of the finest doctors in the country. I knew how blessed we were. I had heard for years what a great doctor Dr. Alberico was and how he was the finest oncologist on the east coast. Everyone who knew "Dr. Steve" and Dr. Walker made similar comments about them. Heather had the finest doctors treating her. She always liked the tv show "The A Team" when she was young and now she had her own "A Team" of doctors treating her. We met with "Dr. Steve" several times before the operation scheduled for February 14 and he went over everything with us. He told Heather to drink all the milk shakes and Ensures she could hold because she needed to gain weight if possible or at least maintain her weight. She had gone from 130 lbs to 98 lbs and looked frail. Heather also met with Dr. Alberico a few times before the operation and he examined her and told her what to expect at some point after the surgery. Dr. Alberico is always extremely busy and patients may have to wait, but they soon realize he is the best in his field. I still don't know how he handles all the pressure and heartbreak, but I think he must feel that he needs to help save as many lives as he can. The tumor was pressing against Heather's stomach and was making her feel full all of the time. She was starting to feel self-conscious about her wait, but I told her when "Dr. Steve" removed the tumor she would be hungry and gain her weight back.

I remember one instance at Sentara when Heather was having some tests done. A man whom I think looked to be in his late 70's stared at Heather and then tugged at his wife and pointed to Heather so his wife would look. I felt like saying something and I hoped Heather had not seen the man. I can honestly say this type of thing never happened with young people. I think young people could sympathize with Heather and probably understood better than old people what it felt like to be different. My parents always told us not to stare at handicapped people or other people who might be different, and I began to understand why I have so much faith in young people. Family and friends held a surprise birthday party for Heather the Saturday night before her operation. Her birthday was February 16, but we knew she would be in the hospital that day. She would be operated on Valentine's Day and recovering from the operation on her birthday. Everyone helped to make sure she had a good birthday even though it was a few days early. Heather also received a lot of support from various churches and organizations. Her good friend from the Coast Guard Credit Union, Tammie Stuck, got Heather's friends and co-workers to call, visit, and pray for Heather. Several local churches like Nansemond River Baptist Church, Faith Lutheran Church, Beech Grove United Methodist Church, Glebe Episcopal Church, Berea Christian Church and other churches put Heather's name on their prayer lists. I am one of those people who believe in the power of prayer. I know the prayer made Heather feel better mentally and she found out how much people really cared about her. I spent a lot of time praying during Heather's illness and I am not ashamed to say I have continued to pray since my childhood. I may not be the best example of a Christian, but I am a believer and I do believe in prayer. I will explain myself later in this book, but please believe me, I prayed as hard as I could for my daughter. A dedicated couple from Beech Grove United Methodist Church, Mac and Carole Clark, began a blood drive for Heather. The Clarks have done this sort of thing numerous times and they are leading members of their church. Mac has been the secretary for his church for many years and he and his wife have always worked hard for the Church's Easter Egg Factory where the members make and sell candy eggs prior to Easter to support needy causes. The Clarks are my model for what I believe true Christians to be.

February 14, 1995 was a very cold day. I awoke early (I really did not sleep much the night before) and warmed the car and put some of Heather's things in the trunk. I was sure her operation would be a success, but there was not a thing I could do except be there for her. I knew it would be a long day and I knew I could not think straight until I knew Heather was safe. We arrived at Norfolk Sentara very early that morning and my mother, Doris and Donna joined us shortly thereafter. The medical staff took Heather in and prepared her for the operation. Everyone from Sentara was friendly and treated Heather like a princess. The operation lasted nine and a half hours and we received several updates during those hours. Well wishers and friends came and left during the period and Reverend Dick Browder (Lutheran) and a few other ministers lead us in prayer. I left the others several times to be alone and pray in the hospital's chapel. Dr. Wohlgemuth came out at the end of the operation and asked us to sit down. He told us he had to remove one of Heather's kidneys and the team removed the tumor that weighed more than ten pounds.

"Dr. Steve" said we may all be back here in five years, but Heather would be o.k. He said we would be able to see Heather in a short while.

Writing this is extremely difficult and I forgot to mention Dr. (blank), who was a kidney specialist and surgeon and was the doctor who removed Heather's kidney. Heather and I met him a week or so before the operation early one evening at Sentara. The doctor wanted to examine Heather himself and he also wanted to speak to us. He told me Heather had some great doctors and they would do everything they could and he patted me on the back and said, "We'll take good care of Heather." Dr. (blank's) compassion was sincere and I really appreciate his kindness. We walked into the recovery room and I saw Heather. She could not speak because she still had a ventilator, but she raised a finger on her right hand to let me know she was o.k. I knew she had been through Quite an ordeal and I knew she needed to rest, but I had a hard time leaving her. Everyone assured me she was o.k. and said we also needed to get some rest. Heather spent the next several days in the hospital recovering. She had been cut from the top near her armpit diagonally across to her waist. Janice told me about the incision and told me a lot about Heather's condition because she understood things because she was an R.N. Pastor Browder would often remark about how everyone got along and focused on Heather's well being. Norma had always been very nice to Heather and her mother (Janice). She opened her home to my daughter and I will always be grateful for what she did. She gave Heather nice clothes and spent a lot of time with her. She did the things a natural mother would have done.

Heather had a lot of company during her stay in the hospital and her appetite was coming back and she was getting stronger. I kept telling her she needed to get stronger so we could go to nearby Doumar's Drive In. Doumar's was one of her favorite places. The Doumar family invented the ice cream cone and still use the old machine. The restaurant has been featured on the Food Network on several occasions and the Norfolk eatery is a local landmark. The drive in offers inside dining and old fashioned curb service. Heather and I ate at Doumars several times when we went to Norfolk for doctors' appointments, exams, or tests. She liked the curb service and she liked the pineapple milkshakes and sandwiches. I tell people to enjoy the simple things in life because you don't always realize how precious they are. I got to the hospital early one morning and a young, sleepy, doctor was sitting in a chair watching over Heather. The internist was Dr. Steven Katz and he really impressed me. He was very friendly and helpful and we talked a little about Heather while she was still asleep. I thanked Dr. Katz for being there for Heather that night and I believe he had been beside her for some time. Dr. Katz said "It's been all my pleasure" and he left us. Donna told me that Dr. Katz kept up with Heather's progress and always wanted to know how she was doing. I think he took an interest in Heather because he wasn't that much older than she was and he could relate to what she was experiencing. Years later Dr. Katz returned to Norfolk and I believe he is now a heart specialist.

Tammie, Heather's friend from her job, brought her a big surprise, while visiting one afternoon at the hospital. Tammie knew Heather, like most girls then and now, was a big Brad Pitt fan and she somehow got in touch with the actors agent. She described Heather's condition to the agent and he came through for her. Tammie received a huge poster of Brad's latest movie. The actor had written a nice, personal message to Heather on the poster and autographed it. Heather had a fit over the poster and I would like to thank Brad Pitt and his agent for what they did for my daughter. She treasured her special poster. I was estatic the Saturday my father and I went to the hospital to bring Heather home. We loaded the car with flowers, plants, gifts, and candy and many other things. There was barely enough room for the three of us in the car. It felt so good to be taking Heather back to Driver. She would stay with my parents so my mother could watch over her.

Heather would have a two week break before she would begin taking her radiation treatments at Norfolk Sentara. She would need the time to heal and get some rest before starting the eight week stretch of treatments. I only have nice things to say about everyone Heather and I came into contact with at Sentara.   The doctors, nurses, aids, practical nurses, orderlies, aids, housekeepers and everyone working in the hospital were great. I will always remember what many of the black nurses, aids, or other hospital workers would tell Heather and me at the hospital. They would help us and then say "God is able". These three words have stuck with me since that time in the hospital and those words were truly a gift.

Heather and I met with Dr. Walker who would be her Radiation Doctor or radiation oncologist.   Dr. Walker described the procedure to us and said Heather would have one treatment each morning and one each afternoon; Monday through Friday. Dr. Walker reminded me of the "Doogie Howser" t.v. show because he looked so young.   Heather had finished one stage of her treatment (surgery) and she was now moving on to the second step of her treatment. During radiation, she would be surrounded by patients daily that were in the same predicament she was in. Everyone was in the same boat. Some patients may have had leukemia, some had lymphoma, some had prostate cancer, some had breast cancer, some had sarcomas, and any other forms of cancer. Some patients were children, some were middle aged, some were elderly, some were Caucasian, some were oriental, some were African American, and any other ethnic or religious denomination. My point is that all these people were equal in that treatment and they were all pulling for each other. I met and saw people during Heather's eight week stretch of treatments who I will never forget.   Thanks to Mrs. Mary Sheppard who took her treatments in the morning prior to Heather's turn. Mrs. Sheppard drove herself to the hospital each day because her husband did not like to go to the hospital. Mrs. Sheppard was probably in her late 60's, but she could relate to Heather and she encouraged my daughter each morning. She always told Heather how good she looked and how pretty her smile was.

Near the end of Heather's treatments, Mrs. Sheppard was told by her doctor that her cancer had spread to her brain. She came out of the office and told Heather and me what she had been told. She was naturally very distraught and worried and said goodbye to us and left that day without taking a treatment. I think of the young (about late 20's) black woman who worked at a lunch counter in Norfolk. We saw her everyday and she always had that sweet smile and talked to us. The young woman was told that her leukemia was worse and she would be sent to Richmond, VA for some different treatments. I pray that she made out all right and I am glad I got to meet her. An elderly lady of eighty-four walked up and down the hall greeting patients each day. She told Heather to think positive because she had been treated sixteen times for various types of cancer and she was now in her seventeenth treatment and she was determined to beat it again. I must admit that the hardest thing I had to deal with was watching the children. The radiation technicians would secure a very young black boy to the table for treatments so he could not move. The child would scream and I felt badly for him. The little guy might have thought he was being punished, but what had he ever done in life to deserve such fate. I hope the little guy made out and is now a healthy young man. I wish the best for the little children who have lost their hair or are in and out of the hospitals. I also feel bad for their parents. I used to think to myself and feel fortunate that I spent so much time with Heather. I would think about the parents of very young children who had cancer. I was lucky to spend twenty-two years with my daughter, and I knew many of these parents would not be as fortunate as I was.

Like my father always said, "There is always someone a lot worse off than we are". I would stop at a Seven Eleven most days after Heather had completed her last treatment of the day. She usually wanted a "Slurpee" and she felt like they made her feel better. The "Slurpees" did seem to pick her up some and my mother would later go through a similar spell while she was going through dialysis. My mother would stop by my store on the days of her treatments and I would give her an A&W root beer. My mother was convinced the root beer made her feel better. I would often take Heather out to eat after her morning treatment and she really enjoyed eating at the Shoney's and Spaghetti Warehouse in Norfolk. She was eating more and getting stronger even while receiving the radiation treatments. She got upset with herself one day because she left her doggie bag with the remainder of her club sandwich on our table.

We spent one afternoon riding around Virginia Beach and looking at the shops, ocean, and sand. Heather had always been fond of Virginia Beach and especially Nags Head. Like most kids, she was crazy about the water and it carried over in her paintings she later did. We had many happy times at the beach. Heather completed her radiation treatments and returned to Sentara the following week to have another MRI. Dr. Wohlgemuth called me a few days later and gave me the results of the MRI. I could tell by his voice that he was very sad and disappointed, but he tried to remain upbeat. The doctor told me another tumor had already formed in Heather and we would have to try something else. "Dr. Steve" asked to speak to Heather and he explained things to her. Heather was trying to hide her feelings, but I knew what she was thinking. My mother was in the den and she and I were also trying to hide our feelings and be strong for Heather. Heather was supposed to start chemotherapy in a few weeks, but we did not know what to expect. Everyone knew Heather's surgery was recent and she was just starting to get her strength back. None of the doctors, family, friends, clergy, or anyone else expected a new tumor to form so Quickly. We all knew Heather had a very aggressive form of cancer, but this was unbelievable. We took Heather to see Dr. Alberico (oncologist) the following week and he said he needed to start the chemotherapy as soon as Heather was fit enough to begin. That never materialized.

Heather tried her best to maintain her weight and fight, but the cancer was too aggressive. She would be in and out of the hospital during the next several weeks, but I knew she was slipping away. Heather reminded me about the dream she had early on in her fight with cancer. She dreamed she was in the living room of our old blue house (my grandfather's house that I bought from him) and she saw a light in one of the front windows. Heather told me she could see Sherri (my sister) on the other side of the window. Heather told me Sherri was surrounded by light and it seemed like she was made of light. She said the light was extremely bright and Sherri was very beautiful. Heather said Sherri motioned with her hand for her to follow her. Sherri then smiled and disappeared. My close friend, William Jones and his wife, Nancy, visited Heather many times at the hospital and my mother's house. William and Nancy were Heather's godparents and they were always good to Heather. They always visited her every Christmas morning and Heather thought the world of them. Heather had grown up around William because he was a close friend of mine and my parents and he was always there for her. I will speak more about William and Nancy later.

During Heather's last stay in the hospital, a female doctor took me aside and asked me if Heather really understood how sick she was. I assured her that Heather knew, but was not the type of person to complain or bring other people down. I did not get mad at the doctor because I knew what kind of person my daughter was. A former neighbor of ours and still a good friend named Rodney Wagner had spoken to me a few days earlier about Heather.

Rodney works as a camera man for the Christian Broadcasting Network and he is a very sincere Christian. Rodney told me he had known many good people in his life, and he said that if any person he had ever known was an angel; it must be Heather. I agreed with Rodney and not because she was my daughter, but because she was such a good person.

Dr. Alberico visited Heather her last Saturday in the hospital and he told me he just told Heather she could go home on Monday. He told me she might not live till Monday, but he would make sure she got home if she did survive. I told Dr. Alberico that I appreciated everything he and all the other doctors had done. I also told him Heather would live to go home and I knew deep inside that was what she wanted. Heather wanted to be in Driver with friends and family. We did take Heather home on Monday and people from everywhere visited her at my mother's house Monday afternoon and evening. She was tired, but she smiled and thanked everyone for coming to see her.

Something happened a few weeks earlier that I will never forget. As usual, we had stopped for a "Slurpee" on the way home from the hospital after her afternoon radiation treatment. When we pulled into my parents' driveway, Heather became nauseated and got sick in the car. Heather apologized to me for getting sick and I told her it was only a car and she meant everything to me and the car was only a "thing". I told her I used to clean her when she was a baby and this was just a reminder of the "old days." I had spent many hours with Heather during her illness and maybe that's why things worked out the way they did and why I left the Shipyard in 1986 when my mother offered my brother and me the opportunity to manage the stores. Most of the time, things may happen for a certain reason that is out of our control. I don't think I could have spent as much time with Heather had I remained in the Navy Yard. I spent many nights on the small couch in Heather's room because she did not want to be alone. I don't think anyone wants to be alone when they are very ill and may need help and especially if they suspect or know the illness may be fatal. Believe me; these are things I needed to do as a parent and I felt strange when people said I was there for Heather when she was ill. When you really love someone: you don't need praise for helping that person, you tell yourself you wish you could have done more.

Heather was very weak and tired on that Tuesday, May 16, 1995, the day after she came home from the hospital. It was as though she had said her goodbyes on Monday and was now truly slipping away. I told her again that I truly wished it could be me instead of her. I also told Heather I loved her and she would never be alone and not to fight anymore to please us, but to be at peace. My mother and father, my brother and his family, my sister Holly and her husband, Jim, Janice, Jerry and Doris (My aunt and uncle), Norma and I, and Jesse surrounded Heather early that evening. Holly's husband, Jim, was a fire chief and paramedic on Sentara Norfolk's medical hellicopter known as the "Nightingale." Jim monitored Heather's vital signs. Jesse held Heather's hand and Jim checked her heartbeat and pulse and nodded and said she was gone. Heather lifted her head and looked at me and said her last word "thanks". The next hours and days would run together like a blur. We wanted Heather's funeral to be special and we decided to have taped music like we did at my sister Sherri's funeral. Dick Browder, the Lutheran pastor, had known Heather for some time and had visited her many times at the hospital and at home. He offered to do Heather's service and I appreciated his gesture. The viewing was very well attended and I saw many people I had not seen for some time. My old friend Kenny Benton and his wife, Carol, were there and I knew it was hard for them because Heather was so close to their kids. Heather touched old and young people during her short life and many of them came to pay their respects. My brother, Gregory, operated the music at the funeral the next day and we played "Pavane For A Dead Princess" as people gathered. I remembered this music from President John Kennedy's funeral and I still think it is a great piece of music. It fit Heather's life. We played the "Tears for Fears" song "Sowing the Seeds of Love" next. I mentioned earlier that Heather was a big "Tears for Fears" fan and their song described Heather because the main thing she had done Throughout her short life was to sow the seeds of love. She spread love everywhere she went to everyone she met. I told the funeral director, Joe Hurf, about the line I wanted on Heather's marker and he really outdid himself. The marker is adorned with a girl about Heathers' age at her passing. The girl has just taken her hand out of the vase and appears to be scattering seed. The marker is inscribed with the words "Sowing the Seeds of Love." Thanks to Roland Orzabal and the band for giving Heather and the rest of us so much great music and thanks to Heather for sharing that music with her dad. Pastor Browder did a great job and when the rain came in he said it was a day that even the angels cried. He knew Heather personally and he captured the meaning of her life and he talked about how her illness had brought so many people together. He mentioned how grateful Heather was for all the prayers, love, and support. Many people came up to me at the end of the funeral and expressed their condolences. I greatly appreciate their kind words and prayers and I thank them for everything. My old friend, Lee Carr, stood by and waited to talk to me. Lee was not a touchy kind of guy usually, but he hugged me tightly and told me he knew how much I loved Heather and if he could he would have taken her place and given up his life for hers.

Lee had lost his brother and father and he understood how I felt. I knew he meant what he said and I knew that is the way things are with friends. When your friend hurts, you also hurt. I am not complaining because many people have been through some of the same things I have, but losing your daughter, your sister, and one of your best friends in two years is hard. It seems as though I lose a little bit of myself each time I lose someone I love, but I lost a lot of myself those two years.

Chapter 18
"The Family" and My Friend Matthew Hargrave

My grandmother, Nannie, had lost a daughter during the 1920's, my mother had lost a daughter, (Sherri) and I lost my daughter. At least three generations and perhaps more on my mother's side of the family had lost daughters. Beyond that, I had joined a group of people that I never dreamed I would be connected to: Parents who have lost a child. I decided to refer to this group of parents as "the family" because we all may not be genetically linked, but we have been uniQuely linked by circumstances or fate that we had no control over. It does not matter what age we are, what race we are, what our economic status is, what language we speak, what our upbringing was, what our education level is, or any other characteristics. We are all connected and only we can understand fully the implications of our loss. It does not matter if we are male or female; we experience the same feelings as a mother or a father when we lose a child. We are all in the same boat and we are all "family". Like any family, we many not handle our loss the same way. Some "family members" may turn to drugs or alcohol, some "family members" may turn to religion or spiritualism, some may turn to groups or organizations for help and others may seek solace alone. The pain affects "family members" in different ways, but that loss or pain is the thing that separates us from everyone else. I have talked to enough parents who have lost a child to believe my observations are true. You Quickly realize how similar your feelings are when you meet another person who has experienced the same fate. Unfortunately, I have also experienced much of this first hand. I may not have been my mother's "Pet" or "favorite", but losing Sherri and then Heather brought us closer together. We understood each other and knew the pain we each felt. I know my mother felt the same way I did and we would often say it is a pain one would not wish for anybody. Many people would tell me after Heather's passing that they did not know how I handled her loss so well. That's because they only saw the exterior and did not realize how I felt deep inside. They don't know about the sleepless nights and the internal grieving. My mother's father was a rock, but I guarantee he suffered when my mother's sister passed as a child. How many times have I Questioned or blamed myself for Heather's cancer? The farmers planted and sprayed the field behind our back yard. Should I have been smart enough to know that the chemicals or sprays could cause cancer? Did I bring asbestos home on my clothes I worked in at the shipyard and the asbestos could have gotten on Heather's clothes in the wash? Should I have controlled more of what she ate? The Questions go on and on. Heather is usually the last thing I think about before I fall asleep at night and the first thing I think about in the morning. Her passing has left a big void or emptiness in my life and I never know exactly when those feelings may overcome me.

Some days I wake up depressed and can't wait for the day to end. Holidays have an empty feeling when you have lost a child. You reminisce about the things you and your loved one did on those days. I am very fond of Easter, Thanksgiving, and Christmas and I like to see people excited on Christmas, but I struggle through these days. Nothing is the same after you lose a child. I have not been to Busch Gardens Williamsburg since Heather passed and I don't know that I ever will. I get an eerie feeling each time I pass the park and I remember how much Heather liked Busch Gardens. I sometimes get the same feeling when I see a movie Heather and I watched together. I saw the movie "Eddie and the Cruisers" recently and I thought about Heather the entire movie.

I mentioned earlier about the feelings I get when I see someone who favors Heather or Sherri. I sometimes get emotional at Christmas time when I see young blonde haired girls who remind me of Heather. Seeing them makes me yearn for my daughter and wish she was living a normal, happy life and all of this was just a terrible dream. I got to know a local grade school teacher who came into my store one day. The teacher mentioned that her nineteen year old daughter had been killed by a drunk driver during the past six months. I told her about my sister, Sherri, and Heather and found out the more we talked, the more we had in common. The teacher came to the store several times and one Friday, I could see she was very upset. She told me the day was the one year anniversary of her daughter's passing and I understood why she was upset. The anniversary of your child's passing is difficult enough without having external problems. The teacher told me her principal had verbally abused her that day. I asked her if the principal knew the day was the anniversary of her daughter's passing and she said the principal did not. I told her if that ever happened again to let the other person know how difficult that day is. Those of us in this situation are not asking for a free pass, or sympathy, but we know the only individuals who truly understand are those who have been through this. I'll admit that I was like most people who think they can fully understand these feelings. I always felt badly for those who had lost a child, but unfortunately I had to learn firsthand. People are kind and feel bad and we appreciate that, but there is no remedy to take away all of the pain. I am a bid Edgar Allen Poe fan and I can relate to many of his feelings as well as his poetry and short stories. I have read that he lost his parents and many other loved ones to consumption which is now known as T.B. (tuberculosis). Poe had experienced enough casualties of consumption to recognize the symptoms of the dreaded disease. Poe was watching and listening to his wife play the piano when he noticed droplets of blood dripping from her nose. He knew that was a symptom of consumption and knew in his heart that his beloved wife would pass away the same manner as so many of his other loved ones. Her death was the final blow to Poe's heart. Legend has it that Edgar Allen Poe would either get drunk or intoxicate himself on Opium and lie on top of his wife's grave during some snow storms or heavy rains. Today, someone would probably be carted off for Psychiatric evaluations if they did what Poe did. To me, I think Poe was trying to protect his wife even in death. How can I judge him when I understand the hand he had been dealt in life? He had suffered so much before his wife's death that his despair left him without any hope. His writings are an insight to the depths of his pain and suffering. Most people have family, friends, or organizations that help them with losses, but I am sure things were much different in the 1800's. Life expectancy was much shorter and many families lost loved ones, but time has not changed the pain of losing a loved one. Edgar Allen Poe was a great writer and he was a very intelligent man. He had attended West Point and also the University of Virginia. Poe may have been a tragic figure and he may have died in borrowed clothes, but I tend to believe he was also a noble person. He knew how to love. I experienced some various emotions when my close friend, Lee Carr, died. I experienced some anger when he was injured and I was angry when he passed. I wondered how Lee could have allowed himself to be placed in a position where he could become injured. We had been close friends for a very long time and we had been friends through thick and thin. Didn't he know we had always been there for each other and I needed his friendship more than ever after Sherri (my sister) and Heather passed? I also experienced feelings of relief when Lee passed because I knew how he always felt about being a burden on others and I felt the same way about myself. I was relieved that he would not have to struggle or suffer to survive each day of his life and depend on others for everything. I watched my mother struggle for years with her health and I watched my father grieve for my mother after she passed. I will grieve for my daughter, Heather, for the rest of my life but I "gotta believe" my loved ones and friends are in a much better place. Life at times is very hard and Quite often terrible things happen to good people. Everyone wonders at times why some cruel or sinister person seems to never miss a beat while some good person struggles or even dies. I don't have the answer and I really don't think any psychiatrist or theologian understands these Questions of life. My beliefs and my feelings maybe simple, but I tend to think we often make life harder than it should be. My philosophy was explained years ago by baseball's New York Mets relief pitcher, Tug McGraw. Tug was the father of country singer Tim McGraw and he was Quite a memorable pitcher and character. The Mets had been a terrible team for most of the 1960's and an interview asked Tug if he thought the Mets could really finally win a World Series. Tug did not explain his philosophy about the Met's chances for winning the series, but he summed up his beliefs in three simple words "You Gotta believe." Tim should write a song about his dad's words because they are true about baseball and life. We all need to believe.

Matthew Hargrave

I drove to Lee Carr's house one beautiful spring afternoon after some afternoon classes in 1970. I looked around and did not see Lee's car and a fellow with no legs wearing a ball cap came over to my car and told me Lee was not at home. The fellow, Matthew Hargrave, was Lee's stepfather. I had met Matthew a few times before when the family lived at Reids Ferry, but I had never been around him much. Matthew and I got to talking and the conversation somehow turned to baseball. Matthew asked me if I played and I said I had played most of my life and I had played catch that afternoon with a college friend who had spent some time in the minor leagues. I opened the trunk and showed Matthew my baseball glove. He told me he had used a first baseman's mit most of the time because first was his main position. I asked him where he had played ball and he said Richmond of the International League was the last place he played. Being a life-long Yankee fan, I knew Richmond was the Yankee triple-A affiliate for several years. I could not believe I was meeting someone who had rubbed elbows with my favorite Yankees. Matthew had been to spring training with guys like Mickey Mantle, Elston Howard, Yogi Berra, Whitey Ford, Gil McDougald and the "Old Professor" manager Casey Stengel. I had a million Questions for Matthew and I didn't know what to think when he asked me if I wanted to play catch. He went into his wood working shop and returned with an old glove. Matthew fell right into a groove and played catch with little effort. I was amazed, but it was only the first time Matthew Hargrave would amaze me. Matthew and I took a short break and sat on the grass and talked more baseball. He went back into his shop and returned with a bat. He asked me if I wanted him to hit me some fly balls and I could not wait to see how he hit.

The yard behind Matthew's house was very deep and fairly wide. The yard ended at a gigantic metal barn. The yard was about to become the Yankee Stadium center field for Matthew and me. Matthew began hitting me fly balls. His legs may have been amputated from the knees down, but Matthew still hit a baseball like he did when he was a six-foot, two inch first baseman. Matthew was as lean as a "fango", but the ball exploded off his bat. Matthew hit fly balls to me for a long period of time and he yelled out "Good One" each time I made a good catch. I was the happiest I had been since my little league days. Matthew had me move in closer and he started hitting me ground balls. Fielding the grounders made me feel like I did when I played short stop in little league. I was sad to see the sun going down, but I could see that Matthew was enjoying himself as much as I was. That spring afternoon lead to a great friendship. I became a regular visitor and guest at Matthew's home. We would sit out on the old, back screened in porch and listen to Yankee games on the radio. Matthew and I would listen to announcers Phil Rizzuto, Bill white, and Frank Messer describe the play by play. Matthew suffered from a disease known as Buergers Disease. The disease causes the arteries to constrict and decrease blood circulation. The doctors originally amputated one of Matthew's fingers and later another finger. They eventually amputated his two legs. I learned one of the most important facts of life from Matthew. Handicapped people are not seeking pity and they are as competitive as anyone will ever know. When you become friends with someone who is handicapped, you begin to understand the person and don't think of them as being different. I learned as much from Matthew as I would have learned from a great educator with two good legs. I introduced Matthew to my old little league coach, Jimmy Wilder. The two hit it off really well and Mr. Wilder asked Matthew to help him coach his present little league team, the Cubs. He accepted and the two men were a great coaching tandem. Mr. Wilder, like Matthew, had also spent some time playing professional baseball in the minors. He had been a second baseman at Greenville, North Carolina and both men were real students of the game. I coached the Bennett's Creek Yankees and we played Mr. Wilder's Cubs in the best two out of three league championship in 1973. The Cubs beat us in extra innings in the third game, but I was proud of "my kids" and they played with a lot of heart. I knew the Cubs were like their coaches, Mr. Wilder and Matthew, and were very competitive. We fought them tooth and nail and I guess if we had to lose, it was better to see two good baseball men like Jimmy Wilder and Matthew Hargrave win. If I was any coach at all it was because of what I learned playing for Jimmy Wilder. Matthew and I had helped coach the local Colt league Nats with Coach Wylie and his son Steve during the 1971 season. We had a great time coaching together and all the boys thought the world of Matthew. Matthew and I helped Mr. Wilder with the Cubs the following year (1972) and the two men became close friends. Reading these paragraphs, one might think I speak of youth baseball as if it is as important as major league baseball. It is to the kids and many of the coaches who participate in it. I agree that many coaches treat the game as if it was life or death and put too much pressure on the kids. Most coaches help instill a lot of good values in their players and give them many fond memories to look back on later in life. It's funny how the older you get the more you miss the simple things in life. I miss baseball, but I also miss playing gin rummy with Matthew. He was hard to beat and Thomas, William Jones, Dale, Bobby, and I were not very successful playing him. He was the same playing poker and I figured he must have played a lot of cards during his baseball days. We all had some great times playing cards with Matthew. Matthew was very good natured and I played many jokes on him and he did the same to me. One year about two weeks before Halloween, I bought a mask and decided Matthew should be my first victim. I waited until about 8:30 and I parked my car down the road from Matthew's house. I snuck up to the house and looked through one of the work shop windows and saw Matthew inside working on some furniture. I had trouble holding the laughter, but I managed to put the mask on. I stood before the window and began to make some strange noises. Matthew saw me and I'll never forget his reaction. He did not move and he began to yell for his wife, Mae. Matthew had trouble speaking her name and it sounded like Maaaaaaaae. He was so frightened that I could not continue because I began to laugh so hard. Many of my friends got to know Matthew and we would often drive over to the school ball field and play pick-up games. It did not take long for everyone to find out that they did not need to cut Matthew any slack because he was handicapped. We always let someone run the bases for him but that was the only concession we made. He was always in his element when he was on a baseball field. Matthew spent countless hours working with me. He would hit fly balls and grounders to me for hours at a time. He did not let up on me and he slammed ground balls to me at very close range. I may have been a good player in little league and later a terrible player in high school who lacked confidence and a good pair of glasses, but I now had someone who believed in me. I was really into baseball again and so was my old friend Tommy Knowles. It's a shame we had not known Matthew a few years earlier. Still, I would not trade the time I had with Matthew for anything. I even miss running into the old barn and pretending it was a Yankee Stadium wall or the Green Monster in Fenway Park.

Tommy, Matthew, Steve Wylie, and I attended some professional tryouts (Mets and Reds) and we did good, but none of us had good speed. Many teams were switching to astro turf by the early 1970's and they were looking for players who could run. The Cincinnati scout told us he was only concerned with speed because the Reds organization would teach a player everything else. I guess things really worked out for the best. I would not have been able to spend as much time with Matthew and my other friends if I had played minor league baseball. I tried very hard and I wanted to make it for Matthew, but some things are not meant to be. I also knew my days with Matthew would be limited because of his illness. Matthew and I went to Met Park in early April 1974 to see the Yankees and the New York Mets play their final exhibition game before heading north to begin the regular season. We had seen the two teams play the previous year, but this game would be much different. I had bought seats on the third base side that were adjacent to the field and the Yankee bull pen. Matthew spotted an ex Yankee ball player and he called out his name and asked for an autograph. The fellow ignored Matthew and I felt sorry for my friend. Third base coach, Gene Michael, told the fellow to sign the autograph for my friend and he begrudinally signed. I knew a fellow, Ronnie Stephenson, who had grown up in Kinston, N.C. where Gene Michael had played for the Pittsburgh Carolina League team. When I told him this story he said he was not surprised because he knew Gene Michael and said he was a very nice man. The Yankee shortstop, Celine Sanchez, came over and signed Matthew's program and my program as well. It seemed as though many of the Yankees had seen the incident and felt bad that a Yankee shunned a man with no legs. I could not believe my eyes when I looked across the infield and saw Yankee greato Thurman Munson and Greg Nettles walking toward Matthew and me. They also signed our programs and spoke to Matthew and me. I believe the former Met outfielder, Ron Swoboda , came over next to sign autographs for us. The great former catcher, Elston Howard walked over to see Matthew and signed autographs. "Ellie" had been on many of the great Yankee teams and he seemed like the kind of fellow I thought he was when I was a kid. Most of the Yankees came over and signed autographs for us and spoke to Matthew. I was very proud of those guys and I was really proud to be a Yankee fan. I was watching the Mike Francesca Show on the Yes Network and callers were talking about Thurman Munson. It was the anniversary day of Thurman's passing and people were telling stories about the great Yankee Captain. I started to call in and tell Mike what my experience was that night. Thurman Munson should be enshrined in the Baseball Hall of Fame. He was a great catcher, a great hitter, a great captain, and a great representative for the game of baseball. Thurman lead by example on the field and he did so that April night in Norfolk, Va. The last Yankee to come see Matthew was the Yankee manager, Ralph Houk. The "Major" had been the manager and leader of the great "61" Yankee team. Matthew and I were talking to the man who had managed Mickey Mantle, Roger Maris, Bill Skowron, Yogi Berra, Whitey Ford, Elston Howard, Tony Kubek, Bobby Richardson, Hector Lopez, and many more of my boyhood heroes. The "Major" was Quite a guy and he acted like he had all the time in the world to visit Matthew. The two men talked and I said, "Mr. Houk, Matthew played for the Yankees in 55 and 56 in Richmond." The "Major" asked Matthew if he knew Johnny Blanchard and Matthew told him he once roomed with Johnny. The two men talked baseball and talked about the mutual friends they had made along the way. I think the "Major" enjoyed talking to Matthew. I was very impressed with Ralph Houk and the Yankees that night and I would like to thank them for what they did for Matthew. I know why the Yankee players played so hard for Ralph Houk and as a fan I do believe there is magic in those pin stripes.

Dale Holland invited some of us to a New Year's Eve party Dec. 31, 1974. Matthew, Steve Wylie, Janice, and I were at the party, but Matthew and I were glued to the television set. A rumor was floating around that the Yankees were about to sign Jim "Catfish Hunter." The announcement was made that "Catfish" had indeed signed with the Yankees. Matthew and I were ecstatic and we felt the Yanks were back on track again. We were very anxious for the season to begin and we had both liked "Catfish" as an Oakland A. He was from nearby Hertford, N.C. and he was also a class person. Jim Hunter was signing autographs at Rice Nachman's Department Store one Saturday morning before the baseball season began. I took Matthew to see "Catfish" and we both got his autograph. We both had a good collection of Yankee signatures due to the fact we had good seats at the Yankee-Met exhibition game in Norfolk.

Matthew and I also had another common link between us. We were both die-hard Washington Redskin football fans. I began watching the "Skins" with my Uncle Cecil when I was a small boy and am still a fan today. Matthew was also a "Skins" fan, but the more time he spent around me, the more fanatical he became. We spent Sunday afternoons and some Monday nights together watching the "Skins" on television. Matthew, like me, became familiar with most of the Redskins roster and he began to "live and die" with the Skins. 1971 was a big year for Redskin fans. George Allen became the new Washington head coach and he brought several of his former Los Angeles Rams players to D.C. with him. Jack Pardee, Myron Pottios, John Wilbur, Tommy Mason and Bill Malinchak were some of the ex-Rams. The Redskins roster was filled by so many ex-Rams that some people referred to the "Skins" as the "Ram Skins". George Allen added players like Billy Kilmer, Ron McDole (the "Dancing Bear"), Roy Jefferson, Diron Talbert, Speedy Duncan, and some others to the line-up. Combining these new players with "Skins" holdovers like Sonny Jurgensen, Len Hauss, Paul Lavey, Larry Brown, Charlie Taylor, Bobby Mitchell, Jerry Smith, Pat Fischer, and other players made the Redskins a very good football team. The Washington Redskins were no longer the laughing stock of the NFL. People like Howard Cosell were beginning to praise them and Howard was famous for stating "they bend, but they don't break" when he described the Redskin defense. Coach Vince Lombardi had started the Redskins in the right direction in 1969, but he died of cancer and the Skins needed new direction. George Allen brought players, respect, direction, and national acclaim to the Redskins and their fans. Those were great seasons to be a Redskin fan. The "Skins" were called the "over the hill gang" and the great Larry Brown was leading the league in rushing yardage. Signs and posters hung everywhere in RFK Stadium. One sign stated "We are not only over the hill; we are in the Valley" as the Redskins won. Coach Allen told the team that "45 men together can't lose" and the fans believed in those players and the fans became the "twelfth man". The "Skins" played the San Francisco 49ers in the playoffs after the 1971 season. The "Skins" played hard, but lost the game. The Washington Redskins had not appeared in a playoff game in over forty years and the fans were hungry for a championship. The "Skins" played the 1972 season as if they were on a mission and they were. They annialated the hated Dallas Cowboys in the NFL championship game and the undefeated Miami Dolphins would be their opponent in the Super Bowl. The Redskins were favored to win the super bowl, but Larry Csonka and Bob Griese had other plans. The "Skins" defense played hard, but the Dolphin defense lead by Manny Fernandez played as hard. The "Skins" lost the game by a score of 14 to 7. I was emotionally crushed, but Matthew cheered me up by talking about baseball and the spring. Like so many Chicago Cubs fans say, "Wait Till next year." I can recall many good and sad times I had with Matthew, but everything changed in September of 1976. The Yanks were winning, but Matthew's health was deteriorating Quickly. I did not want to face reality, but I knew what was coming.

Thomas and I went to see Matthew in the hospital one night. Thomas was trying to cheer Matthew up and he began to tease me. Matthew took his right hand and firmly grabbed my forearm. He then told Thomas not to be too hard on me because I was "his buddy". I definitely felt something that night when Matthew grabbed me. I knew at that moment it would be the last time I would ever see Matthew and my feelings were right. Matthew passed away the following day.

Losing Matthew was the toughest thing I had been through since losing my grandmother, "Nannie". The pain was nearly unbearable and I felt "lost" for a long period of time. I tried to stay busy and work hard at work, but I thought about Matthew a whole lot. I mentioned earlier that many people went out of their way to try to make me feel better after Matthew's passing. I know they meant well and I appreciate their efforts and maybe I had helped Matthew at times. The fact is that Matthew was like a big brother to me and he was a friend. Matthew did more for me than he ever knew. He gave me things that can't be bought or measured. Real friends don't keep track of favors and never discourage you and that's the way things were for Matthew and me. I will never forget Matthew and I think about him nearly every day. Forty-six years is a short time to live, but Matthew had accomplished a great deal in those forty-six years. I have never fully recovered from his loss and I never will. I do take comfort in the fact that I was lucky to know him and I was even luckier to be his friend.

The Yanks played the Kansas City Royals for the American League Championship in 1976. The series began a few days after Matthew's passing and I constantly thought how he would love to watch those games with me and see the Yanks back on top. I cried when Chris Chambliss hit the home run to clinch the playoffs against the Royals. I thought to myself that Matthew somehow knows this and he is very happy for his Yankees. Somehow he saw that home run and he was ecstatic. I sometimes think about all the things in baseball that Matthew might have missed. Did he miss Reggie Jackson's World Series three home runs against the L.A. Dodgers and did he miss Bucky Dent's home run in the one game play off with the Boston Red Sox? Did he feel the sorrow the day Yankee catcher Thurman Munson perished in his plane? I think maybe Matthew knows all these things and he probably even kno ws about Derek Jeter, Jorge Posada, and Andy Pettitte. I may not have known Babe Ruth, Mickey Mantle, Joe DiMaggio, Roger Maris, or any of the other Yankees, but I knew one Yankee and he was my heroe. Matthew Hargrave was and will always be my favorite Yankee.

Chapter 19
Good Friends and Great People

Easter Vaughan

I mentioned Easter Vaughan earlier in this writing, but she was one of my favorite people and I need to write some memories of Easter. She walked into our lives soon after my mother gave birth to Holly and Sherri and she left her mark on everyone in our family. Easter was family. Easter raised thirteen children of her own and there was not a thing she did not know about babies or child rearing. She was a big boned black lady who had a Quick smile and a sweet disposition. Easter was a God send to my mother, and I don't know what my mother would have done without her. Easter had worked part time for Mr. and Mrs. George Cornell and Easter's family lived near the Cornells. She helped other local families also. Mrs. Cornell was my seventh grade teacher and the couple thought so much of Easter that they later built her a new house. I stated earlier that Easter referred to my baby sisters as "her babies." I think back to the days Easter would push my sisters down the road in a double carriage. Easter was also like a mother to my brother and me. I mentioned my mother's health problems and along with my father's drinking, she was one of the most stable people in our lives. Easter liked my father very much and she always called him "Mr. Red." My father also thought a lot of Easter and he often referred to her as "Easter Lilly". Easter was a "jewel" and I don't think anybody who ever knew her did not like her and everyone thought the world of her.

Easter was homemaker, cook, protector, confidant, and a third parent for us kids. The entire family functioned better when she was in our home. We all missed her when she was not in our home, and we kids all realized that Easter's children were very fortunate to have such a good mother. I know Easter could tell when I was having a difficult time as she always told me everything would be all right. I heard a few times that Easter and her husband would have their differences and perhaps she had some of the same feelings I had. I often wondered how anyone could mistreat such a good person. Easter was well known for her homemade cinnamon rolls and I have never tasted one as good as the ones she made. She would make our family a patch of rolls every Friday and I would sit in class on Friday afternoons and think about Easter's cinnamon rolls. Easter knew how much I liked the cinnamon rolls and she timed her baking so the rolls would be warm when I got in from school. I miss Easter's cinnamon buns and would truly love to have a batch of them, but I do have a lot of good memories. I miss Easter very much and feel like she and Sherri's path have crossed. I pray that I will see Easter again someday. I believe someone you love and know greets you when you cross over to the other side. I have always felt that Easter greeted my sister, Sherri, on the other side. She probably smiled at her and said "Baby, every things all right."

Henry Wallmeyer

I entered the Norfolk Naval Shipyard Apprentice School in July 1973. The apprentice program combined on the job training with college courses such as English, Mechanical Drawing, Physics, Public Speaking, and Mathematics. The purpose of the apprenticeship is to mold individuals working in various crafts into individuals who can teach or lead others in that craft and to also coordinate work with other crafts.

Apprentices also took many trade theory classes which helped them perform the various aspects of the craft. Electricians, welders, pipefitters, painters, riggers, sheet metal workers, machinists, Ship fitters and other apprentices were taught by instructors who had knowledge of these functions and had performed them in their craft. I was a pipefitter apprentice and I studied silver brazing, mechanical joint make-up, flange make-up, blue print reading, various piping systems, shipboard terminology, and many other aspects of pipe fitting. Words like starboard and port or forward and aft soon replace right and left or front and back. Two o'clock in the afternoon becomes fourteen hundred hours. I mentioned many of the large shops or crafts at Norfolk Naval Shipyard, but there are many other crafts that are just as important. Crane operators, eQuipment operators, pipe insulators, wood workers, radiological controls, test engineers and codes, and many other specialized crafts are part of many shipyards. I began my apprenticeship in pipefitting working for a supervisor named, Tommy Tise. Mr. Tise was a good man to work for and he put me with a very experienced mechanic named Bohannon. "Bo" was a former navy chief and he knew his way around the carrier, the Saratoga. I enjoyed working with "Bo" and he taught me a great deal. Tommy Tise's gang was made up of very good mechanics who were older and more skilled and a few young men and a few apprentices. Tommy had worked with many of the men in his gang before he made supervisor. Fellows like "Bo", "KoonDick" Morgan, Robertson (Robby), and J.C. Croom were very experienced pipefitters. I finished my time with Tommy Tise working with a fellow named Gary Tester. Gary liked baseball a lot and he had coached for several years and he and I got along great. Gary was a very intelligent person and he taught me a great deal. We would be reunited a few years later in the nuclear section of the pipe shop. My apprentice class was sent to Tidewater Community College for the winter Quarter. Many of my classmates were military veterans and many had served in Viet Nam. Students who were eighteen or nineteen years old and fresh out of high school made up the remainder of our class (the class of 77). A couple of incidents involving apprentices happened during our time on the college campus. We had a few professors who were not particularly enthralled with teaching the apprentice students. One professor became angry with a student in the back of the class and threw an eraser at home. The professor missed his target and the powder filled eraser grazed the head of John Bailey who had been a marine and had served in Viet Nam. John's hair was a little long and was already turning grey and the eraser left a white spot on John's head. The eraser ricocheted and hit a black student named Alphonso King in the head. Alphonso had an Afro and he had also served in Viet Nam as a marine. The two men looked at each other and then looked at the professor. I thought things might turn from bad to worse when Alphonso and John got out of their seats. The two stood for a few seconds and then got back in their seats. Needless to say, the professor showed a bit more respect to apprentices after that incident. John and Alphonso went on to have very successful careers with the Civil Service and both of them are great guys.

1974 was the age of streaking in our country, and we had a streaker in our class who figured he could make a little hustle with the craze. He took five dollar bets that he would streak around the entire Tidewater Community College Campus. We were in a class and heard a loud motorcycle outside. Everyone looked out the windows and saw a streaker with a helmet on riding a motorcycle. No one admitted the streaker was an apprentice and the fellow won the bets and avoided punishment. I enjoyed the college classes and I did not have to take English either Quarter. I submitted one paper the first day of class and the instructor called me to her desk when the class ended. The instructor asked me if I had been to college and I told her I had but had not finished and gotten a degree. She asked me how much English I had in college and I told her I had one year of English Composition, one year of British Literature, and classes in Creative Writing. The instructor told me I could take a study hall that Quarter because I would be wasting my time taking the class. The same thing happened in my next English Class and I was given another study hall. I was able to help some of my classmates in classes like English and Mathematics. I knew how it felt to be falling behind because of my days of high school algebra, but I was lucky enough to finally grasp algebra and trig. I bet my high school teacher, Mrs. Johnson, would never think I would be able to help others with algebra. I felt fortunate to know I could help some of my classmates and I had even considered changing my major to secondary education in college. The college courses were a big part of our apprenticeship and our jobs were on the line in the classroom as well as at work in the shipyard. Some guys flunked out and some were able to find other jobs in the shipyard.

I have a lot of respect for my classmates who served in Viet Nam. None of them complained or were bitter, and none of them resented guys like me who did not go. They had seen horrors that most of us will not see in our lifetimes and the only thing they wanted was to settle down, make a decent living, and raise a family. I recall walking in the shipyard with a friend of mine named Ron Nelson. Ron had been in the infantry in Viet Nam and he was accustomed to flying on choppers or hellicopters in Viet Nam. The chopper would take the troops where the enemy was and would later retrieve them. Ron had the habit of stopping and looking to the sky each time a hellicopter flew overhead in the shipyard. It was a survival instinct for Ron and it is probably something that will remain with him the rest of his life. Ron once told me how hard it was on him to lose buddies in Viet Nam, and he said most of the time he just wanted to get even. Ron is a very easy going, well mannered guy and I am glad he is my friend.

Alphonso King used to tell us stories about some of the things that happened to him while serving with the Marines in Viet Nam. He told us he was sent back home with a body one time. Alphonso said the body moved slightly (natural movement) and he thought he would have a heart attack. Alphonso also told us about a trip to Saigon. He and some buddies came upon a restaurant that supposedly featured authentic soul food on the menu. Alphonso and his buddies ordered pig's feet. They thought the pig's feet were sort of large and tasted different. Another serviceman told them the pigs feet were really water buffalo feet.

John Bailey drove an orange Plymouth Road Runner and he liked to hunt and fish. A few of the guys once told me John had some flash backs on one of the hunting trips. He never complained and I know that John is the kind of person you want on your side. He is very loyal and dependable and deserves the best in life. I have a lot of respect for John Bailey. Our apprentice class returned to the shipyard in the spring of 1974. Each apprentice returned to his shop for reassignment. We usually met in the training classes of our main shop and waited for someone to take us to our new supervisor and work station.

I knew from past experiences that you can't always judge someone from past experiences or first impressions and that was certainly the case with my new supervisor. I had seen Henry Wallmeyer before at the time clocks where the shipyard workers checked in and out of work. I never checked out early or got in line early, but I had seen Mr. Wallmeyer nab some fellows and he gave them an earful. I was a little intimidated by Mr. Wallmeryer and I goofed up the first day I worked for him. His gang was working out of the $O^2 N^2$ plant on the aircraft carrier John F. Kennedy. Aircraft carriers are like floating cities and I could not find the $O^2 N^2$ plant when I returned from lunch. Mr. Wallmeyer had already started his safety meeting when I finally found the $O^2 N^2$ plant. He told me the gang always started back to work after the Whistle sounded. I said "Yes Sir" and I told Mr. Wallmeyer I had gotten lost and I wouldn't let it happen again. I guess Henry Wallmeyer knew I was sincere and he told me things like that happen when you begin working on large ships like aircraft carriers, and it is fairly easy to get lost. Mr. Wallmeyer was already teaching me and he did it in a way that stuck with me. I never got lost on any ship again after that day. A man does not have to be a great coach like Vince Lombardi or a great general like Omar Bradley or Colin Powell to have a positive affect on men or help mold their character. A pipefitter supervisor can accomplish as much as Coach George Allen did with his aging Redskins, if the supervisor is a leader and has the respect of his gang. Henry Wallmeyer was that type of man. Henry Wallmeyer was thin and wiry and he suffered with emphysema from years of smoking cigarettes. He was practical, yet highly intelligent and I will tell anyone that Henry Wallmeyer knew his job and taught pipefitters the right way to do things. Mr. Wallmeyer would explain the systems to the worker and he would explain how various components such as valves worked and what their function was. I enjoyed working for Henry Wallmeyer and I enjoyed going to work every day when I worked for him. He had a bunch of good guys in his gang and all of them did things the "Wallmeyer Way" and all of them knew their jobs and were fast to pass their knowledge on to others. Henry Wallmeyer really knew how to communicate with young people and most of his gang were younger fellows. He had a few "veterans" like "Sawyer" from North Carolina and Harvell and they were also good mechanics to work for. I worked a lot with a fellow named Bruce Johnson who had served an apprenticeship and had left Tennessee to work in the shipyard. Bruce was a very conscientious worker and he is a very devout Christian. Bruce also taught me a lot and he was a fine person and great to work for. He even gave me some tools that I would need in our trade.

Gary Richardson was the other apprentice in our gang and he and I still see each other occasionally. He worked with a former apprentice named Jimmy Lee and Jimmy was also very helpful and knowledgeable. Stanley Swadzyk was another former apprentice in our gang and I still see Stan once in a while. Ray

Vann had long blond hair that hung to his waste. Ray always reminded me of Jim Dandy of the rock group "Black Oak Arkansas." Ray had know Henry Wallmeyer most of his life and Ray thought the world of Mr. Wallmeyer. Henry Wallmeyer judged a person by the way they acted and did their job; not by the length of their hair. Sadly, Ray passed away years ago. I enjoyed knowing him.

I also worked a lot with a mechanic named Henry Martin. Henry was a character, but he was a hard worker and I got to know Henry inside and outside the shipyard. Henry was fun to be around. Bruce Johnson, Jimmy Lee, Henry Martin, Stanley Swadzyk, Ray Vann, Sawyer, Harvell, Jordan and Taylor all got along with each other and there was never any animosity, or jealousy, or back stabbing among these fellows. I knew I was lucky when I worked with these guys and all of us knew we were working for a very special man.

The O_2 N_2 plant gang really was like family and the sailors we worked with were like "extended family." Chief Bolen was the navy chief we worked with and the chief often told me he thought I would have made a great sailor. He said I knew how to follow orders and that was very important. Chief Bolen was like many of the chiefs of his times who thought Admiral Zumwalt was ruining their navy. We worked with a second class petty officer named George and a couple of lower ranking petty officers, Dusty Rhodes and Zero. Zero was the kind of guy you would never forget. He was from New York and he looked like a young Jerry Lewis. Rhodes came to work in the shipyard when he finished his navy enlistment. I was very shocked when I received my evaluations form Henry Wallmeyer. I was hoping to get all satisfactories which was typical for doing your job and progressing. Mr. Wallmeryer graded Gary Richardson and I both with all O's. O's meant that the apprentice was outstanding in his performance and the supervisor had to write a letter to the shop superintendent explaining why he thought the apprentice was outstanding. I thanked Mr. Wallmeyer and he told me Gary and I had earned our grades. He told me he had two good apprentices and he told upper management he intended on "keeping them." I was very happy and I wanted to show Henry Wallmeyer that I was very proud to be one of "Henry Wallmeyer's Boys". Mr. Wallmeyer always told each new man that all he asked was to give him seven good hours a day and he could take his breaks or whatever as long as he obeyed the Shipyard rules and stayed out of trouble. This was never a problem because "Wallmeyer's boys" had so much respect for him they would never do anything to try to make him look bad. Every member of the gang enjoyed working for Henry Wallmeyer and every man knew Wallmeyer would back them up if need be. I can't recall all of the many conversations about the shipyard and life in general that Henry Wallmeyer and I had. Mr. Wallmeyer had two sons of his own that were about my age and I can only say that he sure knew how to relate to me. Mr. Wallmeyer could pull wrenches and explain his point of view at the same time. He may have been an experienced shipyard "old timer", but he had the mind and "get up and go" of a young man. I guess that's why he related to so many young shipyard workers. Henry Wallmeyer never forgot how it was to be young and inexperienced and he was there for anyone who needed him. He lead by example and he was a man's man. I came up with my own theory about the people who had worked for Henry Wallmeyer for any length of time and my years in the shipyard proved me to be right. Anyone who worked for him knew how to treat people and how to get a job done the right way. I would ask future supervisors if they knew Henry Wallmeyer and if they told me they had worked for him at some time, I knew I was working for someone who knew his job. A fellow who abuses, belittles, or takes advantage of his workers will never accomplish what a supervisor who can relate to and communicate with his people will. I worked for fellows like Butch Writtenberry, Paul Adams, Bill Pruett, and others who had worked for Henry Wallmeyer and they were great people to work for. These men had been influenced by Henry Wallmeyer and knew how to earn the respect and trust of their people. I'm not saying that someone had to work for him to be a good leader, but it sure helped. Our general foreman, Mr. Rowe, came onboard the carrier one day and told Henry Wallmeyer I was to report to the main shop for SubSafe School the next morning. Mr. Wallmeyer asked me if I wanted to leave his gang and work on submarines or did I want to stay with him and learn all I could? I told Mr. Wallmeyer that I was happy working for him and I would spend my entire apprenticeship with him if the superintendent would let me. Henry Wallmeyer told me he was going to fight it and he was going to find a way to keep me. Mr. Wallmeyer told me not to attend the class the next day and said he would get things straight with Mr. Rowe. The third day he told me Rowe had ordered him to send me to the class and I needed to report to the main shop. I went to the class as soon as I could, but I was a little late because I was working on the USS Kennedy during the first part of the morning. The instructor, Bruce Neel, asked me where I had been the first day of class. He wanted to know if I had been sick or if I had not been notified. I told Bruce that I knew about the class and I had been working on the Kennedy. I said I stayed on the carrier because Mr. Wallmeyer told me to. Bruce Neel looked at me and said, "Parker, you are going to find out that Henry Wallmeyer does not run Norfolk Naval Shipyard." The entire class laughed at me, but I thought to myself what the shipyard would be like if Henry Wallmeyer was running it. I would work for Bruce Neel in the nuclear department about a year later. He is a great guy and he was also a good man to work for. I would get to know Bruce Neel very well and I brought that day up to him a few times. I returned to Wallmeyer's gang after the class ended and Mr. Wallmeyer told me he would keep fighting to keep me. He told me "I'm not going to let them take you to submarines and ruin you". I did eventually leave Henry Wallmeyer's gang and went to work on nuclear submarines in the sub-safe section of the pipe shop. Leaving Henry Wallmeyer and his gang was my saddest day at the shipyard. I felt like I had left my family.

I got to enjoy working in sub-safe and I worked a lot with a fourth year apprentice named David Wise. Wise was very conscientious and hardworking and I learned a great deal about sub work from him. He became the head of a shipyard unit called the tiger team. The tiger team is a group of mechanics from various trades that travel wherever they are needed in the United States or outside the country to work on naval vessels. David was head of the team for several years and he transformed the team into an elite unit. I would get angry any time I would hear someone in the yard complain about David Wise or how he did his job. I always told them I worked with David in sub-safe and he deserved his job because: a. he knew his job b. he was very intelligent c. he was one of the most conscientious people I knew in the shipyard and worked his way up the ladder. I would see Henry Wallmeyer fairly often while I worked in nuclear. I had to make trips to the far end of the shipyard where the main pipe shop was located. Mr. Wallmeyer became foreman of the pipe shop after his health began to fail more rapidly. I would go to the shop to pick up material or have pipe bent or for many other reasons and I would make it a point to see Henry Wallmeyer. This was as advantageous to the shipyard as it was for me. Mr. Wallmeyer would tell the shop people to get me whatever I needed and to take care of me right away. He would say, "I know him very well and I know he is going straight back to work and get the job done". I always felt like I was letting Henry Wallmeyer down if I eased up and I had too much respect for him to do that. Henry Wallmeyer retired from the shipyard and later passed away from the many health problems he suffered with. He left the shipyard and life having made the world a better place and he touched many people.

When I see some of the fellows who also worked for Henry Wallmeyer and we always talk about him and what he meant to us. We probably sound like war veterans who had served under men like Robert E. Lee or Douglas MacArthur. I think of Henry Wallmeyer Quite often and he would understand if I used one word to honor him. Thanks!

Here and Now

Many people told me that recounting my own personal tragedies and those of people I care about would be very therapeutic. I can say it has been therapeutic, but it has also been difficult. My father told me a few years before my mother and he passed, "Son you're at the age where you will go to a lot more funerals than weddings and it just gets harder and harder." I know what my father meant. The fifteenth anniversary of my daughter's passing is four days away and I have already been in that "funk" for days. I know people who have gone through this know what I mean. They also know that losing the most precious thing in your life does not exclude us from more pain and suffering. It may be worse because we fully understand how precious life is and we feel for others who must also suffer. A neighbor, Ronnie Brett, stopped by yesterday morning and asked me had I read the morning obituary in the newspaper. I don't read them as a rule, but I do occasionally. He told me that a friend of mine, Jimmy Griffin, had passed away. Ronnie did not know all the particulars so I thought I would call my father's close friend, George Cooper, to get more information. George was Jimmy's uncle by marriage and I called him to find out more about Jimmy's passing. George's wife said he was not feeling well, but she would call him to the phone if I needed to talk to him. She had known Jimmy since he was four years old and said he died in his sleep. Jimmy was always a busy fellow. He umpired high school and college baseball games in his free time and he was very involved with the Portsmouth Invitational Tournament which annually features some of the best college basketball players in the country. Jimmy knew more jokes than anyone I have ever known. He could also tell some very interesting stories, and they were mostly humorous. I will miss Jimmy and I will miss talking baseball with him. Jimmy would stop by our store about once a month over the years and I looked forward to his visits. He was red headed and he really related to my father who had red hair while growing up. I considered Jimmy a good friend and I'm saddened by his passing.

I had a message on the phone yesterday afternoon from an asbestos attorney. The attorney was calling to find out if I knew a William Ray who had worked at Norfolk Naval Shipyard. I tried to return the call and I left a message. The more I thought about William Ray, the more I began to remember him. We always called him Ray because that was normally a first name. I remembered Ray as a tall, thin, black fellow who always smiled. He was very easy going and I believe he was in my apprentice class. I knew him years ago, but after a short time I could picture him as if it was 1973 again. I called the lawyer back this morning and he said the message described William Ray the same way some of the people he had talked to described him. The lawyer asked me about some of the old ships Ray and I had worked on such as the Kennedy, the Forrestal, the America, etc. He told me William had died from asbestosis in January 2009. I feel for his family and the world has lost a good man with a beautiful smile.

One more setback has occurred in the past week. A friend of mine named Robert Daniel is watching his ninety three year old mother, Kathryn Jones, live out her final days. Doctors recently took Kathryn off life support and removed her feeding tube. She is slowly passing away because nothing else can be done. She is brain dead and her wish was to die at home. I have known Robby's mother since I was a child in Port Norfolk. She worked behind the counter at Covert's Drug Store and she served me many lime-aids during my childhood and teenage years. She was a pleasant, hard-working woman who worked and took care of a family. Kathryn visited my store numerous times over the past several years and we enjoyed talking about good old Port Norfolk. I watched my daughter and mother slip away and my heart goes out to Robby and his wife, Janie. He has been a good son and he has always been there for his mother.

I recently attended a viewing for a friend of mine named John Coffey. John was the Nuclear Coordinator for the nuclear pipe shop when I went Nuke in the fall of 1975. He interviewed me for the nuclear program. I will always be eternally grateful for a few things John did for me. I once had a bad night (3rd shift) where nothing went right. I was disgusted with myself and thought I may not be good enough for nuclear. I went to John Coffey's house the next afternoon when he came home from work. We sat in his car for well over an hour and he explained to me that things in nuclear are not always under our control. John said, "I could leave nuclear if I felt like it, but he would like for me to stay". I listened to John Coffey that afternoon and I really appreciated what he told me. He was a pleasant man with a little bit of a sQueaky voice and he sure knew how to encourage people. I felt like telling John's son at the viewing that I often felt like I was talking to Mickey Mouse, when I talked to his dad. That was a good thing because I grew up with Mickey Mouse and felt secure when he spoke. I felt the same way about John Coffey.

I spent four years away from the shop while I was working in the Radiological Control department of the shipyard. We worked a great deal of overtime and the job (to me) was not very conducive to family life. I also felt that our department head was not looking out for his own people. He once asked me what certain people I had worked for were doing down on the waterfront. He wanted to know how much time they spent with some of the female workers. I told him I was busy working on the ships and I did not know what they were doing, but they had treated me well. I felt he should go on the job and find out for himself what he wanted to know. I am very easy to get along with, but I do have a hard time working for someone who I don't respect. I will do my job, but I draw the line when people are too lazy to do their own job and don't take time to know their own people. How can you ask people to sacrifice a great deal of their private and family life and turn around and harm the very people who are sacrificing so much for you? I had worked for people like Henry Wallmeyer and I was not accustomed to that kind of behavior. I informed the branch head that I wanted to go back to the shop and he asked me if I thought they would take me back and I told him I didn't know. He then asked me if I knew John Coffey and I told him I knew John very well. The branch head called John Coffey and told him about me and then had a strange look on his face. He said, "John wants you back today, but I can't let you go now, I have to hold you for thirty days". I went back to the pipe shop in thirty days. I appreciate what John did for me and he was one of the nicest people I met in the shipyard. John and his wife would come to my store in later years to buy fresh vegetables during the summer. They were a good couple and I miss seeing both of them. I will always miss John Coffey, but I often hear his voice when I think of him. That friendly voice says, "Hi Pal" and I feel better.

Tommy Bond

I met Tommy Bond for the first time on Christmas Eve 1974. We were in the back of the Sub Safe building in Norfolk Naval Shipyard. Tommy had had a few drinks and he was showing David Wise and some of the guys how he could dance. I did not know that day that I was meeting one of the most talented and intelligent people I would ever know. Tommy could joke around like he did that Christmas Eve, but I would find out in 1975 what a deep and caring individual he was. Tommy was born in the projects in Norfolk, but he did not let being poor discourage him or make him bitter. I began working with Tommy in Nuclear in 1975 and I think everyone in nuclear knew him and liked him. He had served in Viet Nam and Tommy had graduated from apprentice school when I met him. I remember the first night I worked with Tommy. We were working on a table in the nuclear repair building when the inspector showed up. Tommy told the inspector the number of the manual we were concerned with, the page number, and the paragraph. I thought I would never make it in nuclear if you had to know all these things as well as your job. I did not know at the time that Tommy had a photographic memory or something close to it. Tommy was eager to help apprentices as newcomers and he was one of the best mechanics in nuclear. It's eerie to find out how much people have in common or how much pride they have, but working or playing (sports) side by side helps you really understand another person. The sailor on a submarine does not care if the mechanics who worked on his ship were white, black, Hispanic, Native American, oriental, or whatever as long as they did their job right and he is safe on his ship. I worked with many outstanding black mechanics on submarines and I worked with many outstanding white mechanics on submarines. Tommy Bond, Bill Sledge, Smoke Dennard, and Vernon Hardy were some of the great black mechanics I worked with in nuclear. Norman Parker, Mike Pledger, Garry Dowdy, and Frank Sondjes were some of the great white mechanics I worked with in nuclear. I bring this issue up because all these guys I mentioned and many more are individuals who were conscientious and are guys that I am glad I worked with. All of them helped me and many others like me. They took pride in their work and they all wanted to see the job done right. Tommy Bond never thought "I'm smarter than this white guy and I didn't get to go to college." He thought there was no room for error and he wanted me to be the best I could be and he would help me. Smoke Dennard never thought, "I'm hip and I don't owe this guy anything." Smoke knew he was an experienced mechanic and he was glad to show someone how to have pride and do his job the right way.

Some of us would periodically stop at Al's after work and have a beer together. The crusty old bar was located outside one of the shipyard's main gates and many "yard birds" have tried to solve the world's problems in the bar. I believe a great deal of "bonding" went on at Al's because some people can relax when they get away from the shipyard and the stress. I worked with Tommy Quite often because of a supervisor named Paul Adams. Paul is a great guy and he and the guys who worked for him were friends as well as co-workers. Paul had worked for Henry Wallmeyer as an apprentice and I'm sure Mr. Wallmeyer had influenced him. Paul was a disciple of Henry Wallmeyer and he knew that if you took care of your men, your men would take care of you. Paul knew he only had to mention that he was being pushed or a job was extremely "hot" and his men would do whatever was needed to get the job done. He was honest with his men and his men were honest with him. I have been on jobs with other supervisors and Paul would come up to me on a Friday afternoon and say, "Pal, you're back with me on Monday morning. The Silversides is coming in and I told the office who I wanted. I got Tommy, Dooley, Benton, Norman, Smoke, and some of the other guys. I told them I needed the best to get the job done and you guys are the best." I felt proud to be included with such a good group of guys and to be "wanted" by Paul. It was the way I felt while I worked for Henry Wallmeyer. It is a great feeling to have someone who has faith in you and you don't want to let that person down. You don't want to let your "mates" down either. I am not going to lie and say I enjoyed every single minute that I worked in the shipyard. It could be a very stressful job and you might have to switch shifts at any given time. We also had to attend many classes in nuclear and the more Qualifications you had, the more was expected of you. I did get an education that I could not have gotten on a college campus. I worked with guys who had to put their lives on the line for their country and had seen things I would never see and done things I would never be asked to do. I have had deep conversations with these guys and I am glad to have worked with them. I have worked with guys who had to struggle for everything they got in life. Many did not have parents who could afford to send them to college and for some the shipyard and apprentice school were ways to have a better life than their parents. I met a few veterans while I was in college, and they generally studied harder than most students and blended in Quite well with the student body. I met Denny Strickland at Old Dominion and he was an air force veteran who went to college when his enlistment ended. I met several of the same type of individuals in the shipyard. Guys who were always striving to learn more and do more.

I had some very good discussions with Tommy Bond and it reminded me of the ones I had with Lee, Bobby, Dale, and Thomas years before. We talked about writing, books, movies, and society. Tommy could usually shed more light on a topic and I began to see some things from a different perspective. We did our jobs, but we had some good conversations during lunch or after work. Tommy and I were from different backgrounds and areas (Norfolk and Driver), but we had a lot of things in common. We both were big Washington Redskin fans and we both liked comedy and practical jokes. I remember working for Paul one October day. I was working with Tommy in the nuclear repair building and he was silver brazing some pipe joints. Paul stopped by to see us and see how the job was going. Sweat was pouring off Tommy due to the heat from the brazing torch. He finished the brazing work and turned around and told Paul, "I'm glad we have a holiday tomorrow, because I need some time off." Paul looked puzzled and he said, "What holiday falls on October 31?" Tommy Quickly replied that it was Halloween. Paul told Tommy he hated to be the one to tell him, but Halloween is not a federal holiday. Tommy had somehow convinced himself that it was.

One of the funniest instances that I have ever seen happened one Friday night while I was working with Tommy. Work was slack that night and the two of us were cleaning some flexible couplings in the repair facility. We noticed the third shift custodian was having trouble staying awake when we entered the building. Jeff was normally the third shift janitor, but he was asked to stand in as custodian that particular night. He was probably in his sixties at that time and he probably did not know everything about the custodian job. The custodian's primary job was to check everyone who entered the repair facility because it was a restricted area. Jeffries (Jeff) was supposed to make sure the person entering the building matched the badge picture and the person had the proper badge. The building had a code entry set of numbers and most people knew the code, but some people did not know the code and had to check with the custodian for entry. No one is supposed to fall asleep in the shipyard, and especially someone guarding a restricted area. We were working in the flash area of the building when Tommy noticed Jeff was trying to doze off. Tommy went to the phone and called the beeper that lay on the custodian's desk. Jeff jumped up like he was shot from a cannon and began to walk throughout the building. He came over to Tommy and me and asked us had we seen Simmons that night. Richard Simmons was the day shift supervisor responsible for the repair building. Jeff told us he thought Simmons was in the building and he was trying to get him fired. I don't know how in the world Tommy and I kept a straight face. Tommy and I continued cleaning the couplings and we noticed Jeff was dozing off again. Tommy called the beeper again and instructed Jeff to put the beeper in his shirt pocket and told Jeff he was already in trouble for dozing off. Jeff sat still and he stared at the beeper for a minute and then placed it in his shirt pocket. Jeffries made the rounds throughout the building and visited us again. We assured him we had not seen Richard Simmons and he was probably asleep at home. Tommy and I went to see Paul who had his office in another building nearby. When we left the building we saw Jeff placing a bushel of collards in the trunk of someone's car. Tommy Quickly hurried back in Paul's office and called Jeff's beeper. Tommy told Jeff on the beeper that he better get back to the building immediately and he would probably be fired that morning. Jeff headed back to the building walking as fast as he could while Tommy and I laughed. The night was turning to day, but what a night it had been.

Paul had a period of time when he was having some personal problems with his former wife. I believe it had something to do with visitation with his daughter. Paul had a lot on him at that time. He was taking care of his mother, trying to be a father to his daughter, and he was stressed out at work. I don't know any particulars, but I know Paul was still a great guy to work for and we were all worried about him. He had done so much for all of us and we wanted to let him know how much he meant to us. Paul had taken some time off from work and had not returned. A group of us decided we needed to call him and find out if there was anything we could do. Tommy Bond was the first to call Paul. The next day at work, Tommy told me how down Paul was and that Paul didn't think he could come back to the shipyard. He was deeply hurt and didn't know if things would get any better. Tommy said I should call Paul. I called Paul and he thanked me for calling. I told him that Bond, Dooley, and all the other guys missed him and wanted to work for him again. He told me Tommy had called and he told me he thought of Tommy as a brother. He said he missed us, but he needed some time. Paul said he would always love us. Paul did come back to the shipyard and he went back to his old job as training supervisor. We would always see him when we had classes and we were just happy that he had come back to work.

Paul left the shipyard again. He got a job with the City of Norfolk and I heard he was doing well. I don't know why Paul left the yard and we have never discussed it. I know my father always said you can never judge another man till you walk in his shoes. I knew Paul Adams well enough to know he did what he had to do. Paul has visited me several times throughout the years and he is doing well. He liked his job with the City of Norfolk and he even remarried. The last time I saw him he was still the Paul Adams I knew and respected. Paul Adams was and will always be a man I care deeply about and will always admire. I'm glad I worked for him, but I'm happier he is my friend. Tommy Bond made planner/estimator and we no longer worked together. I would however see him before work at the snack bar some days. He would ask me how the guys were doing or we would talk about our Redskins.

I heard some terrible news when I returned to work after the Christmas break of 1983. Someone told me that Tommy had an aneurism Christmas night and passed away. I was in shock and a state of disbelief. Tommy was so full of life and was such a good person. He was the father of two children. A good friend of Tommy's named Clayborn came to see me and we talked about Tommy. Clayborn summed up Tommy's life as good as anyone could. He simply said, "Tommy touched a lot of people." That he did!

McKinley Morrison

If someone ever asked me to name two people I have known who overcame adversity and heartache to become men that others could look up to and admire would be an easy Question for me. The first person would be McKinley Morrison and the second would be Tommy Bond. I was lucky enough to be good friends with both of them. McKinley, Mac, always looked like he never got enough sleep and he probably didn't. He was a burly guy you had to get to know to find out how intelligent and sincere he really was. Mac had served in the air force in Viet Nam and went to apprentice school at Norfolk Shipbuilding and Drydock after he completed his service time. Mac and I had been in the same gang on second shift when we worked for Bill Pruitt. I had worked for Bill before and I always enjoyed working for him. Bill was the same type of supervisor Paul Adams was. He was there to encourage you and he was always fair and honest with his mechanics. Bill had to go on day shift for some time and he alternated Mac and myself as stand-in supervisors. Mac always gave one hundred percent on every job and he was a very good mechanic. We respected each other and we worked hard for each other because we both had a lot of pride. Mac's father left the family when Mac was young and he always promised his mother he would take care of his two brothers. He worked a part time job to help put his brother, Johnny, through law school at Washington and Lee University. Johnny Morrison is now a retired judge. Mac also worked second jobs to help his other brother. Mac's mother must have been a wonderful person because she did an outstanding job raising three boys by herself and he loved his mother with all his heart. He instilled those same values in his daughter and son. I mentioned earlier that I left the Radiological Control department and returned to the pipe shop in 1982. I spent a few months working on nuclear submarines. I worked for Gary Dowdy who I had worked with when I was an apprentice. He had moved up to General foreman and he had a good group of guys working for him. The shop moved me to a Quality Control Office and I was working for my old friend, Bill Pruitt, once more. McKinley Morrison was working in the same office for another one of my previous supervisors, Bruce Neel. I enjoyed working for Bill and Bruce and I was very glad that I had gone back to the pipe shop. I felt like I was back home. You find out what a man is all about when you work side by side with him five days a week for four years. I would learn things about McKinley Morrison that

258

made me respect him more than ever. We developed a deep friendship and McKinley Morrison is one of the best people I have ever known.

Mac had a good friend outside the shipyard named Jerry. Someone told me that Mac would either take Jerry to his dialysis treatments or make sure he had transportation to them. Mac was there for his friend who had kidney problems and he was there for many other people.

Mac and I worked together in a tiny brick office that was situated in front of the nuclear work building. Mac kept track of the exposure records and radiological records for the nuclear pipe shop. He was a whiz in mathematics and he was completely thorough in his job. I have seen many supervisors and general foremen come to Mac for help or advice. Mac listened to a small radio throughout the day as he worked on his paperwork. He asked me early on if I wanted him to change the channel from a local soul station (WRAP) to another station. I told him I liked the station and my sister worked for WRAP one time and she always said how nice the people were at the station. Mac was surprised when I reeled off some of the names of the WRAP disc jockeys. I will never forget a daily song disc jockey Bobby Gee played during our lunch break. The dj used the old Impression's song "People Get Ready" for a backdrop to his own version of the song. Bobby would refer to the train in the song as a train steaming throughout our Hampton Roads area. He would say something like "The train is now in Suffolk, VA the peanut capital of the world. The train is stopping at Planters Peanuts to pick up some more passengers. Mrs. Jackson is very well dressed as she is wearing some very nice perfume." The song went on and on with different descriptions and Mac and I enjoyed the song and wondered what the DJ would come up with next. I will never forget some of the phone conversations Mac had with his son after school. Mac would sometimes phone home to find out if his son had started doing his homework. If his son was not working on his homework, Mac would often say, "You better be working on that homework or I might have to work on your hind parts." I had access to a set of four Redskin tickets each season and Mac was usually one of the guys who went with me. We always had a great time and the Skins won most of the time in those days. We went to one Friday night preseason game and a few Monday night games. It usually took three and one-half hours or better to return home and everyone was tired and sleepy after night games. Mac would nap, but he would always share the driving time with me.

In 1986, My mother approached my brother and me about operating the family stores in Driver. My parents were taking care of my grandfather and my mother did not have time to operate the stores, take care of things at home, and take care of my grandfather. Her own health was not too good and she had worked in the stores since she was a child. I told my mother I needed about a month to make a decision. I liked my job and I enjoyed working for Bill Pruitt and I had thirteen and a half years in the Shipyard. I was close to Mac and I would have been happy to work with him for the remainder of our shipyard careers. It was a hard decision and I realized the stores had been operated by my family for nearly one-hundred years. I knew I had to take a chance because I could not accept the thought of my parents having to sell the stores. I left the shipyard and my brother and I began operating my grandfather's general store known as Arthur's General Store in Driver. Mac would come out to the store and visit me and we stayed in touch. Mac was promoted to supervisor and left his old job as man ran custodian. He began working on ships again and I didn't see him very often. I would ask other shipyard people I knew if they ever saw him, but most of the time they said they would see him but did not get the chance to talk with him. Mac found out he had diabetes and I heard later that it caused him to go blind. I feel badly because I wish I could have been able to help him or take him places if he needed transportation. I had a lot going on with my sister being in the hit and run accident, my daughter having cancer, and my mother's failing health, but I wish I had known all that was going on with Mac. Someone who knew Mac and me stopped by the store one day and asked me if I knew Mac had passed away a few weeks earlier. I felt as though I had been hit by a ton of bricks. I told the person I did not know this and I needed to call Mac's wife and tell her how sorry I was about his passing. I did call Mac's wife, Evelyn, and told her how much I thought of Mac and what a good person and friend he was. I was sincere when I told her I would miss Mac very much. The old saying that "the good die young" seems very true. For me, the saying holds true for my daughter (Heather), my sister (Sherri), my friend (Matthew), my friend (Lee), my friend (McKinley) and many others. I don't like to use the words die and dead because they are too final and I don't believe people "die". They continue to live on in the hearts and minds of those they touched. Mac and I used to joke with one another and say one day we would be retired and meet at a mall a couple of times a week to watch the people and world go by. We never got to do that or the other things seniors do, but we did get to spend some time together. I was very fortunate to have McKinley Morrison as a friend and I will always remember him. I pay tribute to Mac each time I pull out my old "Impressions" greatest hits album and play it. I listen to songs like "It's All Right" and "People Get Ready" and I think of him. I believe he knows this.

Fly Yardbird Fly

I have many fond memories of many of the people I met at Newport News Shipbuilding from 1971-1973 and Norfolk Naval Shipyard from 1973 to 1986. My affiliations and friendships with them make me proud to be a "yard bird." Thomas (Tom) Chapman is an old friend and mentor who I stay in touch with. "Chap" took me under his wing when I was an apprentice and he put a lot of faith and confidence in me and I will always be grateful.

Apprentices were supposed to spend two weeks in the planning section, but I stayed much longer. Chap wanted to go to Planning/Estimating School and he convinced John Coffey I could handle the job alone. He promised John he would check on me each day to see how I was doing and he did. Chap has two sons and he made sure both of them strived to excel in education and life. Michael has a high level job with NASA and his brother is a career army man and is being considered for the rank of general. Michael was going to Virginia Tech when I worked with his dad and I have to say that Chap was always proud of his boys. Tom Chapman is a very intelligent and motivated individual who has a great personality. He finished a career in the navy before going to work in the shipyard. Chap was well liked and respected by everyone who knew him in the shipyard. I was lucky to work with "Chap" and he educated me far beyond the shipyard. He treated me more like a son than an apprentice boy and I am indebted to him. I think the world of Chap and he taught me more than any professor or teacher I had in school. As a "yardbird", I heard all the jokes and comments about shipyard workers and federal employees. How many times did someone ask me if I was going to the shipyard to get some sleep or rest? Someone else would ask how long you had worked at the "gravy yard." I would have liked to have taken some of those people up the mast of an aircraft carrier or the bottom of a dry dock in February on a six degree night. Maybe these people would like to spend eight or twelve hours inside a damp and slippery tank. They might even enjoy being on top of a carrier flight deck on a cold January day with fifty mile an hour winds blowing. The bottom of the dry dock beneath a submarine on a cozy one-hundred degree day is a nice place to be. The sand blasting grit, water, paint fumes, welding fumes, etc. are bonuses. Most "yard birds" take their jobs seriously and feel great compassion for the sailors and fleet they serve. When did a "yard bird" sell secrets or information to a Russian spy or someone else? When did a "yard bird" sabotage the ship or eQuipment he was working on? Tommy Bond used to call me on the office phone during lunch hour if he and I were on the same job, but different shifts. He wanted to know how the job was going and if we had any problems. Tommy did this because he cared about the job and he cared about his craft. "Yard birds" work on the most expensive and sophisticated eQuipment in the world and they know that. The U.S. Navy places many of its finest sailors on nuclear vessels. The shipyard does the same. A ship comes into a shipyard for updates, repairs, or overhauls. "Yard birds" play a huge part getting that ship out to sea and making sure she comes back to port after her deployment.

William Jones

William Jones and I attended church with our parents at Glebe Episcopal Church in Driver and we were always in the same Sunday school class. I was about two years older than William and I was two years ahead of him in school. William's father, William Wellington Jones or "Billy", was an attorney and later became a judge. William's mother, Elizabeth, was a home maker and the organist at Glebe. He had a younger sister named Mary Margaret. William and Mary Margaret spent much of their free time studying and practicing music. William studied piano and Mary Margaret played the harp and is still a professional musician. She has played with different symphonies. I got to know William much better when he started high school at John Yeates. He was becoming more outgoing and I remember him trying to play jokes on my friend Bobby Harrell. I believe William began to get out more often during his junior year at Yeates. He went with me one afternoon to visit Matthew and from that point on William was a regular in our circle of friends. He already knew Lee's younger brother Harvey, but he would soon be a fixture in the circle that included Tommy Knowles, Matthew, Lee, Thomas, Dale, Bobby, and me.

William wasn't a very good baseball player in the beginning, but he became close to Matthew and worked with him to become a good baseball player. I mentioned earlier that many of our activities centered around Matthew and like the rest of us; Matthew became a trusted friend and ally for William. There was no better friend or role model. William and I became very close and we both worked at Planter's Peanuts one summer. We took turns driving to work and William actually had a very good time working at Planters and he continued making new friends and becoming more confidant and outgoing. He did not care what sort of job he had at the plant. He wanted to prove he could do anything anyone else could do.

William entered the College of William and Mary after graduating from Yeates and we still got together during weekends, holidays, and summer vacation. I went to a few William and Mary football games and I met some of William's college friends. Many of them referred to William as "Joe College." I introduced William to Bob and Mae's niece, Sheryl Tilson, who I knew from Port Norfolk. The Tilsons left Port Norfolk and moved to Glouchester, VA when Sheryl was young, but we visited them fairly often with Mae and Bob. Sheryl was very intelligent and beautiful. She had no problem getting into William and Mary and she had been a cheerleader at Glouchester High School. Her parents, Libby and Paul, were great folks and Sheryl was a lot like her mother, a very sweet person. William finished college and moved back to Driver with his parents. His grandfather passed away and he inherited his grandfather's house. I knew Williams grandfather, Captain Roy Jones, and his wife who was a Quaker. William's grandparents were fine people and everyone in Driver liked them.

I think William's father probably wanted him to study law, but William had other ideas. He came to see me one night and told me he was in a real dilemma.

William said his father had set up a job interview with a local bank. He told me working in a bank and wearing a suit every day was the last thing in the world he would want to do. William told me his cousin Woody Jones asked him if he would be interested in working the trucking farm with him. William asked me what he should do and I asked him not to tell his father about our conversation. He told me he really wanted to work outdoors and thought he might like farming. I told him what I thought my father might have told me, and that was to do the kind of work that made him happy. I told him the world was full of people who dreaded their jobs, but some people love their jobs and can't wait to go to work each day. I told William he had to do what he thought was right for him. William went to work on the farm and I have seen few people who enjoyed their work the way William did. He enjoyed working with the farm hands and Woody was like a big brother to him. He worked long grueling hours in the hot summer, and things were sometimes slow in the winter. Woody and William grew butterbeans, corn, cantaloupes, snap beans and a variety of vegetables during the summer and kale and collards in the fall and winter months. Woody operated a produce stand on the farm and people would come from miles away to buy farm fresh vegetables. He was a very astute business man and he made many good investments, but he was a very caring and good hearted person. Woody gave William a lot of insight on handling his personal finances. William and I had a lot of fun together and he also spent a lot of time at my parent's house. He used to tell me how my father reminded me of someone like Davy Crockett. William was amazed with the number of people who knew and liked my father. He spent a lot of time hanging out with my father and he was like another older brother to my two sisters. People who knew William well were fascinated by the amount of food he could eat. He really enjoyed my mother's home cooking and he was not shy at the dinner table. My father teased him a lot and used to say things like, "William, I'll go out to the shed and get you a shovel to eat with if a fork is not big enough." William would laugh and continue eating. He would also drink several glasses of iced tea. William tried a lot of different foods while working on the farm, and there were not many foods he would not eat. Some of his old college class mates would be amazed if they saw William eat chitterlings, cheese sauce, hog jowls, hominy, dandoodles and some of the other foods he ate. We all partied a little and drank our share of Jim Beam, Rebel Yell, Ripple, beer, Boone's Farm and the various "flight fuels." I mentioned earlier that Bobby was our designated driver and we were not a hazard to others. William was one of the boys and he enjoyed the "fellowship" and conversation. We were in a club one night shooting pool and a VietNamese waitress started a conversation with William. She asked him what he did for a living and William told her he was a farmer in a little place known as Driver. The waitress visited William the next day and said she came out to see his farm. William tried to explain to her that he worked with his cousin on the farm and that he did not own the entire farm. He said he was polite, but he did not want Woody or his father to think he was bringing girls out to see the farm.

William met his future wife, Nancy Clark, while he was having dinner at "George and Steve's Steakhouse" which was about four miles north of Driver. Nancy was working at the restaurant part time while completing her education at Old Dominion University. William was impressed with Nancy and her parents owned a farm; so the two had a great deal in common. Nancy was also bright and caring. She was exactly the kind of girl William was hoping to find and the two began dating. William and Nancy married and I would use the old saying that "they were a match made in heaven" to describe their life together. I was William's best man and the wedding was very nice. William had served as an usher when Janice and I were married ten years earlier. I mentioned earlier that William and Nancy were my daughter's (Heather) God parents and we could not have chosen two finer people. Nancy and William were both good to Heather and she loved both of them. They were an important part of her short life and I will be forever grateful to them. William became a Mason and the lodge became very important to him. He started an annual plant sale to raise money and he was a tireless worker in the lodge. William was already known for his good deeds and he never sought recognition or praise for helping others. No one knows how many people William helped during his lifetime. I received a phone call from my sister, Holly, the afternoon of June 5, 2006. She told me William had suffered a massive heart attack and her husband, Jim, had brought him back with artificial susitation. Jim is a fire chief and was once an EMT on a hospital hellicopter. William had eaten his lunch a few hours earlier on the front porch of my store. He had been discing the field next to Holly and he needed electricity to operate an electric drill to remove a broken bolt from his tractor. Before returning to work, William said he noticed Holly had a few outside receptacles on the outside of her house. He asked me if I thought Holly would mind if he used her outside receptacle. I told him she would not mind and to run his extension cord to her power.

After talking to Holly, I told Joe Sandige (a friend of mine and William's) what had happened and I asked my friend, Lee Roy Schmidt to watch the store while we checked on William. We hurriedly walked down to my sister's house. A terrible feeling came over me when I saw William lying in the driveway where fire fighters were trying to resuscitate him again. He looked so helpless and lifeless lying on the ground and I was praying that he would somehow survive. I knew the situation was bad, but it was much like the situation when I found Lee. I saw one of my best friends lifeless and my heart and mind were telling me two different things. An ambulance transported William to Obici Hospital and paramedics worked on him during the transfer. William passed away during the trip and Holly met Nancy at the hospital and did her best to console her. A few days later I was doing something I have done far too often in my lifetime. I was once again a pall bearer in a close friend's funeral. I have been a pall bearer at Matthew's funeral, Lee's funeral, Reverend Bob Bennett's funeral, William's funeral, and several other funerals. It has been an honor each time, but it is very hard taking a friend to his final resting place. Many lives are affected each time a good person passes on; and many people are affected several different ways. Friends and acquaintances can usually remember the good times or the way the person touched their lives for a long or brief time. Loved ones like parents or spouses are affected every way imaginable.

I know how Nancy feels and I have gone through many of the same things. She expected to have a long life with William and I expected to see Heather marry and have children. Nancy's world and life revolved around William and my life revolved around Heather. Nancy knows there is no time table for healing and her heart will never be completely mended. Nancy lost a brother and I lost a sister. Both of us lost our parents in recent years. We are both doing the best we can, but some days are more difficult than others. Nancy does not have any other siblings and she has had to face many hardships without family to lean on. I do have Holly and Gregory to confide in about our losses and I can't imagine how hard it would be to not have them. Nancy has a sister-in-law and nephew and they are an important part of her life. Nancy is a special person and I truly wish happiness for her. She has poured herself into her work and friends and that is good. Nancy has faced more than her share of tragedy and she knows that life is not always fair. I guess William Shakespeare thought of people like Nancy or me when he wrote, "It is better to have loved and lost than to have never loved at all."

Woody Jones

I have mentioned Woody Jones a few times earlier in this book and I am happy to say that he was one of my best friends. Woody was a huge, strong fellow and stood about 6'5", but he was really a gentle giant. I knew woody from the time I was a small boy. We both attended Glebe church and I sat in the back of the church with my father and Uncle Cecil when I had grown too old to be an acolyte. Woody would also sit in the back of church and I would usually talk to him after the service. Woody was single and he and his mother lived together in the family farm house. Woody's father, Harry Jones, was ill much of Woody's early years and Harry passed away. Woody worked his father's share of the Jones farm while he attended high school and The College of William and Mary, Norfolk Division. Woody had started working the farm as a boy and worked it his entire life. I mentioned earlier how much my other friends like Bobby, Lee, and Dale like Woody. Woody was like a highly intelligent version of Hoss Cartwright from the old "Bonanza" television. He was the kind of fellow people liked to be around and you always felt safe in his presence. He was self assured, powerful, inQuisitive, sensitive, thoughtful, and women thought of him as lovable. I remember the time Woody, Dale, and I went to a Club in Norfolk. The area was frequented by a lot of sailors and one navy Chief got on Dale and I as we entered the building. We both had long hair and the chief asked "how are you ladies doing tonight?" Woody came in after parking the car and the chief changed his tune when he looked at Woody. The chief told us he was only joking and told us to have a good time. We all figured "No harm, no foul." We were always safe with Woody. We had some very good discussions with Woody and I learned early on that he was someone who really cared about his fellow man. He was older than us, but he always thought young. Woody could identify with the struggles of the time and the sacrifices many young people were making. He worried about the servicemen in Viet

Nam. Woody was not just a rural farmer worrying about his farm, his crops, and his own life. Woody and I shared many of the same ideas about politics, religion, and life. We were Episcopalians and we did not believe we had to speak in tongues or do charitable deeds in front of others and praying in a closet was as important as praying in a synagogue. Woody Jones was a devout Christian. A Driver friend and resident, Severn Warrington, went through school with Woody and grew up on the farm next to Woody. Severn recalled how Woody stutered in school, but never stutered when he talked to him and another friend. Woody did not stuter when he talked to me and he never did when singing hymns in church. Woody faced many adversities and hardships in his life, but he was always constant. He was very dependable and he was a "rock." He was a "rock" for his church, his community (Driver), his family, and his friends. I vaguely remember Woody's father, but I knew his mother Quite well. I often hear what a good man Harry Jones (father) was, but I knew firsthand what kind of woman Mrs. Jones was. She was kind, considerate, giving, and lovable. She loved Woody with all her heart and he was always her "little boy". It was a pleasure knowing her. Woody met Marie Futrell and the couple fell in love and married. Woody used to tell me that Marie had given him a nickname. Marie called Woody "Mr. Big Stuff" after the hit song of that time. I miss many things about Woody, but I think I miss his humor and laughter as much as anything. I can still see him laughing at something Dale or Bobby did that was funny. He would say "Oh my word" and follow with a hearty laugh. It was the sort of thing that made the rest of us feel good. Woody and William worked with various chemicals and fertilizers on the lands they farmed and we will never know what lead to their health problems. Woody fail ill with cancer, but he fought back and recovered for a few years. Woody passed away and William continued to farm for a few more years. He was not the same after Woody's passing and he was grieving for his cousin much of the time. I had seen my father go through the same thing when my mother passed and it is hard to watch someone you care about grieve. Those of us who knew William told him Woody would want him to go on and have a good life with Nancy. I know how hard it is to go on and it is not as easy as one would think. Most people believe time will heal everything and that is often true. Time will not always mend a broken heart and many people lose a lot of their will and drive when they lose someone they love. Bereavement groups and other great organizations are not the remedy for some people. William worked side by side with Woody for several years and they shared the good times and bad times together. William no longer had Woody as the steady influence and William felt as if he was lost without him.

The little village of Driver and farming changed about the same time. Many farms were sold and houses replaced corn and soy bean fields. The people who moved here are nice and they are good neighbors, but it is very hard for many of us who have been in Driver our entire lives. We miss the farms, the fields, the livestock, the wild life, and especially our old friends and neighbors. William told me several times that he wanted to continue farming until 2011 because that would be the 300th anniversary of the Jones family farming the land in Driver. Not many businesses or corporations in this country can boast of selling their products for 300 years. Woody and William have passed on and so has a way of life. I miss my two friends and I will be thinking about them a lot next year when 2011 rolls around. I sure wish they were going to be here for their anniversary, and perhaps they will be looking down on old Driver. I miss seeing Woody or William riding down Driver Lane on an old dusty tractor. I miss them waving to me as they passed by and feeling like everything was alright in Driver.

BMW's, Navigators, HumV's, and golf carts now travel the old roads once traveled by tractors and mud covered farm trucks. I know this is progress, but I really miss the old days. I miss the old way of life and I miss the people who were part of that life.

Chapter 20

Good Bye OLD FRIEND

2007 and 2008 were definitely not the best years of my life. I found I had prostate cancer during the summer of 2007 and my urologist, Dr. Miley Walker of Suffolk, told me to take thirty days to decide which type of treatment I might prefer. I was pretty naïve when it came to prostate cancer and I really thought it was always very treatable and it was not a big deal. I read the book Dr. Walker gave me and I also called the American Cancer Society to find out more about prostate cancer. I had read four books and done Quite a bit of research when Heather (daughter) developed cancer, but my opinion about prostate cancer changed Quickly. My grandfather had prostate cancer when he was 89 years old and the doctors told him not to worry because he would die from something else. He died of pneumonia at the age of 91. I soon learned there were slow cancers, moderate cancers, and very aggressive cancers like the one Heather had. The American Cancer Society is a great organization and the people go out of their way to help you. If someone you speak to is not able to answer the Questions you may have, they will put you in touch with someone who can help you. I can say from my own cancer treatment experience that the Cancer Society is an organization made up of dedicated people who truly want to help others.

Today most people are weary and skeptical when it comes to any level of government or many organizations or agencies. I thank God there is an American Cancer Society and I am glad there is someone who can help answer your personal Questions that you did not think of while you were talking to your doctor. I am not saying that everyone who knows someone with cancer should call the Society at the drop of a hat, but the staff is there for people with serious Questions and doubts. I have talked to staff members as long as thirty minutes and I have felt more educated and secure each time I talked to someone. The best part of the name of the American Cancer Society is the word American because that word describes what the Society is all about and what other organizations should strive to be like. I thank the American Cancer Society and wish everyone associated with them only the best because they deserve it. I went through eight weeks of radiation treatments during the months of October, November, and December of 2007. I had been with Heather during all of her treatments, but this time I was an inside member of the fraternity of Cancer patients. This time I was not only an "outsider" or observer, but I was personally having the same emotions and concerns the other patients were having. I was in the same boat and I knew firsthand what it meant to have other patients "pulling" for you. The radiation technicians were super and they have the type of job where they have to be "On" everyday. Operating a store, I know you cannot allow your personal issues to affect your job. My father told me many times that customers have their own problems and issues and they sure don't need to hear ours. I will always be grateful to Gayle, Sheryll, Beth, and Lisa and the other people at Obici. My oncologist, Dr. Archie, is the best and I am glad he is my doctor. I breezed through radiation treatments and finished a few days before Christmas which was a great present. My right hip had been hurting for months, but it had nothing to due with the cancer or radiation treatments. I went to my primary physician, Dr. Thankam Pillai, who had been my doctor since she arrived in the area in 1978. Dr. Pillai sent me to have X-rays and she called me a few days later to inform me of the results. Dr. Pillai told me I had the bones of an eighty year old man and part of my hip was worn down and that was causing the pain. I was taking pills for the pain, but surgery would be needed to solve the problem.

Monday, April 28, 2008 was one of the worst days of my life. My good friend, Lee Roy Schmidt, was watching my store while Cynthia and I rode to the nearest Food Lion to pick up a few groceries. Cynthia stayed in the car and I went inside the grocery store to pick up the groceries. I noticed the store lights were flickering on and off and the lines were not moving because the computers kept resetting. I finally got through the check-out. Cynthia drove up to the front of the store and told me to hurry and get in the car. My sister, Holly, had called my wife on the cell phone and told her a bad tornado had just hit Driver. My Store, The Driver Variety Store, had been demolished by the tornado. My heart sunk and I felt sick to my stomach, but I asked Cynthia if Holly knew if Lee Roy was o.k. She said he was, but the ambulance was taking him to the hospital to check him. My good friend could have been killed, but he heard the freight train sound and dove under a clothing rack. A fellow, Harry Lee Gutelius, who runs the feed and seed store down the street pulled Lee Roy out o f the rubble. We pulled into Driver and the village looked like a bomb had been dropped on it. My store lay in a pile on the ground and the store (The Harmony House Antiques) two doors down only had one wall standing. Power and phone lines lay everywhere and debri covered yards and store lots. My brother's house (My grandfather's old house) had been hit by the tornado and several windows were blown out and the front porch was gone. The house which was built in 1830 suffered a great deal of water and wind damage. The poarch on the front of my brother's store (Arthur's) was destroyed and wind and water had scattered merchandise throughout the store. Two other buildings owned by my family had roof and exterior damage. The old metal building next to the Knot Hole Station was also struck by the tornado and demolished. Driver had been severely crippled, but thank God no one was killed or seriously injured. I had two dogs at my store and they both got loose after the tornado. I found Rocky and Buddy in my neighbor's yard across the street from my house. Buddy was frightened, but he was o.k. Rocky was in a state of shock. A teenage boy named Cameron Powell was working at my brother's store the day of the tornado. Cameron saw Rocky on the side of my store and thought he was injured. He picked the dog up in his arms and carried him to my neighbor's yard. Cameron is a very brave and kind young man. The police were making some residents evacuate their homes due to the downed power lines. I told the officers I needed a little time to move my dogs and we would take them to my mother-in-laws home. My wife gathered our two cats and placed them in pet carriers. Mosby and Rocky (the two cats) were frightened by the tornado and were hiding under the bed in our upstairs bedroom. We took our animals to Cynthia's mom's house and we all spent the night there and waited until we were allowed to go back home the next day. We returned home and our dog Rocky spent the day lying outside and many people stopped by and petted him. Rocky took a turn for the worse on Wednesday and Cynthia and I took him to the Vet. The vet told us he would check him over and give us a call in a few hours. The vet called us back and said he had found out that a small tube to Rocky's kidney had been severed during the tornado. He said our dog was being internally poisoned and the vet suggested we have Rocky put to sleep. We had no choice.

Lee Roy was trying to console me and he told me he was glad I was not at my store during the tornado. He said I probably would have been looking for my dogs when the tornado hit and I could have been killed or injured. Driver had police protection for the days immediately following the tornado. Virginia State Police, Virginia Beach Police, Portsmouth Police, Norfolk Police, Hampton and Newport News Police, Suffolk Police and some other departments watched over the homes and stores in Driver and they all did an outstanding job. The City of Suffolk had damage in several areas of the city and one police department could not cover so many large areas. The police actually caught a few people vandalizing a couple of homes. It is bad enough to have your house and property destroyed or damaged and having to worry about someone stealing what you do have left. Driver has always been a safe and Quiet neighborhood and we did not need thieves praying on us.

The Village of Driver was the site of a media blitz for the next several days. Hellicopters flew over head and television station trucks became a fixture. Media from Richmond and other cities joined the Tidewater media in the tornado coverage. A friend and former neighbor, Rodney Wagner, visited me a few days after the tornado. Rodney is a camera man for CBN and he was in Red Chia during the tornado on an assignment. He was watching CNN China in his hotel room when he saw my store and Driver on television. Rodney called out to the other members of the film crew and told them the tornado hit the village he once lived in. The crew watched the television and Rodney described to them where my store and other buildings were located. The old store was shown on television throughout the world. I had been interviewed so many times that I did not know if I was coming or going and it was the same for many of the other Driver Merchants. We were not given the o.k. to remove the store merchandise until Thursday; which was three days after the tornado. I think Reverend Tom Potter pestered the police until they relented. Reverend Potter is also a chaplain for the Portsmouth Police Department and he can be very persuasive. I don't have enough time left on this earth to thank Tom Potter for all the good he has done for me, my family, and many others. Anyone who knows the Reverend realizes he exemplifies what Christianity is all about. I have always believed that true ministers are "called" by God and Reverend Tom Potter is a perfect example. I have known Rev. Potter for several years and I have seen many of his good deeds. He will meet families at the bus station and try to find employment for the unemployed mother or father. He will feed people if they have not eaten. Reverend Potter jokingly told me about a fellow he met at the bus station and helped to find a job. The Reverend asked the man if he was hungry and the fellow said he was very hungry. The Reverend spent about fifteen dollars at Burger King trying to fill the fellow up. Reverend Potter brought a group of disaster relief workers to Driver and helped me and many others in the village clean up the destruction caused by the tornado. A local fellow named Steven Wright brought storage units to my store as we needed them. Reverend Potter's Disaster Relief Team, some of the girls who work for my sister Holly, and friends filled up four pods with merchandise we were able to salvage.

Another response group associated with The United Methodist Church came from hundreds of miles away to help in the clean up. My yard was covered with limbs and other debri, but the response team and neighbors cleaned my yard and several others. Members of Beech Grove united Methodist Church opened their fellowship hall to residents and workers and offered meals throughout the day. Power workers, police officers, relief workers, city workers, merchants, and local people affected by the tornado dined together and the fellowship was very special. Beech Grove Minister, Brian Sixby, held services for the workers and the community. Brian was very instrumental in bringing the community together and providing spiritual guidance during a very trying time.

Berea Christian Church also prepared meals for workers and the community. The Red Cross, The United Way, the Driver Ruritan Club, the City of Suffolk, and numerous organizations offered food, help, and repair funds to those affected by the tornado. Our local delegate in the Virginia State Legislature, Chris Jones, obtained Pods for people whose businesses and houses had been damaged. Food Lion and Farm Fresh were two super markets that gave food to feed the workers and community. Looking back, it was probably a good thing I was so busy trying to recover some of my merchandise that I did not have time to dwell on my loss. I now know what it is like to instantly lose cherished personal items and things passed down from previous generations. I was lucky to find some pictures of my father that were taken throughout the years. I lost one of the last video tapes of my daughter and I keep hoping it will be found in a box or bag of other items that were saved. Pictures, child hood toys, my grandfather's old pipes, and countless other items will probably never be located. I now know what it is like to lose a painting your daughter did when she was six years old. I no longer see tragedy and devastation on the nightly news the way I once did. I always felt bad for people and hoped they would be o.k., but now it hurts my very soul. I now know what a helpless feeling loss of loved ones, pets, and even keep safes can be. I lost one of my dearest friends the day I lost my store. A great-great uncle, Wade Brinkley, built the Driver Variety Store around 1910. The old girl missed her 100th birthday by less than two years. I could never duplicate the old store or the memories she helped to create. My store may have been wooden with a tin roof that leaked during heavy rains, but she was a gem and losing her will hurt me the rest of my days. I have a lot of fond memories of the old store and the people I met in the store during my times as a child, teenager, and adult. No one could ever duplicate the Old Driver Variety Store or recapture the essence of the building. A large front poarch extended from the front of the building. I have seen pictures of old gas stations with columns or posts that support the poarch and these were very similar to the store's poarch. People have told me over the years that whoever built the store had some engineering skills because there was always a gentle breeze flowing through the poarch. The poarch was a place where shoppers or visitors could mingle with local folks and possibly learn something about life in the country or small village. The poarch was a constant and the seasons of the year had very little affect on "poarch gatherings." The old woodstove situated in the back half of the store drew people to it on cold days like a light draws a moth. Men would huddle around the stove for hours spinning yarns or talking about farming, hunting, or fishing. The men would step aside if a child or woman needed to stand by the fire and warm up. Most of the world's problems were discussed and debated beside the old metal stove. Every day that I opened the front door of the store was a new adventure. I truly never knew what to expect each day. I did not know if I would be busy or if business would be slow. I didn't know if I would meet someone who would become a friend or see an old friend whom I had not seen in a long while. The old store taught me that anything is possible.

I miss the intangible things of the store as much as anything else. I miss the smell of the hardware, the paints, the turpentine, the clothing, and all the smells of an old store. I miss the gentle morning breeze coming through the side windows each morning. I miss the sun glistening through the big front windows and darkness peaking through on fall and winter days. I miss the holiday seasons at the store. I miss the old fashioned large Christmas tree bulbs hanging along the store roof and poarch roof. The green, red, orange, blue, and white bulbs gave an old timey feel to the store and village. My wife, Cynthia, collected snowmen and used them to decorate the inside of the store's large front windows. Some were made of wire and were round like huge snowballs and some were made to look like large blocks of ice. All of the snowmen had hats and were decorated with eyes and noises. Women were constantly trying to talk me into selling one or two of the snowmen, but they had become a big part of the Christmas season at the store. The tornado carried some of the snowmen away and the others were destroyed. We also lost two small artificial Christmas trees that meant a great deal to us. My wife decorated one tree with hummingbird ornaments and figures to honor my mother and her connection to hummingbirds. She decorated the second tree with small red birds because everyone called my father by his nickname "Red" and my wife always called him "red bird." It was a good way to remember my parents during the Christmas season. A good friend of mine named Joe Sandige helped me decorate an old red tractor each Christmas season. Another friend of mine named Tommy Thomasson would park the old tractor on the drive way in front of the store and Joe and I would decorate it with white miniature bulbs. The doctors discovered a malignant brain tumor in Joe's head about the same time I was diagnosed with prostate cancer. We talked about getting our radiation treatments at the same place, but Joe became very ill Quickly. Joe passed away in November, 2007 and I know I will always think of him: especially when I am helping decorate for Christmas. A couple of strange incidents happened before the tornado destroyed the store. I would save old bread and feed it to the sparrows and thrush that lived near my store. I did not see any birds on the day of the tornado and I wonder if they knew the tornado was coming and stayed away. I was outside the store and looked through one of the windows and saw a tiny hummingbird on the other side of the glass (inside the store). I called out to the other fellows on the poarch and we all watched the tiny bird in amazement. The little bird was not afraid and finally flew out the store's front door after several minutes inside. That was Sunday afternoon and the store was destroyed twenty four hours later.

I miss my mother-in-law, Jackie Butterton, visiting my old store. Jackie is a very special person and I think the world of her. She and my wife would come to the store and sometimes spend three or four hours dusting and cleaning the store. My wife would make me stay outside because she knows I am a packrat and I don't like to throw things away. Most people get excited about Thanksgiving and Christmas, but all holidays are special to Jackie. She decorates her mantle with villages and bears that play Christmas music during Thanksgiving and Christmas. Jackie decorates with eggs and singing rabbits on Easter and hearts and valentines on Valentine's Day. Jackie loves for kids to come to her house on

Halloween and they look at her living room decorated with ghosts and goblins. She takes great pride in her decorating and I guess my wife's sister, Theresa, got her skills from her mother. Theresa is a professional interior decorator and stays very busy in Florida where she and her husband, Kenny Shea, live. Jackie always brought candy to my store on Halloween and Valentine's Day and my customers looked forward to coming to the store on those days. She would stay at the store and hand out candy and leave a bowl of candy on the counter for anyone who came later. As I am writing this, my wife and her mother are at Dr. Hubbard's office in Norfolk. Jackie has had breast cancer twice and so has Cynthia. We found out last Wednesday that Jackie has had a recurrence of breast cancer and has some spots in her lungs. Naturally, my wife has been distraught since last week and she is extremely close to her mother. Jackie is eighty-four years old and she is extremely energetic. She still drives and cooks most meals and cooks huge holiday meals for her family. I am a country boy and I am crazy about Jackie's deviled eggs and I enjoy all of her cooking. She even grows her own collards for Christmas. Cynthia has watched me go through the pain of losing my parents and I have tried to prepare her for a day that will come. I can't imagine a world without Jackie and I know how hard it will be for Cynthia, Theresa, and their brother Gray. I know it is extremely hard when it is a loved one you are very close to and see often and your entire life suddenly changes. I hope with all my heart Jackie will be all right. My right hip deteriorated more after lifting and moving merchandise after the tornado. I could not stand on my feet very long by June and I had trouble walking. I went to see a specialist my wife goes to.

Dr. Jamali looked at my x-rays and told me he considered me disabled and I would end up in a wheel chair if I did not stop pushing myself. I was worse off than I thought and I believed I was doing great having been through prostate cancer. Dr. Jamaili asked me did I know what a forty-hour work week is and he said he knew anyone who was self-employed usually worked excessive hours. I had been working since I was thirteen and I accepted the fact I would operate the store for as long as I could. I had no idea a tornado would destroy my store and threaten my lively hood. I like Dr. Jamali and he is a fine doctor, but the insurance company would not pay for one of the procedures he recommended for me prior to surgery. I was still trying to recover from the tornado and I was operating my business in a small tent on my lot. There was no way I could afford a $12,000 to $15,000 medical procedure. Dr. Louis Jordan performed my hip replacement in early December, 2008. Everything went smooth, but I could not drive or lift anything for six weeks. I had physical therapy at home and a nurse saw me three times a week and checked my vitals and took blood. I felt great after the replacement. My hip felt so much better than it had before and I really did not need pain medication. I was going to build my store back and things looked like they would work out.I really found out some things after I lost my store. Many vendors and companies were easy to deal with and I paid every cent to companies like the power company, hardware company, etc. The local power company, Dominion Virginia Power, was extremely helpful and offered to put up a temporary pole and help me any way they could. A few national companies said they would cut my rates (advertising) and to call back in a month to see what could be done. I called back for several months untill I was finally told I would have to pay full price for services I did not use. I operated my store for four months in 2008 (Jan-April), but I was charged full price for an entire year. My word was my bond with customers when I had my store. I did things a lot like my grandfather and father did when they were in business. We live in a time where the customer does not come first or "the customer is always right." We live in a world driven by greed. My lawyer has been trying to settle with my insurance company for two years now. I would work with the insurance company, but it seems as if they don't feel they owe me for my building. I was obligated to pay my premiums and I did, but the insurance company seems to be able to do things at their own pace. I feel like they would be very happy if I would just die. I'm easy, but not that easy.

My store was a place of solace for me and I miss the peace and stability it offered. Beach Boy, Brian Wilson, wrote a great song in the 60's called, "In My Room." I felt the same way about my store that Brian did about his room. I spent more time in my store after Sherri (sister) and Heather passed and it was a place like Brian described as a place "I can tell my troubles to." It was a place that protected me and offered hope. Many times I would return to the store after closing and going home. I would sit in a chair in the store and think about many of the things that happened in that building and think about how good she was for me. I know how the captain of a ship feels when he loses his ship and sometimes wishes he had gone down with her. I might be crazy, but I have many of those same feelings about the Variety Store. I don't have a death wish and losing the store was similar to losing a loved one. I don't know how many times I have asked myself if things would have been any different had I been in the store at the time or if there were things I could have done differently since I knew every inch of the store. The best way I think I can do the Driver Variety Store justice is to briefly describe some of the people who loved her like I did and like me became a part of the store's mystiQue and fabric. She did her job and she did it well.

I hope anyone who reads this does not think I am enamored with every human being I meet and I enjoy spending time with everyone I meet. I genuinely like most people and I do hope I have my father's trait of looking for the good in everyone. I am not rich, but I am very wealthy when it comes to friends. Starting with "Nanie" and continuing on with the Driver Variety Store, I have met some very good and very interesting people. My PSA numbers for my prostate cancer are up (9.7) but I am very hopeful. The health insurance my wife and I carry went up to $1,500 a month ($18,000 yearly) and I can't switch because I have cancer. I now know what a mess our health care system is and I don't know how people afford insurance. How much more can people take? Who can you trust? Who cares? Who runs our country; the government or corporate America? It sure looks like "we the people" don't get much say.

I think I'm probably good for two more chapters and they are very important to me and I hope they are important for others. I must first describe and honor some of the great "friends" I met at Driver Variety. I hope to do a good job and show why the old store was so important for so many people.

Chapter 21

More Close Friends

Ray Gurnsey

I took a creative writing course at Tidewater Community College in 1976. Ray was a classmate and I thought it was neat that a fellow his age would have such a thirst for knowledge. I had no idea that we would become good friends eleven years later. Ray walked into the Variety Store one morning and we somehow started discussing writing and poetry. I told him I remembered him from the creative writing class, and he told me he had continued writing. Ray went to his car and returned with some of his poetry. The poetry was very good and I was very impressed with his creativity. Ray was one my favorite people. He was congenial, wise, witty, astute, gentle and the type of fellow my Grandfather Arthur would refer to as a "high toned gentleman." He was in his eighties when he started coming to my store two or three times a week. Everyone looked forward to his visits. Ray was born on the Sioux Pine Ridge Reservation in South Dakota and I liked finding out more facts about Sioux culture from Ray. I am a big admirer of Crazy Horse and many other great Sioux warriors. Ray grew up poor, but he was very proud and determined to make something of his life. Ray once told me he had always wanted and organ and thought he could teach himself how to play one. I took trumpet lessons as a child and I knew how much time and practice it took to be good. Ray bought some instruction books and taught himself to play his new organ. I should have known he could do anything he set his mind to. Ray was one of those people who seem to make every minute of their lives worthwhile. I mentioned the thirst he had for knowledge, but he had an even bigger thirst for life. He did not finish every project because of his age, he simply ran out of time. Ray always worried about his wife's health and I was very surprised when his wife called me and told me he had passed away. Ray packed a great deal into one lifetime and it was my pleasure knowing him and being his friend.

Mr. Bell

My father had known Mr. Bell for several years, but I first met him at the store in 1987. He was a big, non assuming man with a big heart. The old store was full of old pictures and calendars that Mr. Bell thought would enhance the store. Mr. Bell drove an older green Dodge station wagon and usually carried his four small white dogs wherever he went. He loved his dogs and he liked to see people take time with them. I believe the dogs were great comfort for him and were a healing force in his life. Mr. Bell had been a tail gunner on a B-17 and saw a lot of action in Europe during World War II. He would face something more terrible after the war and it would alter his life. Mr. Bell and his wife were the parents of a boy after the war. Years later, the child was walking in downtown Richmond one day when a driver lost control of his car and went up on the sidewalk. The car struck the boy. He survived, but he was mentally challenged and was placed in a care facility. Someone told me the accident was a Strain on Mr. and Mrs. Bell and he never spoke about his wife. He did tell me that he went to Richmond Quite often to visit his son when Mr. Bell was younger. I often wondered how Mr. Bell remained so gentle and pleasant after everything he had gone through. Like so many other people, the only thing left was to make it through life the best way he could. I didn't see Mr. Bell for about a month and someone told me he had passed away. I was worried about his dogs, but the person told me he believed someone who liked Mr. Bell was taking care of them. Mr. Bell was a good man and I miss him, but I do know he is at peace and in a better place. Much had been taken from him, but he is now rewarded.

Frank Nelms

I only wish that I had completed this book before Frank Nelms passed away. He loved Driver and was always telling me he wished I would write about the village and its people. Frank was very much like my father in regards they were both local legends and neither of them ever met a stranger. Frank also grew up poor in Driver and he lost his mother at an early age. Frank had his own contracting company (paving) and he did very well, but he never forgot his roots or what it was like to be down. Frank loved the ocean and sea about as much as anyone I have ever known. He was probably happiest when he was deep sea fishing or boating on the Inter Coastal Water System. People who went to sea with Frank will tell you the stories he would tell later were not fiction, but were very real. Frank bought a marina down at Hatteras, N.C. many years ago. He was an outsider from a village in Virginia when he first set up shop in Hatteras, but it wasn't too long before the islanders knew who he was and discovered the "old country boy" from Virginia was all right. Frank told me many stories when we were standing by the old woodstove. He and my father were both operating gas stations in Portsmouth during the 1950's. My father drove to Frank's station one afternoon and told him about a good poker game to be held that night. My father and Frank left for one of the local "watering holes" and did Quite a bit of drinking before going to the poker game. Frank said he did not even remember playing any poker that night, but he had proof. Frank told me he woke up the next morning still fully dressed. He said money was stuffed in every pocket and he must have had a good night of poker. Frank said the fellows my father and he played cards with must have been some honest men. I would often feel bad for Frank during his last years. I knew how much he loved the water and how much he missed fishing and he enjoyed talking to people who came in the store and were preparing to go on fishing trips. I honestly thought Frank had been out to sea the last time. Frank's health did improve and he was able to boat and fish some more and he was happy again. Frank passed away a few years ago and Driver is not the same without him. I can still hear Frank asking someone "Mister, do you know a real good sea story?" Frank and Jo Nelms were fixtures in Driver and the couple was always available when someone from Driver was ill or someone had passed away. Frank deed a lot of good and charitable things and never mentioned them and Mrs. Nelms has kept up that legacy. Frank may have bragged a little about his fishing skills, but he never bragged about helping people. He was a darn good fisherman, but he was also a very special person.

Rev Robert "Bob" Bennett

Reverend "Bob" Bennett came to Driver in 1965 as pastor of Berea Christian Church. Rev. Bennett bought a house in Driver after his tenure at Berea ended and he continued to preach at a church in Walters, VA. The Rev. and Mrs. Bennett raised their only child, June, in Driver. As an army seargent in World War II, "Bob" Bennett was involved with the French invasion a few days after the Normandy Invasion. He often told me that many of his fellow soldiers referred to him as "an old man" because he was twenty three years old and most of them were younger. Reverend Bennett had a distinguished military career and was wounded in action. Driver is a very old village, but no minister here or most other places will have the impact Rev. Bennett had on Driver. He was an active member of the community from the moment he arrived until the moment he left us. The Reverend was an active member of the Driver

Volunteer Fire Dept. and was also chief for several years. He was on the department's board of directors when he passed away in his late eighties. Rev. Bennett was also a member of the School Board for several years and served as a substitute teacher Quite often. My class had the Reverend for a teacher a few times and believe me no one was about to act up. Everyone respected Rev. Bennett. At the time Reverend Bennett came to Driver, the three local ministers were friends and knew and visited community people no matter which church the family attended (Episcopal, Christian, or Methodist). Rev. Bennett visited everyone in the hospital and he married and buried many, many people who were not members of his church. He did these things his entire life in Driver. I know most people in Driver always considered Rev. Bennett to be "our minister." He married Cynthia and me, he married my sister Sherri, he buried Sherri, and he touched every family in Driver. Rev. Bennett was your neighbor, your confidant, your friend, and he was always accessible. He was always "among his flock." Rev. Bennett and Frank Nelms were close friends and both men had been fixtures at the Driver Variety Store for years. Bob Hosier was a retired tugboat captain who hung out with my father at the store Quite often. His wife was a very faithful member of Beech Grove Methodist Church, but Bob was skeptical of most ministers. Rev. Bennett wore a dark suit most of the time because he made so many hospital visitations. My father, Bob, and a few others were sitting out on the store's poarch when Rev. Bennett walked up. Bob looked at "Preacher" Bennett and said, "It's Johnny Cash, the man in black." Everyone, including Rev Bennett laughed out loud. Rev. Bennett knew the jest was done in admiration and he became very proud of his new label. Rev. Bennett conducted Bob Hosier's funeral and the pastor told the story of how he became known as "Johnny Cash" and "the man in black" by everyone in Driver. Rev. Bennett passed away weeks after Frank Nelms passed on and I was very honored to be a pall bearer. Driver was very lucky to have Rev. Bennett and the village will never be Quite the same without him, but he sure served her well. No words we could ever say would fully describe how we feel about "Preacher" Bennett. Like Heather said when she looked at me for the last time, Thanks.

Stanly Clark

Stanly Clark was from nearby Portsmouth and he had known my father since he was a boy and my father operated the old Amoco Service Station. My father knew everyone in Stanly's family and Stanly was close to everyone in our family. He moved to Wonderland Forrest in the 1960's and built a new house. Stanly only lived about one mile from my parents and he visited them Quite often. He and my father did a lot of things together and Stanly hung out at the Variety Store with my father when he wasn't working for Frank Nelms. He would often join in the poker games with my father, Frank Nelms, J.W. Nelms, William and a few others. Stanly could do about anything he wanted to do. He could do electrical work, carpentry, plumbing, siding and sheet metal work, auto repairs, operate heavy eQuipment, and anything else that needed to be done. He was a jack of all trades and someone you could learn a lot from by being around him. Stanly once told me the Marine Corp doctors told him he had a very low IQ and should consider making a career out of the Corp. I told him the doctors were either kidding or were trying to convince him to reenlist. Stanly was not only smart, he had more practical sense than most people I have known. Stanly also had a very sad side to his life. He never married and my father once told me Stanly truly loved one girl and was crushed when she married another fellow. Stanly would sometimes go on drinking binges and drink for weeks straight. He would eventually get straight, but no one ever knew how long it would be till the next binge. People would sometimes get angry with Stanly because they felt alcohol was destroying his life. I honestly did not know if he drank to somehow punish himself or he was like Edgar Allen Poe and was so hurt and lonely inside that he sometimes could not cope with life. The thing I really admired about Stanly Clark was the fact that he was always a champion for the underdog. He took a fellow called "Shorty" into his home and looked after him for years. Raymond Pumphrey ("Shorty") was about 4'8" tall and he had grown up as an orphan in West Virginia. He somehow found his way to Portsmouth, VA and worked odd jobs such as grass cutting, painting, and any job that would pay him some sort of wages. "Shorty" did not have much of an education, but he was honest and willing to work hard. Stanly took "Shorty" in during the 1970"s and he made Shorty wear clean clothes and take care of his personal hygiene. Shorty began to take some pride in himself and he finally had someone in Stanly whom he could trust and look up to. He called Stanly "Big Brother" and he felt like he had a big brother to help him. Shorty was a sincere, innocent little person in his own right, but Stanly offered him a home and more importantly, confidence. Many people began to not look at Shorty's stature and began to look at him as someone who had something to off others. Years ago, "Shorty" would tell people he had once been a Merchant Marine sea captain, a West Virginia State Trooper, or a horse jockey in Kentucky. He wanted others to think he was somebody and he was important. Like anyone else, Shorty wanted to be accepted. I don't think Stanly would mind me including Shorty in his remembrance. The two men were opposite in many ways, yet loneliness had made them "brothers." Everyone liked "Shorty" and joked with him, but few took time to think what it must have been like to go through life not knowing who either parents were. Were they poor and could not afford another mouth to feed, were they worried that their child's size would cause problems, or did they simply not want the child? I have this habit of separating people I know into two categories. To me, the world is made up of takers and givers. Many people have much to offer and much to give, but they give very little. Others have very little or even nothing at all, but they manage to keep on giving. Kind words, good deeds, encouragement, time, smiles, laughter, etc. are some things that can be given that don't cost anything. Stanly Clark and "Shorty" Pumphrey were always givers. I miss the intellectual conversations I had with Stanley and I did not always agree with him, but I respected him. Stanly was a true believer in the old saying that "there's good in everybody" and he was willing to spend hours proving it. Stanly was able to bring out the better Qualities of many people and make them better. He once told me he was worried depression would get the best of me when Heather passed, but he said I did the right thing by throwing myself into the store and work. Stanly was completely honest and I leaned on him at times. He simply understood. Stanly was stricken with colon cancer about 2001. He recovered and lead a normal life for about a year and the cancer reoccurred. He pretty much let nature take its course during the last bout and he suffered Quite a bit. I called Stanly a lot and asked if there was anything he needed or anything I could do. He always told me to keep calling him, but not to worry about coming to see him. I knew early on that he did not want me to see him the way he was and I appreciate that. Stanly wanted me to picture him on the store poarch sitting on an old chair debating someone. That's the way I remember him. Neighbors took turns taking care of "Shorty" after Stanly's passing, but everyone knew he did not know what to do without "Big Brother." A passing car hit "Shorty" one afternoon as he was travelling on his bike. Shorty was seriously injured and spent a few months in the hospital. Tough little "Shorty" bounced back one more time and went on just as he had after Stanly had passed. Shorty was riding with a fellow one morning who was taking his wife to work at Chesapeake General Hospital. There was a car accident and "Shorty" had a heart attack and passed away. Shorty may have been small, but he is some one few of us will ever forget. Like Stanly, Shorty lives on.

Doug Sadler

I knew Doug Sadler from the time I was thirteen years old and working at my grandfather's store. Mr. Sadler came to "Arthurs Store" once a week to buy his groceries. I knew that Mr. Sadler also had an invalid wife and invalid daughter at home to take care of. Doug Sadler was a very forthright person and you usually knew where you stood with him soon after he met you. He served under Gen. George Patton and fought in the Battle of the Bulge during World War II. He once told me his outfit was stuck in the same spot for thirty days and the G.I.s wondered how General Patton was fairing. Mr. Sadler never complained about the things he had to do in and out of the service. He worked at Norfolk Naval Shipyard after the war and he worked and took care of his wife and daughter both when they became ill. He was a very disciplined man who put God, Country, and Family first and in that order. I liked Doug Sadler and because of an old airdale dog named Willie Nelson, I learned a lot more about Mr. Sadler. Willie was the town dog, but he spent more time with people at the Driver Variety Store than he did anywhere. He was at the store every morning when I opened up and he was always there for closing time. Willie had a great sense of things and the dog took a liking to Mr. Sadler. Mr. Sadler picked this up and he began to come out to the store to visit Willie. He would bring Willie dog biscuits and scraps and Willie would follow him every time he made a move. Mr. Sadler went across the street one day and bought an ice cream sandwich at Arthur's. He came back to my store and opened the ice cream and gave it to Willie who was estatic. The pair was inseparable after the ice cream sandwich, and anyone could see how fond Mr. Sadler was of "Willie Dog". Mr. Sadler did get angry with Willie one time. As usual, Willie patiently waited for Mr. Sadler to arrive and the dog rushed to him as he pulled up. Mr.

Sadler petted Willie, talked to him, and went across the street to buy an ice cream sandwich. Mr. Sadler gave Willie his ice cream, but the temperature was a little cool and Willie disappeared. Mr. Sadler wondered where Willie had gone and he finally saw the dog burying the ice cream sandwich in the ground. He yelled, "Willie old boy, that's your last ice cream sandwich." Doug Sadler patched things up with Willie and the two were as close as ever. Mr. Sadler didn't show up for a few days and someone told us he had passed away. Everyone, especially Willie, was saddened by the news, but we all realized that a very good man would finally have some peace.

Luther (Willie) Willey

I have known Luther Willey since the day in 1987 that he brought a twenty pound propane tank to Driver Variety Store for me to fill. I did not know that day that I was meeting someone who would become a close friend of my parents and my family as well. Willie was born in Weldon, N.C. on April 28, 1928. His family included five boys and two girls and his father passed away when Willie was two months old. The older boys tried to operate the farm, but Willie's mother was stricken by tuberculosis. Mrs. Willey was placed in a sanitorium when Willie was six year old and started school. Willie visited his mother each time family members or neighbors went to visit her. Willie's mother never got to come home and she died after a few years. Willie went to live on a farm with an older sister and her husband. He worked on the farm more often than he went to public school and survival was a struggle. Willie loathed the hot work in the tobacco fields and barns and he was involved with the other farming his brother-in-law did. He worked on the family saw mill on rainy days and days not suitable for farming. He often says he never entered the farm house in fall or winter without carrying an armful of wood for the house. Willie told his brother-in-law that he was going to leave the farm when he was eighteen and his brother-in-law told him he would not survive on the outside. Willie asked him what difference it made, because he was going to work him to death if he stayed on the farm. Willie left when he turned eighteen. Willie went to Norfolk, VA. in 1946 and got a job on the old ferry that transported cars from Norfolk to Portsmouth and vice-versa. He met new people and he had his own money he earned. Willie was finally happy. Willie got a better job on the ferry and he enjoyed his job, but someone told him Norfolk Naval Shipyard was hiring and the job offered benefits and security. He applied for the job in the Yard Transportation Department and was hired. Willie operated various types of heavy eQuipment at the yard, but his back was permanently damaged and he could no longer do the same type work. Doctors operated on him, but they were unsuccessful in mending Willie's back and he was left disabled. Willie moved his family to Florida for several years and moved near Driver in the mid 1980's. He got to know my father and my parents and Willie and his wife Berniece became good friends. Bud Yost and his wife, June, also became friends with the Willeys and the three couples went out to eat together Quite often and socialized together. The couples often went to a buffet on Wednesdays at O'Connors in Ahoskie, N.C. My father spent a great deal of time with four Ahoskie ladies one afternoon. He was born in Ahoskie and he was having a good time talking to them about people they all knew. While my father was socializing, Willie told the waitress to make up a phony bill for the ladies and to bring it to my father after they had left the restaurant. The waitress did as reQuested and told my father the four ladies really appreciated him paying for their lunch. Willie said my father stood up from the table and said he never laid eyes on the women until that day and did not offer to pay their bill. Everyone at the table roared with laughter and my father learned to stay at his own table instead of wandering about a restaurant.

Willie, Bud, and my father loved to hunt together and the three of them were happy when they were together. Bud passed and my father passed a few years later. Willie tells me often that he misses them and things are not the same without them. Willie and I will leave for Smithfield early some mornings before I open up my rented shop. We go to the thrift stores and different places and have breakfast together some mornings. We often talk about the past and the people we both knew. I see Willie nearly every day and we are the best of friends. I am fortunate to know him and don't know how things would be without him. I do know that it will be like losing my father all over again and I will miss him very much. Maybe he will join my father and Bud at the "Happy Hunting Grounds."

Leroy Schmidt

I will never forget the day Leroy Schmidt walked into the Driver Variety Store. I had seen him at some village meetings and other places, but I did not know him. I knew he liked to give politicians a fit and would stand up for what he believed in. I knew he could be loud and sometimes radical, but I had the feeling he was sincere. Leroy bought a jacket and hunting boots that day and he began coming into the store a lot. I felt like he was different from the person I saw debating politicians. Leroy had many of the same feelings I had, yet he was not afraid to voice his opinions and he was very passionate. He did not care what people thought about him and he was determined to be himself. Leroy was born on a farm in Burkville, VA. in 1943 and he had two sisters. He attended the University of Richmond for a year and was drafted into the Army in 1963. Leroy served in Viet Nam from 1963-1966 and was stationed at An Khe and Pleiku. Leroy was involved in a great deal of combat in Viet Nam while in the infantry. He had some horrible experiences and he still suffers from his service time in Viet Nam. He has spent some time at the Veteran's Hospital in Hampton, VA and he still visits and helps Viet Nam Veterans. Leroy attends many of Suffolk's City Council meetings and he is often the voice of "the man on the street" or the common man. I have been in grocery stores or restaurants with him and I have seen people of all ages come up to him and shake his hand. They say things like, "Stay on them Leroy" or "Keep it up Leroy and don't stop." Leroy researches his material before he speaks before City Council and his facts are usually accurate. Many think he should run for public office, but I think he is happier being a "watch dog." I have seen Leroy befriend many people throughout the years and he genuinely cares about other people. He has told me many times that he is glad I did not have to go through what he did in Viet Nam. Many vets feel like Leroy and don't begrudge others that did not have to make the sacrifices they did. I am grateful to Leroy and the other Viet Nam Vets. Leroy can be hard headed at times and he can also be meek as a lamb. I can't remember the number of times when he finished arguing with someone and ended up saying, "You're right, you're right." A big man can admit that he is not always right. Leroy was in the Driver Variety Store when the tornado hit and luckily he dove under a rack of clothes and was not hurt or killed. We could have easily lost him that day, but he lived to "fight another day." When people ask me to describe Leroy, I usually say he can be a handful but he has been like a big brother to me. He was there for me when I lost my parents and he was always available when I needed him to watch my store. We have shared the pain of losing many mutual friends during the past years. Leroy lost his wife, Sandy, a few years ago. My wife and I have been on vacation with Leroy and Sandy and have done other things with them. Sandy was confined to a wheel chair for many years, but she was a fighter and tried to live life to the fullest. Leroy and I have shared many of the same tragedies of life. He lost his mother and one of his sisters a few months ago. Leroy watched their health deteriorate and he knows that terrible, helpless feeling. He still remembers his father, L.W., with much fondness and admiration years after he passed. Leroy came from a very good family. I knew his mother and have met and talked to his sisters. Mrs. Schmidt always told me to "look out for Leroy" after she had visited me when she was in town. She loved her children dearly and she was a great person.   I care deeply about my friends and loyalty goes a long way with me. A good friend today will be a good friend tomorrow. If I was in a battle or if I was in a foxhole, I would want Leroy to be with me. I know he would not cut and run when things got tough. He would be there.

Severn Warrington

Severn Warrington is the descendent of a family of farmers that farmed land in and around Driver for over two hundred years. I have known him since we moved to Driver in 1957 and my mother's ancestors have known the Warrington family for two hundred years. During his teenage years, Severn reminded me of James Dean when he was driving around Driver in his 1956 Thunderbird. Like James Dean, Severn liked fast cars and racing. He looked the part with slicked back longer hair and sideburns and he could have fit in with the cast of "Rebel Without a Cause." Severn began working on his father's farm when he was a boy and he still remembers the times a few hundred migrant workers would come to Driver to help harvest crops. He worked the long hours on the farm and he bought an old truck and sold fire wood during the winter. Severn has a sister named Catherine who worked at my grandfather's store when she was in high school. Mrs. Warrington sold eggs, melons, corn, and other items to my grandfather for resale at Arthur's Store. Mrs. Warrington would also trade for goods that could not be raised on the family farm. Mr. Warrington was stricken with cancer when Severn was a teenager and the boy operated the farm and still attended school. Severn loved his parents very much and he will never forget his father having to take radiation treatments. Severn has told me many stories about his drag racing days and his adventures with his friend and fellow Driver teenager, John Whedbee. The two knew the highway from Driver to Chuckatuck (6miles away) so well they outran the Virginia State Police from Chuckatuck back to Driver. Severn and John cut their car head lights off when they reached Driver and hid behind Driver Elementary School. The Division of Motor Vehicles was Quite different during the 1950's. Severn would be issued a speeding ticket on a Friday night and he could go to Grandy's Gas Station and pay the fine to Claude Grandy on Saturday morning. Severn's father passed away and his mother decided the family should stop farming. Severn went to work at Jake Gutelius' grainery and he worked long hard, hours. He later decided it was time to enter the military. Severn joined the Air Force and went to San Antonio, Texas for basic training. He studied Russian and was in intelligence, but he had trouble with the language and was placed in the air police. He liked his new job. The Air Force sent Severn to an air base in England and he met his future wife, Wendy. The pair married and Wendy came to Driver a few months before her husband was discharged from the service. My mother and Wendy became close friends. Severn later bought a house two doors down from my parents in Driver and Wendy gave birth to a son, Cliff, and later a daughter, Kim. The Warrington children grew up with my sisters, Sherri and Holly and our families have always been close. Severn and Wendy split up in the late 1980's and both remarried. Severn's wife had pancreas complications and passed away. Daughter, Kim, moved to England and met a nice English fellow and married him. She and her husband Lawrence have four children, three boys and one daughter and the daughter is named after my sister Holly. Severn spends six months a year in England with Kim and her family and he spends the other half a year in Driver. He and Kim's family take and go on a cruise for two weeks each summer. Severn's son, Cliff lives in Leesburg, Va. and has one son and one daughter. He visits them when he is able and he talks about his grandchildren Quite often. Severn spends a lot of time with us at the store (the rented building) when he is in Driver. Everyone who knows him knows he thinks the world of his family and Wendy. Severn talks often about making his home in England and leaving Driver for good. He always says that his children will never live in Driver again and they don't have a lot of interest in the antiQues and things he has collected. If Severn does move away, it would mean the end of his family's long history of being Driver residents, but the Warringtons like the Nelms, Jones, Arthurs, Hurfs, and other families will be remembered for many years.

Pat Mims

I have known my friend Pat Mims for several years. He reminds me a lot of Lee Carr. Like Lee, Pat is very bright and he has a kind of Quiet confidence. He works very hard and he was always there for his mother after his father passed on. Like Lee, Pat is one of those people you simply like to be associated with. He graduated from the Norfolk Naval Shipyard Apprentice School as an electrician, but Pat is highly skilled in many trades. He can talk about cars, boats, music, politics, life and anything else. Pat is a very responsible person and he is wise beyond his years. Pat and his wife, Lorraine, have a daughter named Chrissy and a son named Pep. The couple now have three grandchildren and they stay very busy being active grandparents. Pat and Lorraine are very family oriented and they dearly love their children and grandchildren. I could never really explain to Pat what his friendship means to me. He was there for me when my parents passed away and he was there for me when I lost my store to the tornado. I can't count the number of favors he has done, like fixing my furnace or rewiring my house. Pat and Lorraine are great friends and they are great neighbors and hosts. I have spent some wonderful evenings at Pat's house standing by a backyard barn fire or listening to some classic rock and talking about muscle cars. Several years ago when my father was alive, Lorraine gave our group of Driver Variety Store friends a name that has stuck. She called us the "Old Farts Club" or the O.F.C. It's people like Pat that make me proud to be a part of that club. I did not get the chance to hang out with my old friend, Mckinley Morrison, like we talked about years ago. Perhaps Pat and I will be able to "hang out" and talk about the good old days and the good memories. I can only say that Pat is a true friend and he is a great person and I will always think the world of him.

Rev. John Ashenfelder

Pat Mims and I have a mutual friend whom we both care about deeply and admire. He is a Presbyterian minister named John Ashenfelder. Pat and I don't just respect the reverend for being a minister; we respect him for being a good role model and a good human being. Knowing Reverend Ashenfelder like I do, I can honestly say he is not a man who likes to "toot his own horn." I met the Reverend years ago when a mutual friend named Don Allison asked me if I could sell a few bikes for a friend of his. Reverend Ashenfelder brought a couple of bikes to my store a few days later and we have been friends ever since. He gave me prices for the bikes, but he said I could give them to children who were poor or came from struggling families. Money was not a factor and that impressed me very much. The Reverend and I continued to sell bicycles until parts were harder to find and kids became interested in other things. He still came to visit me at my store and I was always glad to see him. The Reverend would often drop by with one of his daughters. June is handicapped and she is always smiling. The Reverend seemed to always sense when I needed a little help or encouragement. He would place his hand on my right shoulder and it was like my days as a boy when Reverend Ned Thompsen would do the same thing. I would feel better and would start thinking more positive. If the Reverend could handle all his tribulations, I should be able to handle mine. Reverend Ashenfelder is pushing ninety and is now suffering from Alzheimers. He no longer drives and he doesn't come to the store anymore. I sometimes run into his wife and June at the grocery store and we talk about the Reverend. Reverend Ashenfelder liked to confide in me for some reason and that always made me feel privileged. A few years ago he told me the Bishop asked to meet with him and he went to see the Bishop, but had no idea why the Bishop needed to talk to him. The Bishop told the Reverend he checked into his retirement and found out Rev. Ashenfelder was not receiving what other ministers with such long service received. He asked the Reverend why his salary was so small for so many years. Reverend Ashenfelder told the Bishop he knew his congregation was made up of elderly people and families that struggled to make ends meet. He told the Bishop his church members were loyal parishioners and he did not want to leave them so he never complained. The Presbyterian Church did the right thing and increased the Reverends retirement. Reverend Ashenfelder is from Pennsylvania and he is highly educated in theology, but he has a tremendous amount of common sense. I sometimes feel that many ministers today think they have to take care of church "business" first and the congregation later. The Reverend has never had a big fancy house and many of the material trappings of this life. He does have many friends and admirers and he has touched many, many, people. Reverend Ashenfelder has all the things Money can't buy and I will always be thankful for him. He is the "real deal."

J.C. Strickland

I have met many people who I wish I could have known for several decades rather than five or ten years. J.C. Strickland was one of those people. Mr. Strickland was born in the hills of Western North Carolina and his family was poor. Every Thanksgiving he would tell me how he made home-made sling shots and would kill a turkey for Thanksgiving and Christmas. He said the family could not afford a box of shot gun shells, but he became Quite skilled with a sling shot. J.C. had done about everything a man could do in one life time and he was one of the most interesting people I have ever known. He worked hard and rose above poverty. Mr. Strickland and his brother owned their own electrical company and did electrical work on commercial buildings. J.C. never lost his passion for the outdoors and nature. He was close friends with the great bow designer, Joe Parker. J.C. designed his own bows and was Quite a marksman. He was featured on the John Cameron Swaze outdoors television show years ago.

J.C. hunted all over the world and his home was filled with trophies (wild game) he had hunted. Montana, Alaska, Canada, Europe and Africa were some of the places he had hunted. Mr. Strickland served as an Army train engineer during World War II, and he remained in Germany for a time after the war. He and other soldiers would hunt Seka deer and the Army cooks would feed the German people in the base chow hall. Mr. Strickland told me many times he really liked the German people. J.C. told me the U.S. forces captured German General Gerbels train and Mr. Strickland became the engineer on the train. He said the train was decorated with artifacts and he asked his commanding officer what the troops should do with the relics. The officer told J.C. the soldiers could ship some items home, but he did not want the Russians or French to confiscate them. Mr. Strickland gave me a small chandelier from the train and Pat installed it in our dining room. Mr. Strickland was a very distinguished man with silver hair and rosy complexion. He liked to have a drink in his garage each evening and he called the drink a "hammer." J.C. spent a lot of time in his garage and he always had a project he was working on. He designed and built his own tree stands and hunting ladders. He would show them to hunters who came to my store and he was going to sell them when he got his patents. He had a good time talking about hunting and he was happy when he was in the company of fellow hunters. J.C.'s son was severely injured in Viet Nam. His son was in the Sea Bees and was operating a piece of heavy eQuipment when a mine exploded. J.C told me he probably would have lost his son if his good friend, Admiral Yount, had not made sure J.C.'s son received the needed medical treatment. His son fully recovered from the injury. J.C. had the same type of thirst for life that Ray Gurnsey had and both of them were "high tone gentlemen." Both men encouraged me and both of them may have been elderly but had the drive and ambitions of men much younger. J.C.'s brother was a pilot in the Pacific during World War II and his plane was shot down on the final day of the war. The crew survived the crash, but all the members were executed. J.C. would often tell me what a difference one day can make and he made every day count. Mr. Strickland was stricken with Alzheimers and he eventually went into a home. Mrs. Strickland visited him every day, but she could not control him alone at home. She is a fine woman and it must have hurt her badly to watch the man she loved change so much. Alzheimers is a terrible disease and I have seen firsthand what it can do. Mr. Strickland lived a long and very fruitful life (into his late eighties), but his disease drained him. He was not one to sit in a home and watch the world pass him by, he was a participant. I miss the J.C. Strickland I knew and liked very much; I miss my friend.

Frankie Ward

Frankie Ward and I have been good friends for many years. He probably would not like me writing about him, but he deserves some credit for being a real friend. Frankie called my father "Red Man" and I know he looked up to my father. Frank is not the kind of fellow to make heroes out of other men, but I thinked he liked my father's outlook on life. Frankie is the type of fellow who will do anything for you if you are his friend. He is extremely loyal and he is the type who will do a friend five favors for the one favor his friend did for him, but he does not keep track of favors. Frankie is a very forth right person and he will tell anyone that if he took a drink of liQuor it could be his last. He will tell you that he almost drank himself to death years ago. He had a massive heart attack and nearly died, but he recovered and has remained loyal to the people who did not judge him and waited for him to straighten out. I have learned many things from my friend, Frankie, but I have learned one thing that is as important as anything anyone has ever taught me. Frankie nearly died and he simplifies his life and most people's life when he says "every day is a bonus."

Joel Howell

Joel Howell was another person I wish I could have known much longer. He came from a fine family and he graduated from the University of Virginia, but his character alone would separate him from most people. My father used to say that people like Joel were "100 percent", meaning the person was 100% dedicated to their beliefs, morals, family, religion, friends, and values. Joel was not one to look for a lot of gray areas in life. Individuals were either completely honest or they were dishonest. They were either sincere or they were phony. Joel and I were talking about the Bible one morning and I told him I had read the New Testament a few times. He said he liked God in the Old Testament because he understood completely where he stood with God in the Old Testament. Joel said many people need "fire and brimstone" and that's what they get in the Old Testament. Joel was a very interesting man. He was comfortable working in a nice suit and he was comfortable wearing shorts and a tee shirt while he whaled away on his drum set. Joel handled estates for banks and attorneys during the day and he was a musician at night (his hobby and first love). Joel was stationed on a swift boat in Viet Nam with the Navy during the war. He was stationed in New Orleans after his tour in Viet Nam and he once told me a funny story about his final days in the Navy. A fellow petty officer found Joel one afternoon and told him the Commanding Officer wanted to talk with him. Joel said he needed to change into his uniform, but the petty officer told him the C.O. said to come as he was. Joel met with the C.O. and the officer said he had been looking over Joel's files. He said the Navy was impressed with his education at Virginia and the Navy thought he would make an outstanding officer. He just needed to re-enlist and would then be sent to Officers Candidate School. Joel asked the C.O. if he could be frank with him and the C.O. said yes he could. Joel told the C.O. it took four years for the Navy to think about this and he did a lot of thinking on the swift boat in the rivers of Viet Nam. He was now ready to be discharged and all of the sudden he is important to the Navy. Joel said he appreciated the offer, but he was ready for civilian life. Joel and I both liked soul music and we talked about old rock N roll whenever we got together. I would see him almost daily, Monday through Friday when he would stop at the store before going to work. We would listen to some classic CD's and talk about the Temptations, Four Tops, Otis Redding, Isley Brothers, Marvin Gaye, and many other artists. One of the things I admired most about Joel was the fact that he was a real family man. He and his wife, Chris, were the parents of one daughter named Jamie. Both parents made sure Jamie received and excellent education and they were very active in her school life, social life, and other activities. Jamie was an award winning cheerleader and the family spent numerous weekends involved in competitions. Joel was a great father and he was very proud of his daughter. Jamie is currently a cheerleader at North Carolina State University and like her father, she is very dedicated. I could relate with Joel Quite well because I knew how it was to have only one child. The daughter is always "Daddy's little girl" and Joel and I felt the same way about our daughters, Jamie and Heather. I guess in some way every father hates to see his daughter grow up and leave the "nest" after so many years of being the man in his daughter's life. Pat Mims and I were inside the store one morning a little over three years ago. A bird kept flying into one of the side windows like it was trying to enter the store. Pat asked me if I had a funny feeling about the bird and I told him I did. The phone rang. Chris, Joel's wife, called and told me Joel had passed away the previous evening. She had trouble telling me and I did not want to comprehend what I was hearing. Joel could not be gone, I had seen him the day before and he was fine. Once again that sick, helpless feeling came over me like a dark cloud. I miss Joel very much. I won't elaborate on his passing, but I am thankful he was my friend. He would have fit in very well with Bobby, Dale, Thomas, Lee, and me because he was always seeking the truth. A mutual friend once told me Joel was too honest for the line of work he was in. The world could use more men like Joel. He was an honorable man.

Bill Lauver

Bill Lauver decided one day that he would have his brother, Danny, drop him by the Driver Variety Store. He had recently moved in with Danny and he wondered why so many fellows hung out at the store. It was a good day to make new friends and Bill Lauver was very good at making friends. There were thirteen children in the Lauver family and many of them came to the Driver and Portsmouth area after Bill's brother, Dick, finished his naval enlistment. The family from Bellwood, Pennsylvania soon became an integral part of the community and everyone soon knew and liked the Lauvers. They were honest, hard working people and they all revered their mother. I had known some of Bill's brothers for years, and I had seen Bill, but I never really knew him. I knew some people called him "Big Bill" and others called him "Uncle Bill." It didn't take me very long to find out why so many people liked Bill. I met Bill when he was in his late 60's. He was a big man with a big heart and big smile. The fellows at the store took to Bill instantly and he soon became a member of the O.F.C. He and I soon became very good friends and I sort of felt like I was with Matthew again. Bill's brother, Dick, told me Bill had rheumatic fever and Saint Vitus Dance when he was a young boy and Bill would shake and stutter because of the disease. Years later, Bill was sent to Penn State University to take speech therapy. Bill often told me he got to know Penn State football star Lennie Moore who was later a great running back with the Baltimore Colts. Bill said Lennie was a great guy and he was always nice to him. The Army drafted Bill and sent him to Germany when he completed basic training. Bill was a communications technician and he installed communication lines. He said the sergeant sometimes yelled at him and said, "Lauver get your butt up that pole." The Army told Bill they had made a mistake and he should not have been drafted. Bill told his C.O. that he was drafted for two years and he felt like he should serve his country for the entire two years. He completed his service time. Like Joel, Bill was an honorable man. I have heard many stories about neighbors hiding their house keys and then telling Bill where the key was so he could take the paper in the house when they were gone. As a child, Bill demonstrated a lot of character and responsibility for someone who had some major setbacks. Bill watched over my store like a mother hen and he was always looking out for my best interests. He would go inside the store whenever I got busy and he would talk to the customers. He often told customers, "We probably have what you need."

My father became very fond of Bill and he would usually take Bill with him when he went to the bank or ran errands. Bill once told me, "I know why your daddy took me to Hardy's this morning. Somebody robbed the bank across the street yesterday and he didn't want to go by himself." My father was very tight and he was always looking for a bargain. Bill walked up to the store one morning and asked me; "Have you seen the banana split commercial on t.v.? Your daddy and I are going to get one." A few minutes later my father picked Bill up and drove off to buy the banana splits. The two returned about one hour later and Bill only said "O.K." when I asked him how they liked their banana splits. He was Quiet for a few minutes. Bill placed his thumb and finger apart and told me that's how big the cheap banana splits they bought were. He said he and my father did not save any money because each of them ate three banana splits. I would have loved to have seen their faces when the waitress brought them the first banana split. Bill loved horse racing and his family had been to many horse races throughout the years. I remember Bill was the first person I knew who told me to keep an eye on a horse named "Smarty Jones." He also told me "Smarty" would win the Kentucky Derby and two out of three, but he would not win the Triple Crown. Bill was right. My wife and I took Bill with us for a long weekend in Winchester, Va. in late August. We had a great time and visited Harpers Ferry, Charles Town, W. VA., Antietam, and Gettysburg. Bill knew all the areas like the back of his hand and my wife and I felt like we had a tour guide with us. He did not drive, but he remembered all the routes and shortcuts. The three of us had a ball at the horse races in Charles Town that Saturday night. We bet a little on the horses and also played the slots. Bill decided to go to one of those areas where you could bet on horse and dog races from other areas of the country. I checked on Bill one time and he was betting on three horse races and one dog race at once. I still don't know how he did it. I kept thinking of my father who was still alive at that time and was back in Driver watching the store for me. I told Cynthia we would bring Bill and my father both to Charles Town the following year and we would make the same rounds. I knew my father would really enjoy that. Anyone who has the same type situation should take advantage of the time and not hesitate. We did not get a chance to make that trip because my father passed away in early October and Bill passed during early spring. The Driver Days after Bill's passing was not the same for me. Bill was not sitting next to my mother-in-law (Jackie) at a table in front of Driver Variety Store selling items for me. He was not there wearing a Driver Days sweatshirt and ball cap and he was not there for the kids. Bill's family told me Bill had reQuested that he be buried in his Driver Days sweatshirt if anything happened to him. Driver Days has grown and become special to kids and adults alike, but nobody loved Driver Days the way Bill did. His pastor mentioned that fact at his funeral service. It's strange how life works sometimes. Sometimes you can be nice to someone and a real bond can develop from one simple act. It's also strange how certain people come into your life when you need them most.

As with my friendship with Matthew, I was the lucky one. The small things I did for Bill were repaid tenfold and I really miss him. I have been lucky enough to know a couple people that only looked for the good things in me. If someone asked me right now where Bill is, I would ask them if they have ever seen the great movie, "It's A Wonderful Life." If they had I would ask them if they remembered the angel who was sent to help Jimmy Stewart. The angel accomplished what he was sent to do and he got his wings. Bill Lauver got his wings.

Joe "Little Joe" Sandige

I mentioned Joe Sandige earlier when I was writing about decorating the store. I knew Joe for only a handful of years, but it seemed like I knew him my entire life. Joe would often say that he wished he had met my father much earlier and he had known about the store sooner. Joe was a retired general foreman at Northrop Grumman Shipbuilding and he and his wife moved near Driver. He stumbled upon the store one day and he Quickly fit in. Joe was small in stature, but he was very big in character. Joe was the type of fellow who would help anyone, stranger or friend. I could not count the favors he did for me, my uncle Jerry, William Jones, my sister (Holly), and several others. Joe was very intelligent and very low key, but he was also practical and confidant. Joe found out he had a malignant brain tumor about the same time I found out I had prostate cancer. Joe's health deteriorated rapidly. I visited him at his home and it was sad to see such a good and active man decline so Quickly. Joe passed away that November and I lost a good friend and confidant. He sort of reminded me of my father and he had that same type of wisdom. I truly wish I could have known Joe for many, many, years, but life has taught me to be thankful for the time we do get to spend with good people. I am very thankful Joe Sandige was my friend.

Brian Beverly

Brian Beverly and his friend, Tony Collins, pulled up to the Driver Variety Store on their motorcycles one afternoon six years ago (2004). The two friends are now in their seventies and they are still riding their Harleys. Brian grew up poor and was born in Wolf Pen, West Virginia and raised in Arkansas and Portsmouth, VA. He found out he had a skill for laying brick and he became a brick mason and stone mason. Brian started his own business and worked some large projects in different parts of the country.

Brian worked on the Christian Broadcasting Network building in Virginia Beach, a granite jail in Little Rock, Arkansas, the Hillcrest Medical Center in Tulsa, Oklahoma, additions to Portsmouth General and Maryview Hospitals in Portsmouth, VA., and other jobs in Memphis, Kansas, and several other areas. Brian worked on the fence at Graceland but never saw Elvis. Brian became a regular very Quickly at Driver Variety Store. He served in the Navy and Marine Corp and was once stationed in Japan. He liked the guys who gathered at the store and the fellows liked him. Brian enjoyed talking to bikers who would shop at the store. Brian has fought numerous health problems throughout the years. He recently had an operation at McGuire Hospital in Richmond, VA. and doctors removed a tumor from his pancreas. The tumor was not malignant and Brian recovered nicely. I have seen a lot of people who enjoy motorcycles, but I can put Brian near the top of the list. He dreads the day he will no longer be able to ride his cherished Screaming Eagle Harley Davidson. Brian is ready to take a short bike trip at the drop of a hat.

Brian is the type of fellow who knows a lot about very many things. He knows when something is a good deal and when it is not. He enjoys looking in thrift shops and wholesale warehouses. My wife and I both think the world of Brian and his wife, Doris. I get worried if I don't see Brian for a few days and I call him at home. It is enjoyable to spend time with someone like Brian because he is the same person everyday and he is satisfied with his own life. He does not try to compete with people or need all the material things of life. Brian has a spiritual side within him and he is a very good person. He treats everyone fairly and he gets along with everyone. Like most folks, he likes to be accepted and he always is. Brian is simply a "real" friend.

Charlie Taylor

I met Charlie Taylor more than twenty years ago when he and his family moved near Driver. He was a lieutenant in the Navy when I first met him and he liked to talk to my father about his days in the Merchant Marines. Charlie has lead a very uniQue life. He grew up in Southside St. Louis, Missouri two blocks from the Anheuser Bush Brewing factory. He credits the Boys Club of America in St. Louis for giving him refuge and the skills to make it in life. Without the Boys Club, Charlie says he could have been a different type person and a person on the wrong side of the law. Charlie was a very good athlete in high school and excelled in baseball and basketball. He decided to enter the Navy when he graduated. Charlie had no idea the Navy would become his new "family." Charlie went through diving school and became a master diver. He enjoyed diving and he enjoyed the regimen of the Navy. He was a diving hull technician and he also worked many retrieval missions such as crashed aircraft. Charlie made chief and ran one of the diving schools. He has many, many stories about his navy career and some of them are very funny. He once dropped a keg of beer through his commanding officer's convertible top. Charlie got into a few scuffles during his career and he will be the first to admit he was fortunate to pull twenty three years. He does not like liars or cheaters and his St. Louis roots took over a few times. Charlie received a personal call from Admiral Mike Borda one time. Charlie had done a lot of sea duty and he had been promised shore duty, but was ordered on another deployment. He complained and the word got around. Charlie had made lieutenant by this time and he and the admiral were both Mustangs; which means they were both enlisted men and rose from seaman to Naval Officer. A navy friend of Charlie's passed Charlie's problem on to an officer at the Pentagon and one of the officers under the admiral spoke to the admiral about the dilemma. A lieutenant at the Pentagon called Charlie and asked if he was Lieutenant Charles Taylor. Charlie said he was and the officer from the admiral's office told Charlie to "stand by for Admiral Mike Borda." Charlie thought someone was playing a joke on him, but he figured he better play it straight. Admiral Borda came on line and spoke to Charlie. He told Charlie he reviewed his service record and agreed he deserved some shore time. He also talked to Charlie about the both of them being Mustangs. He told Charlie to never threaten to leave the Navy before his time was up because the next time he would take him up on it and not ask him to stay. Charlie and his wife, Fran, have three sons and the family is very tight knit. Fran deserves a lot of the credit because she often had to raise the boys alone. She is a wonderful person and Cynthia and I like her very much. I often tell Charlie what a good person Fran is and how lucky he is. She is also a terrific cook. Charlie has accomplished a great deal in his life and he has a lot in life to be proud of. He is a good example of the service people who sacrifice a tremendous amount of their lives so we can all enjoy the freedom we have in our country. Charlie has not backed down from many challenges in life and I am very glad he is my friend.

Robert "Stretch" Perrott

I probably had the same reaction most people had the first time I met Robert Perrot. I saw a 7' 1 ½" fellow standing in my parents' store (Arthur's) and I immediately began wondering who he was and where he had played basketball. I had no idea I would become friends with him and I would not even think of his height. Anyone who ever knew "Stretch" soon realized he was a uniQue person and an original. He was not called "Stretch" because he was so tall; but for the outlandish tales he would tell. His tales were harmless and everyone who knew him knew he was a tall fellow who was big hearted and liked everyone, but had a penchant for "stretching the truth." Baseball   fans often chat about "Yogisms" attributed to Yankee catcher Yogi Berra. People who knew Robert "Stretch" Perrott talk about "Stretchisms", which are tales "Stretch" either originated or embellished. "Stretch" came into the Driver Variety Store one morning and asked me if I wanted to hear about his latest invention. He said he had developed an icicle bullet for the C.I.A. He said the bullet could be fired and would immediately melt leaving no evidence. "Stretch" came into the store another morning and asked me if I had heard the sirens in Driver the night before. I knew he would be able to explain the sirens, but his explanation was like something from the "Dukes of Hazzard" t.v.show. "Stretch" told me he was testing the new go cart he had built. He said he had no idea the go cart would do 195 m.p.h., and he lead the police on a wild goose chase trying to catch him. A 7' 1 ½" man doing a 195 m.p.h. through Driver would have certainly been unusual. A fellow came into my store one day while "Stretch" was hanging around. The conversation turned to Viet Nam and the fellow mentioned that he had served in Viet Nam. That was all that "Stretch" needed to hear. "Stretch" proceeded to tell us that he did three tours "in country" with the Special Forces. He told the vet that he was the person who developed the steel shank of the jungle boot. He said he almost stepped on a bungi stick when he first got "in country". He cut open c ration cans and molded them around his feet before putting his boots on. Naturally, the Army liked his idea and boots were then manufactured with the steel shanks. Stretch may have been an outlandish story teller, but he was very gifted mechanically and electronically. He was a whiz working on engines, video eQuipment, ham radios, and many other things. Many people saw firsthand what Stretch could really do when a crew from Richmond was in the area running sewer lines. The crew was working next to the highway when the machine they used to run a long hole beneath the ground broke down. The supervisor was complaining that he had eleven men at a standstill because of the breakdown and it would be hours before a mechanic could come down from Richmond and repair the machine. Stretch overheard the foreman and he said he could fix his machine. The foreman asked "Stretch" what his labor would be and "Stretch" told him $20.00 an hour. The foreman told him to start immediately. Stretch started the machine, looked it over and said he was going to get the parts he needed for repairs. He returned about an hour later and fixed the machine as he promised. He had even picked up an installed a better muffler which would make the eQuipment more efficient. The foreman came over to my father and said, "I have never seen that tall guy before, but he knows his stuff and he saved us a lot of money today. My father often told a story of something that happened with Stretch one day. A college professor came in the store and he told my father he was a mathematics professor at Tidewater Community College. "Stretch" overheard the conversation and he bluntly said, "I could have been a mathematics teacher. I'm a mathematical genius." The professor told Stretch he would like to write out a complicated problem and see if he could get the correct answer. "Stretch" looked at the problem and told the professor he did not need a pencil and paper because he already solved the problem in his head. The professor left and took the problem home to work on it. The professor returned a few hours later and told my father the tall fellow may truly be a mathematical genius. He said "Stretch" had gotten the correct answer. The professor said he had never seen anything like that before. Someone could write a book on "Stretch" and like his life, there would be very few dull moments. A lady once told me that the world would be a very dull place if everyone was alike. Stretch was uniQue. Stretch had to have one of his legs amputated years ago because of diabetes. He called me a few days later from his hospital room and asked me if I had an eye patch and a pirates' hat at the store. He said he wanted to be a peg legged pirate. "Stretch" battled diabetes and the disease finally won out, but he never complained about anything. I have often said the writers of "Saturday Night Live" should have had "Stretch" on the t.v. show. He was a very entertaining fellow and he was a good human being. Things aren't the same without my tall friend "Stretch."

George Boswell

I have known George since the mid seventies and we have been able to remain friends through good times and through trying times. Friendships are like marriages because both reQuire give and take. There has to be something special for two friends to remain close for more than thirty-five years and there is something beneficial for both parties when people remain friends for that length of time. George is an only child and he lost both parents fairly early in life. He did not have siblings to help him along the way. I had two sisters and a brother and it is hard for me to imagine what it might have been like to have been an only child. Only rhymes with lonely; and I think I would have been lonely as an only child. George and I had similar childhoods in many ways. We both had fathers who drank too much and we both had mothers who struggled to make the family atmosphere as normal as possible. We both struggled for attention from our fathers. Each father was a man's man and was admired and respected by his peers. Each was a "buddy" to everyone else, but often a "stranger" to us. I think being an "only" child is a lot tougher than most of us realize. The only child might be catered to or does not have to share much, but he or she has to bear the family problems or short comings alone. The only child probably has to work harder at friendships and relationships. George and his wife, Kay, have one child and I had one child, Heather. Their daughter, Amy, means everything in the world to them and they are great parents. As with Heather; Amy will always remain "daddy's little girl." George and Kay were a lot of help to me when Heather passed. They took me to see the band "Chicago" in Norfolk shortly after Heather's passing. The evening helped ease some of

318

the pain of my loss and George and Kay seemed to understand what I was going through. George is a very generous person and he enjoys giving gifts to others. Sometimes I feel like telling him that people like him for who he is and not because he might give them gifts. I've seen him give money to people less fortunate than he and he genuinely gives from his heart. George and I have had spats over the years about some very silly things, but we always seem to forgive each other. We are both hard headed at times, but we both know how important being friends is. George has one Quality that is one of my favorite traits in anyone. He is extremely loyal and he will be there for his friends when they need him most. He is very reliable, dependable, and thoughtful. George is one person I could count on anywhere or anytime; night or day. George is a Dallas Cowboy fan and I am a Washington Redskin fan. We agitate each other at times and we surely don't agree with each other all of the time, but we have remained close friends because we respect each other and sincerely want the best for each other. George is like a big brother to me and I am thankful for that. George and I have had our disagreements over the years, and we have pushed our friendship to the limit a few times. It is no fun being angry with a good friend and it is often silly, but like everyone else, our feelings are often fragile. Friendship is an investment and each of us has to ask ourselves if our friends makes us a better person. I feel like I am a lot better off with George as my friend and I am glad I have known him all these years. I realize I have been very lucky and I learned about friendship from some very good people. A friend was there for you yesterday, he is here for you today, and he will be there for you tomorrow. No Questions, no demands, no limitations. Just friendship.

Tommy Thomasson

I have known Tommy Thomasson for the past decade or so, and he is one fellow who is now living out his dream. Tommy was a salesman for Fram Oil Filter Co. for thirty years, but he always wanted to be a farmer. Tommy grew up in Collinsville, VA which is outside Martinsville. His father worked at the local Dupont Plant, but Tommy decided to join the Navy after high school graduation. He served in Viet Nam on a ship that supplied other vessels with food and supplies. Tommy is very outgoing and he can tell sea stories with the best of the seaman. Tommy is well educated in many ways, but his passion is acting like a "good ole country boy" and swapping stories. Tommy met his wife, Sue, while the two were attending college at Virginia Commonwealth University in Richmond, VA. They both lived at the same apartment complex and began dating and later married. Sue is a retired school teacher. Tommy got his chance to begin farming after he retired. He bought a piece of property and tends a friend's property. He grows corn, tomatoes, collards, green beans, butter beans, etc. and he buys from other farmers. Tommy has a produce stand on his property, and he sells his produce, pumpkins, cantaloupes, jams and jellies, and other seasonal goods. He is happy wearing his bib overalls and talking to his customers. Like most farmers, Tommy claims to never make any money, but I don't think he would enjoy doing anything but farming. The fellows like to rib Tommy because he spends a lot of time traveling and buying produce. He also likes to stop, socialize, and have a two hour lunch break. I often tell people that Woody and William Jones were truck farmers, but Tommy is a "cell phone truck farmer." The cell phone and his white Ford Pick-up truck are his two most important farming implements. Tommy is a great guy and I have enjoyed his friendship. Travelers would stop in my store and ask for directions. I would begin giving directions and if Tommy was in the store he would take over the direction instructions. Tommy would begin telling the people how to get where they wanted to go, but he often sends them on a more scenic route. He tells them where some interesting sites are and where some good eating places are located. The people usually have no idea where they need to go when Tommy finishes talking. Tommy is a throwback to the way things and people were back in the 1950's. Neighbors and friends helped each other and watched over each other. Things were simpler in those days and life was not so fast paced. Tommy and his produce stand are perfect for good old Driver and I am glad he is here.

Buster Miller

My father and his brothers knew Buster Miller when he was a boy growing up in Portsmouth. I have known Buster since the mid 1980's and I can say he is a man with a lot of integrity and common sense. Buster retired several years ago from the Portsmouth Police Department. He has a tile business and still works as a repairman for the Community College in Virginia Beach. Buster likes auctions and flea markets and his barn is filled with items the "American Pickers" would like to see. Buster, Willie, Stretch, and I used to go to a lot of military auctions. Stretch was known for his stories and Buster was known for his appetite. The auction was held in Williamsburg, VA (about 45 miles away) and we usually stopped two or three times so Buster could get something to eat. He, surprisingly, is not overweight. Buster and I both like to talk about history and the different things that concern the State of Virginia. He is a huge Patsy Cline fan and he still likes to listen to her music. He also researched the Carbel family who once lived near Driver. Carbel was the wife of Confederate General George Pickett who was famous for his charge at Gettysburg. Buster and I both like small towns and old buildings and we both like bargains. We keep talking about going to Gettysburg and Amish Country in Pennsylvania. I would like to go with Buster because he would not be in a rush (unless he is hungry). I have always admired my friend Buster.

Ferrel (F.M.) Malone

Ferrel Malone is one of those fellows you will not likely forget after you talk to him. He is a retired truck driver from Sevierville, Tennessee and he has a very distinctive southern accent. Most people simply call F.M. "Tennessee". F.M. has lead a rural life and it is interesting to hear him talk about life in the hills of Tennessee. His sister grew up with Dolly Parton and F.M. knows several country western singers. He is very proud of his home state and he owns the farm land his family tended. F.M. knows a lot about cattle and farming and he and Tommy are something when they are telling stories. John Denver's hit song "Thank God I'm a Country Boy" fits F.M. and Tommy nicely. They make you realize that our country is rapidly losing a valuable way of life. F.M. is a very personable fellow and there are few dull moments when you are with him. Anyone who thinks the guys from the country are a bunch of bumpkins needs only to meet F.M. His truck driving job took him all over the U.S.A. F.M. makes friends wherever he goes.

Carlton Cobb

Carlton Cobb is one of the eldest members of the O.F. C. He is 88 years old, but he has so many irons in the fire, he is hard to keep up with. We would need a thirty hour day if everyone was as active as Mr. Cobb. Mr. Cobb was born in Shelby, N.C. which is about 40 miles west of Charlotte. He moved to Norfolk, VA. and got a pipefitting job with an engineering firm that did a lot of work at the Norfolk Naval Base. Mr. Cobb served an apprenticeship at Norfolk Naval Shipyard as a pipefitter and graduated in 1950. I graduated with the class of

1977 and Mr. Cobb and I talk a great deal about our apprentice days. We were in different eras, but the craft was the same. Mr. Cobb moved up the ladder and landed a job in the Planning/Estimating Division of the Shipyard. He and his wife began an antiQue business while he still worked at the yard and continued the business after his retirement. The couple bought a camper and worked several shows along the Atlantic Coast. Mr. Cobb worked hard at the shipyard and put his son through the University of Virginia. His son did very well at U. VA. and he is currently a corporate lawyer. His wife is also an attorney and the couple lives in Durham, N.C. Mr. Cobb and I are both baseball fans and we are both New York Yankee fans. He started with the Babe Ruth era and I started with the Mickey Mantle era. We still keep up with our team and we will always be Yankee fans. Mr. Cobb and I both coached little league and we share stories about the kids we coached. He was very instrumental in starting the Simonsdale Little League and I remember riding by the nice fenced in park as a little leaguer. The park had lights and advertising boards like a big league park. I often wondered how it felt to play your games in a park like that. Mr. Cobb coached a fellow named Dickie Balderson in little league. Dickie went on to have an outstanding pitching career at the University of Richmond. He was drafted by the Kansas City Royals and spent eight years in the minors. Dickie thought of becoming a pitching coach, but he went into the executive part of baseball instead. He has been a scout, General Manager, and held other positions in the big leagues. Mr. Cobb is a fine man and everyone thinks the world of him. He knew my father very well and he has made many friends throughout his life. Mr. Cobb is highly intelligent and extremely personable. He even works at one of the local strawberry patches each year for the enjoyment of the work. I see Carlton Cobb, Harry Land, Dave Lochne, Clayton Jensen, Kenny Harrell, and a few others in the store I am renting and I feel like I am a very lucky person. These fellows range in age from the mid-eighties through ninety-four. That's a whole lot of wisdom and also a whole lot of sacrifice to their country. It takes me longer and longer to recover each time I lose one of these friends or any of my other friends. I just keep telling myself that I was lucky to know them at all and each one was and is a gift. I lose a part of myself each time one passes, and I pray that we will all be together again and it will be in a much better place. I thank each one for being a friend and I thank the Good Lord for sending them my way.

Chapter 22
Talking Bout My Generation Hail Hail Rockn' Roll

I will never forget that cold morning in early February, 1959. I awoke that morning to news that left me feeling the same way I did in November, 1955 when my Grandmother (Nannie) Arthur passed away. February 3, 1959 is the date that Buddy Holly died in a plane crash and it truly was "the day the music died." Most people know that Buddy, the Big Bopper, Richie Valens, and the pilot all perished in that late night flight after a concert in Clear Lake, Iowa. I can easily recall how sad the next few days after the crash were. The thing I remember most about the morning after Buddy Holly's death is how sad all of the teenagers looked that day. Every teenager looked as if he or she had suddenly lost their best friend. A few teenagers listened to transistor radios trying to hear the latest news on the three stars, but things were very Quiet that day. I was only nine years old, but I felt the same way the teenagers felt. I knew the three rock n rollers were not much older than the teenagers I saw on the school buses headed for Chuckatuck High School 6 miles away. I knew the three performers, especially Buddy, were very important to them and to people their age all over the country. Like them, I asked myself why this had to happen. I will use an old "Byrds" song titled "He Was a Friend of Mine" to explain my feelings for Buddy Holly. The "Byrds" released the song after John Kennedy's assassination and it describes the feelings the song writer had for the President. One song line states "Though I never met him, I knew Him Just the same; He was a friend of mine." I never knew Buddy, but I knew he was a friend. I had seen Buddy Holly on a few television shows, but I guess I knew him through his music. My mother may have raised me on Mario Lanza, but I could tell by the t.v. shows and recordings that Buddy's music was very important to him and that he loved what he was doing. I also had the feeling that he really wanted others to like his music and younger kids like me were not just "goofy" children but were also his fans. Kids my age felt comfortable listening to songs like "Peggy Sue", "That'll Be the Day", "Raining In My Heart", "Rave On", "Words of Love," and the other Buddy Holly classics. The melodies and lyrics were catchy and we appreciated the songs as much as the teenagers did. I must have felt the same way John Lennon, Paul McCartney, Bob Dylan, Mich Jagger, and so many others felt the first time they heard Buddy Holly and the Cricketts. I believe Buddy Holly had just as much to do with the British Invasion of the 1960's as anyone. I believe that all good things come from God, and I believe that is even true about rock n' roll. Jesus said that Peter was a rock and he would build his Church on him. Perhaps the Good Lord looked down one day and decided the new music the kids were listening to might not be so bad after all. Who would He pick to be the foundation of this thing called rock n' roll. The foundation would not need the looks of a movie star, he would have to be from humble surroundings, he would have to relate to everyone who listened to his music, he would have to be someone who people could admire and trust, and he would love his music and his craft and would enjoy sharing them with the world. The Lord picked Buddy Holly. I am certain there are very many people as passionate about Buddy Holly as I am, and not all of us fully understand how we have been so connected with him all these years. Is it because he was a shooting star with a brightness we had not see before and he never got the opportunity to Share his total gift with us? I truly believe Buddy Holly was an "old soul" and we were lucky to have him as long as we did. I am a big Elvis fan, but comparing Elvis and Buddy is like comparing apples and oranges. Elvis was probably the greatest entertainer who ever lived, but Buddy was what they used to call a "triple threat" in football. Buddy could play music, sing music, and most importantly write music. He didn't start rock n' roll, but he sure brought respect to it. I remember how Buddy's music always made me feel better. I had to practice parallel parking years ago so I would be able to park when I applied for my driver's license. I don't remember how many times a disc jockey would play a Buddy Holly song and I would smile and try harder. I began wearing glasses when I was in the eighth grade and several of my glasses in high school were like the black horned rimmed glasses Buddy Holly wore. I was wearing a pair of Buddy Holly glasses in my senior picture. I always felt I had an easier time wearing glasses because Buddy wore glasses. I still listen to a lot of Buddy Holly music and I still get a lump in my throat whenever I hear "True Love Ways." It is a beautiful love song and I often imagine what Buddy's wife, Maria Elena Holly, felt like the first time he played the song for her. The couple must have been a match made in heaven because Maria Elena has never remarried. My daughter, Heather, was also twenty two when she passed away and I can really sympathize with Buddy's family and friends. If I could talk to Buddy I would tell him one thing "Rave On." Certainly Buddy Holly was a very big influence on me and the people of my generation. We were the "baby boomers" and television was the major influence of my generation and generations to follow. The heroes and the villains of life were brought into the family living room. I did like most of my counterparts and grew with television. As children, we watched shows such as "The Howdy Doody Show" with Buffalo Bob, "Felix the Cat", "The Mickey Mouse Club", "Captain Kangaroo" and other period programs aimed at young viewers. We also like some of the same programs our parents watched such as "The Cisco Kid", "Boston Blackie", "Tarzan", "Roy Rogers", "Jungle Jim", and "Gun Smoke." The shows of that era had one reoccurring theme and that was that the good guys always win. Naturally, the good guy was not good because being good would make him wealthy or popular with the ladies; but because he cared about what was right and he cared about his fellow man. The good guy followed most of the Ten

Commandments. Television became more sophisticated as we grew with it. Playhouse Theater, "The Twilight Zone", "The Outer Limits", "Maverick", "The Fugitive", "Route 66" and other shows made us expand our thinking and take a different look at the world we lived in. Even westerns such as "Rawhide" and "Paladin" were more thought provoking. When people my age are asked about the M & M boys of the sixties, most will answer that the M & M boys were Mickey Mantle and Roger Maris of the New York Yankees. There was another famous pair of M & M boys in that decade named Martin Milner and George Maharis who starred as Tod Stiles and Buz Murdock on the 1960-1964 CBS television hit, Route 66. Route 66 was a well written, hip show that was uniQue for its time. Any eleven year old boy wanted to grow up to be like Buz or Tod and drive a Corvette and travel all over the country. The two were buddies, they usually got the beautiful girl, they were smart, and they did the right things and were good guys. Route 66 is one of my favorite shows and I am still amazed how good it was when I see old episodes. Thomas and I talked about the show Quite often and thought about buying a Vette and seeing the country when we graduated from high school. He told me minutes before my wedding that we could leave that minute and still be like Tod and Buz. Route 66 had many of the elements of real life and the show projected things of life that most people could relate to. Tod was highly intelligent and thoughtful, and Buz knew the type of things someone raised in the inner city would know. Buz was a champion for human rights and he was always ready to go to battle. The prevailing pattern of the show was like most westerns however, Tod and Buz were decent young men and they would always do the right thing. Television always delivered many comedies that allowed us to escape everyday life and dream about fun places and people. They often took us back to times and places where life was less complicated and people were simply trying to get on with their own lives. "Happy Days" made people yearn for the "good old fifties" and the characters were simply trying to find their place in life. My generation was bombarded with every imaginable aspect of life. The nightly news always reminded us how terrible the war in Viet Nam really was and it seemed as if the war was being fought in our living rooms. Many factions had a lot to do with ending the war, but I think American mothers had as much to do with ending the war as anyone. Mothers reached a point where they were tired o f seeing their sons killed or wounded or were tired of seeing their friends or aQuantenances experience those tragedies. My generation had grown up with shows where American service men were supported by their country and given every opportunity to succeed. Sgt. Chip Saunders (Vic Morrow) of the hit show "Combat" was idolized by kids everywhere. Saunders put his men first and he was not about to let his country down. Shows such as "The Blue and the Gray", "The Gallant Men", "The Men of West Point", "Combat", and others instilled patriotism in us and made us proud to be Americans. Our fathers and grandfathers were heroes and we did not want to let them down or let the country down. I will say one thing for my generation and that is that my generation was diverse. Some supported the war, some were against the war, some wanted great changes, and some wanted minor changes, some liked tradition and others wanted a different lifestyle. We did not dress alike and we certainly did not all think alike. Many felt compelled to express themselves and many simply wanted to live their lives. I could sympathize with many of the feelings of the various fragments of my generation. Call me wishy-washy, but I fully felt for the young people who fought for our country and I wanted peace at the same time. The great domino theory was losing steam and Americans were tired of losing friends and loved ones in Southeast Asia. My friends and I were generally in the middle when it came to the politics and expressions of the sixties. We wanted peace, but we were not about to damage a college campus or property anywhere. We believed in marriage, but we were not going to condemn those who lived in communes or lived outside the American mainstream. We could get along with a hippie or someone in the Military. We believed in freedom, but we did not believe we had the right to inflict all our beliefs on someone else. The drafted or volunteer service person of the Viet Nam era was every bit as dedicated and patriotic as today's service people. <u>They</u> did not lose the war and they did everything that was asked of them. We all owe all Military people respect and gratitude for what they have done and will do in the future. Stories about the hardships of Viet Nam veterans began coming out in the 1980"s. Thousands of vets were living in the forests of Oregon and Washington because they felt more secure in the woods than they did in their home towns. Vets were having breakdowns and nightmares caused by the ordeals of combat. I remember reading about vets who slept surrounded by newspapers so they could hear the newspapers crinkle if someone "snuck up" on them or got too close. I went through a spell when I felt guilty for not serving in Viet Nam. I knew I was no better than the 58,000 troops whose names are listed on the "Wall" in Washington, D.C. I would drink too much at times because I have had many opportunities in life and have never lived up to my potential and I wondered how many of them would have fared. I said before that the veterans probably understand my feelings better than anyone. Leroy, Bobby Cooper, Arthur Powell, and several other veterans have often told me they are glad I did not go through what they did and they have never begrudged me for not going. The veterans are very understanding people. I have had some rough spots in life, but I am very thankful for the friends and good times I have had. I did not have to ever see either of my parents enter a nursing home and I had a wonderful daughter for twenty-two years. I still root for the Yankees and I watched the M & M Boys as a boy. Mickey Mantle and Roger Maris were a pair I was actually able to see in D.C. once and I will probably never see another such duo in my life time. I was fortunate to see another set of M & M Boys and they were pretty good players in their own right. Thurman Munson and Bobby Murcer were credits to the Yankees uniform and baseball. Both passed away too soon, but they were both good Yankees and more importantly, good men. I stated earlier that I liked Edgar Allen Poe and many other great poets and writers. I once asked my British Literature professor if the song writers of the 60"s and 70"s would be remembered as the poets of my generation. He said they definitely would and the very good song writers should be appreciated more than they were. I am a big Doors and Jim Morrison fan and listening to the band to me is like discovering stereo. Morrison and Robby Krieger (lead guitar) were great writers and Krieger, Ray Manzerak, and John Densmore were fantastic musicians who I feel will never be duplicated or fully appreciated. I was hooked on the Doors the first time I heard "Light My Fire" and I soon realized that Jim Morrison was a gifted "word man." I feel the same way about the "Doors" that I feel about the "Beatles." I have never listened to one of either's albums or CD's and felt fooled or short changed. I have read many books on the "Doors" and Jim Morrison and I realize the band has a hard core following that will pass the legacy on to others. Jim Morrison was a very intelligent person who truly wanted to be a poet, but could not shake the chains of rock n' roll. I have a friend named Gary Gould who knew Jim Morrison and his family during the time Gary's father served under Jim's father in the Navy. The Morrison family resided in Alexandria, Virginia but also spent a great deal of time in Portsmouth, VA. at the Portsmouth Naval Hospital. Jim was older than Gary, but Gary said Jim was always nice to him. He said Jim's room was filled with books and Jim was either reading or writing. The two families would picnic at a local lake called Lake Ahoy and Morrison was an excellent swimmer. There was similarity between Rick Nelson and Jim Morrison. Both were handsome young men and both were adored by thousands of women and countless fans, but both wanted to be taken seriously for their writing and creativity. Rick Nelson eluded to this fact in his song "Garden Party" when he sings, "You've Got to Please Yourself." Neither artist was comfortable in the box that fans, producers, and critics wanted them to remain in. I guess I could sympathize with Jim Morrison because I felt he was really passionate about his writing and poetry. He sometimes referred to himself as the "freedom man" and I believe he spent a great deal of his twenty seven years trying to free himself of the things that bothered him. I know alcohol can become an escape enabler for anyone who suffers from fears or anxieties. Jim Morrison was a very complex individual and I know that by listening to his music. Countless explanations have eluded to the facts why Jim drank so much and was so preoccupied with "the other side." Writers have stated that Jim's father, Admiral Morrison, was an authoritarian figure to Jim and that may be true since Mr. Morrison was a naval officer, and accustomed to giving orders. Others elude to the fact that the Morrisons spent a good amount of time moving and settling into different environments and that is hard on any child. I personally believe that Oliver Stone's scene in his movie "The Doors" where the Morrison family is traveling west and happens upon a bad accident involving Native Americans is actually a significant piece of Jim Morrison's life. In later years, Jim would describe the accident scene and say that an Indian's soul entered his body. Mr. Morrison basically told Jim to forget what he just witnessed and I think parents generally reacted that way in those days. Today there would be help for a child who had witnessed something so traumatic. Jim read a lot and he probably read about the different tribes, customs, and Indian legends and tied together what he witnessed with what he read. Anyone who reads in depth about Native Americans usually develops a kinship to the first Americans and their culture. Jim may have taken the mental picture of the dying Indian and made him his alter ego or he simply wanted to be a shaman. Many soldiers, like Oliver Stone, were Captivated by the Doors music while in Viet Nam. The Doors music is like Beatles music because so many songs relate to what people have experienced in real life. A listener can relate to drinking with his buddies in the song "Whiskey Bar" or he can visualize a night on the beach in "Moonlight Drive." "The Unknown" soldier made many listeners anticipate the end of the Viet Nam War, yet remember our friends who had died in the war. Jim was a southerner and he could often smile and hide behind his boyish southern charm. He liked Elvis, Buddy Holly, and Otis Redding. He liked to hang out in blues joints when he was living in Alexandria, VA and he carried those experiences into his own, brief career. John   Lennon had a great impact on many lives and so did Jim Morrison. A person can appreciate someone's gift or talent and differ with them on certain issues. I think Jim did often test the boundaries, but I often think I understood him. My parents lived their prime in the days of the great crooner, Frank Sinatra, and I lived during the time of Jim Morrison. One thing can be said for James Douglas Morrison, the great song writer and poet, he did it his way.   Many people of my generation developed an interest in the rights and cultures of the Native Americans during the many changes of the 1960's. I admire the many great men of our great American heritage. Washington, Jefferson, Franklin, the Founding Fathers, Lincoln, Lee, Teddy Roosevelt, F.D.R., John Kennedy, and many others helped make this country what it is.

My Heroe

My favorite American or "heroe" was a first American and I believe he understood more than anyone, what freedom really is. Crazy Horse, the great Sioux warrior and chief, knew what it was like to be totally free and to lose all of your freedom in a very short period of time. Freedom meant as much to Crazy Horse as the air he breathed. He not only lost his freedom, but he had to witness his people lose their freedom. Native Americans knew how to co-exist with nature, but modern man seems compelled to destroy it. Indians were penalized for being content with the same type of life style their ancestors lived for thousands of years. Progress is definitely important, but is the cost always eQual to the gains? Our country is in the process of trying to solve the B P dilemma in the Gulf. I wonder what Crazy Horse would think if he saw all of the wild life dying or being threatened in the Gulf. I am as guilty as anyone, but I think I realize Americans do need change. How much damage have we done to the land and wild life in the past four hundred years? I have no problem with hunting as long as the meat is eaten. There are organizations such as "Hunters For the Hungry" who do an excellent job of helping the poor or needy. I have a problem with hunters who hunt only for the kill and could care less what happens to the meat. To me, that is a crime against nature. Today, we place too much emphasis on material possessions and the trappings of modern life. Family is not as important and we usually admire people who have had success no matter what sacrifices were made. Crazy Horse and other Indian leaders were not admired because of wealth or objects, but because they were totally unselfish. They would give horses or weapons away rather than accept favoritism or gifts because they were leaders. They struggled like the people of their tribe. Crazy horse was light skinned, curly haired, and wore a single feather. He had no need for a fancy headress and did not like to draw attention to himself. He was an Oglala Sioux and he believed the elderly should eat first after a hunting party and the children should eat next. The warrior was responsible for protecting the tribe and providing the food. As a child "Curly" (Crazy Horse) could leave the tribe and travel two or three states and meet back with the tribe. He could follow a bird to water (mud on a bird's claws means water is nearby) and he could watch the clouds or study the environment for clues to where he was. Buffalo and other wild life were very important sources of information. I get very annoyed when people say Native Americans were savages or were placed on reservations because they would not change. Most of us would probably feel differently if our heritage had been destroyed and we were forced to live on a reservation. The Native American suffered because of the same reason many Americans suffer today. The answer is the timeless word "greed". I am a typical American and I enjoy the freedom so many fought and died for and I realize that greed has become a major problem. Most people I talk to have lost faith in our government and no longer believe we have public servants. It seems as though most politicians change after they are elected and their priorities change. I think term limits may become a necessity and something must be done about lobbying. I may be very ignorant, but I wish our government would try to operate without lobbyists. The government employs many purchasers, contract specialists, and the Government Accounting Office and we don't need politicians making deals with lobbyists for the "good" of everyone. I would like the President or any other political figure to set a day for the end of lobbying and suggest that any politician caught making deals is expelled from his or her office. "We get the government we deserve" and each of us bears some of the blame for the mess we are in. I realize people will say that corruption was rampant after the Civil War and many other times in our history. It seems our country is served by individuals who believe our government should be "of the rich, by the rich, and for the rich." I have been involved with a small business most of my life and I am sick and tired of every politician saying "I want to help the small business owner." I have never had a politician approach me and ask me how they could help my business. I may live long enough to see real change and I hope it is peaceful. My generation has seen and participated in wars since our birth and we realize there has to be a better way. I believe the majority should always rule and we need to remind the politicians who they are supposed to be representing. We just need to keep voting and expressing our concerns until they get it right.

My father was born during the Great Depression, but he lived when people believed our country is always right and we will always pick ourselves up by the boot straps. There was apathy, but many believed in F.D.R. and his "New Deal" and most people were thankful for any job they could get. As far as I can tell, the greed of banks, insurance companies, Wall Street and various corporations got us in this Quagmire we are in. Companies and corporations can work employees thirty eight hours a week or less than forty and do not have to give benefits to their workers. The hard working middle income American has been the one who has suffered most and he is getting tired of this situation. I believe in states' rights and believe people generally know what is best for them, but there are areas where the Federal government needs to step in and protect people. During the past several years we have seen more and more deregulation and I don't think that's good for the Average American. The trickle-down economy and deregulation obviously did not work. A farmer does not put a fox in a chicken coop to watch over his chickens nor does he loan his neighbor more money than his neighbor can ever repay. How many people actually understand what they are paying for when they pay their phone bill. You would need a Philadelphia lawyer to interpret most of our bills and I'm not too sure they would figure them out. When I was a boy, the truth and honesty were very important and I know most parents enforced those principles. My father would have used the hair brush or belt on me if I had lied to him. I hate to think what he would have done if I had been dishonest and I knew what the end result would be. We have to get back to those basic principles where a small lie leads to a bigger lie and you don't stick your head in a fire because your friend did it. We can't steal because the banks and Bernie Madoff did, we need to punish them instead and make examples of them. There were many young people of my generation who had many good ideas and were good patriotic citizens. Many realized that money would never make someone completely happy and we needed to try to relate with the people of Red China and Russia. I remember Richard Nixon was instrumental in improving our relations with China. I like sports and I have seen many athletes who lead by example. Jim Brown of the Cleveland Browns, Bill Russell of the Boston Celtics, Walter Payton of the Chicago Bears, Pat Tillman of the Phoenix Cardinals, Cal Ripkin of the Baltimore Orioles and Derek Jeter of the Yankees are athletes who lead by example and were also good citizens. I became a Boston Celtic fan as a boy after I saw the legendary Bill Russell on a basketball game on television. I was impressed with his determination and drive. Many people will say that Bill Russell was the greatest defensive players ever, but he was one of the greats for all his skills. Bill Russell played many games guarding the great Wilt Chamberlain, and Wilt once scored 100 points in a game against the Knicks. "Russ" could score when he needed to, but his primary job was to stop his opponent and get rebounds. How many great players could have handled "Wilt the Stilt" the way Bill Russell did?

Bill Russell never has signed autographs and that is his right. It is his belief and he has many Qualities that are far more important. I read years ago that he did not take any drugs or drink any alcoholic beverages because he did not want to alter what he came into this world with. Bill Russell, like Crazy Horse, has a lot of spirit and he often reminded me of a lion watching over his den. I wrote a paper on Bill in one of my English Composition classes. My professor was a female named Dr. Halladay and I have never forgotten her. She told me she was a big Celtic and Bill Russell fan when she returned my paper. I was pleased when she said she enjoyed my paper, but I owed the thanks to Bill Russell. The South and Driver in particular remind me a lot of the "The Waltons" television show of the 1970's. Earl Hamner, Jr. had experienced many of the things he wrote about and had known many people in life who he patterned his characters after. I remember the "Walton Wedding" television movie where John Boy told Cora Beth that she needed to write about the things she knew best. Some professors, like my friend Bob Arthur, and others have told me I should write. I will admit that I am a big "day dreamer" and my head is often in the clouds, but I did write this because it is what I experienced and I think it is what Earl Hamner or "John Boy" would have told me to write about. I'm probably running out of time, but I began writing a ficticious book about Crazy Horse thirty five years ago and never finished it. I would only hope it would give the great warrior the credit he earned and deserves. He should be remembered and honored for the true American he was, and his name should be synonymous with the word, freedom. I have even thought about a book on baseball (ficticious) and one about Santa Claus. I think of the great writer and story teller, L. Frank Baum, and think how many generations he touched with "The Wizard of OZ." I think Frank Baum may have been a dreamer, but he also had a great understanding of young people. He realized they deserve happy times and will face the burdens of adult hood and life soon enough. Mr. Baum shared his dreams with many people young and old and he left this world a better place.

Chapter 23

"Bye Bye American Pie" and

My Near Death Experience

on Mclean wrote a line in his song about Buddy Holly (American Pie) where he states "the three men I admire the most, The Father, Son, and Holy Ghost." I have to agree with Don Mclean and I have very many reasons that make me feel as I do. I am not the biggest sinner of all time, but I have many personal flaws that I need to correct. I have been blessed throughout my entire life and I have always been provided with whatever I need to get by. I have met many outstanding people and several clergymen who I admire and respect. These clergymen probably don't know how I really feel and I need to be honest. I have had a few spells in my life when I drank too much. I don't know if I inherited the genes or I was simply looking for an escape. Alcohol can make you feel at ease and smarter temporarily, but a drinker reaches a point where he is no longer intelligent, but a boring drunk. My father talked to me a few times or nights when I was drinking and he told me, "Son you will soon find out that you can't save the world." I guess he knew from experience and I should have taken him at his word. I did not let drinking interfere with my work, but I knew when Heather became ill that she needed me and I needed to be there for her. It would have been easy to drink my sorrows away after she passed, but I loved her too much to do that. I believe in marriage and I am one of those people who needs the union of a marriage. I need the friendship and support marriage offers and I like being home with my wife, two cats, and two dogs. I know marriage is something one must continually work at and one party must often give a little more than the other.

I am not proud to say that I have been married three times and I truly thought I would be married for life. I believe I was truly in "love" each time I got married, but it takes two people to make a marriage and it takes two people to destroy a marriage. I have fond memories of my first two wives and I sincerely hope they are happy. Heather was the child of my first marriage and I am glad Janice and I did share her birth and life together. I have had people joke with me and say "three marriages uh; you Qualify as a marriage counselor." The only thing I know is that marriage is not a joke and you need to be best friends with the person you marry. I often feel as if I let God down in my marriages, but I hope he will forgive me. The Father, Son, and Holy Ghost have always been part of my life and I don't see myself ever changing. I can't Quote countless verses in the Bible and I don't attend Church like I should, but I know what God has done for me. I watch the comedian Bill Maher, and I find him funny. I do not, however, look upon "My God" as some great myth or wizard I use to tell my troubles to or help me whenever I'm in a jam. The God I know is real in every sense of the word. He is in the food we eat, the air we breathe, and the world we live in. I believe the people of the world worship the One God, but they believe in him and relate to him in different ways. The Native Americans worshiped the "Great Spirit" and the world is made up of Islams, Christians, Muslims, Buddhists, Jews and many other factions. Most religions embellish many of the same beliefs. My father always told me to never discuss religion or politics at the store because someone would be offended. He also told me more people in the history of the world have been killed in the name of religion than anything else. I know all good things come from my God and I need only to look at the sun, moon, trees, birds, babies, and all the other wonders of life to know he exists. He gave every human who ever lived a thing called "will" and He hopes we cherish His will but he does not force it on us. How many politicians can say that? Many men wrote the Bible and the story is generally the same. If ten people witnessed an accident, each person would probably describe the accident differently. We can accept Babe Ruth because our grandfather saw him play baseball, but many people doubt Jesus even existed. I also believe in God because of the many people I have known in this life. I can't tell you the impact the Father, Son, and Holy Ghost have had on so many people. My God exists in many of my friends and many of them are able to talk about personal experiences. I had a very personal experience in December of 1980 and it only strengthened my beliefs. I was working a twelve hour shift with the Radiological Control Office of the Shipyard and one of my areas of responsibility was the nuclear carrier's hospital. I believe the carrier had recently entered the yard after a Mediterranean Cruise. I remember hearing about John Lennon's death while watching Monday Night Football. Howard Cosell broke into the game and made the announcement. I was in a state of disbelief like so many other young Americans and I could not understand why someone would do such a thing. Christmas was only a few weeks away. I was due to finish my year at work in one week because I saved my leave and had to use it before the new year. I felt like I had the flu, but I did not want to miss any time. I would have a few chills and sweat profusely an hour later. We were short handed and I thought I would rest when I got off early for the holidays. I completed my year at work and went shopping with my wife, Janice, a few days later. We were in a department store and I suddenly felt so weak I thought I would collapse. I told Janice I needed to go home immediately. I went home, took some cold/flu medicine and went straight to bed. Janice was a Registered Nurse and she knew the next morning that I desperately needed to see a doctor. I took a warm bath and became so exhausted that I could not lift myself from the tub. Janice called my father and he came over and lifted me out of the tub. My family doctor, Dr. Thankam Pillai, was on Christmas vacation and a female doctor in Suffolk was seeing her patients. My father helped dress me and lead me to the car and drove me to see the doctor. The doctor examined me a few minutes and told my father he needed to take me straight to Obici Hospital in Suffolk. She said she would call and the staff would be waiting for me. I had contacted viral hepatitis. The date was Dec. 22, 1980 and I could see that my Christmas was ruined, but I really did not know how much danger I was in. I continued to alternate between chills and sweats during the next few days in the hospital and I was still too weak to eat or get up much. I was hooked to I V's and drips and the nurses were constantly giving me aspirin, but I was not feeling any better. I will never forget many of the things that happened in the hospital those days before Christmas. I remember one of the supervisors telling one of the nurses she would have to work Christmas Day. The nurse threw her clipboard all the way down the hall after her supervisor left. I soon found out she was one of my nurses and I was scared to death at first, but she was a great nurse and I liked her a lot. Another nurse would check on me in the middle of the night and she would bring me tall cups of Coke. Those sodas helped me more than she will ever know and I will never forget her. The elderly lady (95) across the hall would yell at me and ask me to come over and visit her. I would talk across the hall to her and told her I was sicker than she was, but I would visit her if I got well first. The hospital can be a lonely place at Christmas, but the second floor staff went out of their way for everyone.

I remember Santa Claus going down the hall to visit the elderly and the children. It took me back to happier Christmases and it helped put me in the Christmas Spirit. I knew the second floor nursing supervisor, Kay Culpepper, because I coached a little league team that played her son's team. Kay is a fantastic person and nurse and everyone liked her. She had trouble sticking me with the needle and she kept apologizing. I have always had trouble because my veins are deep, but I promised her it never hurt.

I became a little worried Christmas Eve night when I went to the bathroom and I noticed my urine had turned dark. I realized this was very serious and I might not get well as Quickly as I thought I would. My father and Jimmy Rust (Thomas' father) visited me a lot in the hospital. Janice, Heather, and William also visited me Quite often. William was a big help to Janice while I was in the hospital and Christmas eve was the night he learned what it was like to be a father. I am so thankful he was there for them. My mother never visited me in the hospital and I remember my father skirting the Question when I asked him. I think the doctors had told her how sick I was and she did not want to see me die. She wanted to convince herself that it was not happening and she might have remembered the lukemia scare when I was very young. I was very weak Christmas morning and my father and Jimmy came to see me early that day. I did not know it at that time, but Dr. Pillai was so concerned that she headed back to Suffolk from vacation to treat me. I recall lying in bed and looking at my tray with turkey and dressing on a plate above the bed on the dolly. The phone rang and it was my mother. She said there were some people at the house who wanted to wish me a Merry Christmas. I spoke to Janice, Heather, my father, my two sisters, (Holly and Sherri), my brother (Gregory), My grandfather Arthur, my grandmother Parker (Bye Bye) and my cousin, Vernon. I said good bye to Vernon and hung the phone up. Native Americans called it "giving up the Ghost" and that is exactly what happened. I have never been as weak as I was prior to that moment and I have never been so much at peace either. I remember telling myself I was dying and the next thing I knew I was hovering near the ceiling and I was looking down at my own body. No medical alarms sounded and no one entered the room. I was not looking at my I V s and I assume everything was still hooked to my body. I remember this very special feeling came over me and I knew I was about to see Matthew Hargrave. There was a bright light and the thing I remember the most is the peaceful feeling.

Matthew was the one who would greet me. I did not want this to end; I was ready. I cannot explain how what happened next happened, but I know it was real. I was not in a tunnel, but something that was much more than a voice and more like a sensational feeling told me it was not my time. In an instant I was back in the bed in my own body. I turned and looked at the night stand beside my bed. I knew there was a Christmas card there that was brought in my room with my Christmas dinner. I opened the homemade card and it read "Thou shall worship the Lord thy God and only him shalt thou serve" Matthew 4:10 I cried like I have never cried in my life. I prayed and then I picked up the Giddeons Bible and went to the New Testament and read more from the Book of Matthew. I did not know why I was spared, but I knew I was. The card was a simple card made of crape paper. Someone had cut out a picture of a pair of hands praying above a single candle and pasted it to the card. The inscription was inside the folded card and the back was inscribed, "The Ladies Auxillary Smithfield Baptist Church." I have always believed that some little, elderly lady made my card. I began to feel much better and I had a strong will to get well. Dr. Pillai came to the hospital that Christmas night. She told me she was going to order a blood transfusion for me and I thanked her for coming home to care for me. I told her I knew I would soon be completely well and I also knew I had been through the bad spell already. I stayed in the hospital until the day following New Years Day. Every nurse, doctor, staff member, and technician was great to me and Christmas of 1980 is one I will never forget for many reasons. It's strange, but I actually had a sad feeling the morning I left the hospital. Dr. Pillai was still making her rounds the morning I checked out and I had something I needed to ask her. I walked over to her and asked her how close I came to dying and she placed her index finger against her thumb and said "that close." I told her she saw me when I was better and it had been a lot closer than that. My mother came to the hospital to give me a ride home. I think she was relieved I was going home and she told me the doctor said I could eat whatever I wanted so she and my father wanted Janice, Heather, and I to eat dinner with them. She would have a second Christmas dinner since I missed the original. It was close to lunch time when I finally left the hospital and my mother asked me if there was anywhere I would like to eat. The food at the hospital was good, but I had only gotten my appetite back in the last few days. I had lost twenty-two pounds in ten days and I told my mother I would like some southern fried chicken and that's what we ate at a local spot called "Grunewalls". The doctor told me it would probably be a month before I could return to work. She told me to be very careful the next few weeks and get a lot of rest. I was still a little weak, but I was a different person (in more ways than one) than the person who left Driver. The Methodist Minister, David Burroughs, lived in the parsonage two houses down from me and we had become very good friends during the past few years. The strange thing was that David and I were born on the same date Sept. 29, 1949. David's wife, Marlene, and my wife, Janice, were also born on the same date and year. I had often told David that I would attend his Church one Sunday and I did a few Sundays after I came home from the hospital. I had not been to church recently, but David's sermon would have a profound effect on me. When the service reached the Sermon, David stated that his sermon was based on the 4th Chapter of Matthew, Verse Ten. I almost fell off the church pew as Matthew 4:10 registered with my brain. Janice must have told David what happened on Christmas Day in the hospital and the significance of Matthew 4:10 to me. I walked down to my parents' store a few hours after church and David walked in a few minutes later. I went outside on the poarch and waited for David because I had something I wanted to ask him. I asked David if my wife had said anything to him about what happened to me in the hospital on Christmas Day. He looked confused and said he had not spoken to Janice and did not know what I was talking about. I ask David why he took his sermon from Matthew 4:10 and he told me he was a loss for something to speak on and he simply opened the Bible and it opened on Matthew 4:10. He read the verse and based his sermon on it. I told David about my experience in the hospital and he listened carefully. He smiled at me and patted me on the back and told me something I will never forget. David simply said "that's the way it works" and I knew he was right. It was that simple. The next several months were strange in many ways. I had been spared and I felt I would know why at some point. What was I supposed to do and how was I supposed to do it? Why me?

I tried to change my life completely at home and at work. I avoided people who smoke, drank, or cursed and I faithfully read the Bible. All this was fine, but after many months I told myself I was separating myself from the real world and that's not what Jesus did. I will tell anyone that dying is very peaceful and you will not be alone. I can't imagine that anyone who has experienced a N D E (Near Death Experience) does not believe in God. I am not an expert on NDEs or religion and I don't even know if I had an actual NDE, but I know what happened to me in the hospital and I know I am telling the truth. I have told people about my experience at different times, but this is the first time I have recounted it on paper. I think it has made me rethink my experience and I think it may be similar to the movie, "It's a Wonderful Life." The angel, Clarence, showed George Bailey (Jimmy Stewart) what the world might have been like if George had not been around and I put myself in George's place.

The following are some important things that I nearly missed.

1. My grandfather fell out of bed a few months after my experience and I heard him yelling the next morning as I was leaving for work. He broke his hip and could not move, and I ran into his door and knocked it in. He could have died that February morning.

2. I walked into my parents' kitchen one night and my Grandfather was choking on a piece of steak. My parents were in a state of shock and I performed the Heimlich Maneuver on him.

3. I found my Aunt Mildred after she had a stroke and I took care of her until the Rescue SQuad arrived.

4. I walked into a Safe Way Super Market on Saturday afternoon and saw a lady fall down in the back of the store. I administered first aid and told the store manager to call an ambulance.

5. I became much closer to both parents.

6. I was there for my parents when my sister, Sherri, was killed.

7. I was there for my mother when she was ill and I am glad to say I was the one my father called on when he needed help with her in the middle of the night.

8. I was lucky to spend the next fifteen years with my daughter, Heather, before Cancer took her (This is probably the biggest reason I did not die Christmas, 1980)

9. I had a wonderful relationship with my sister, Sherri, before her hit and run accident in July, 1993.

10. Finding my close friend, Lee Carr, when he passed. I think that was the way he would have wanted it.

11. Making friends with Leroy Schmidt

12. Making friends with Bill (Uncle Bill) Lauver and Joe (Little Joe) Sandige

13. Marrying my wife, Cynthia

14. Spending as much time as I did with my father, Red Parker and being there for him when my mother passed

15. Being Joel Howell's friend

16. Knowing all the people I have known because I lived

I am not tooting my own horn, but realizing that sometimes it was good that I did not pass away that Christmas. I hope I did not bore you with these words, and I will leave you with one thought. Everyone can pray and prayer is very important. I try to do it every day and this is my prayer.

Dear Father:
Thank you for everything you have done for me and everything you have given me. For the food I eat, the water I drink, and the air I breathe. Thank you for sending your son and our blessed brother Jesus who suffered on the cross for the sins of this world. I pray for the Blessed Virgin Mary and Joseph, the earthly father of Christ. I pray for the Saints, angels, arch angels and everyone who spreads your good word and good will. I pray for St. Matthew, St. Catherine, St. Fillemena, St. Stephen, St. Francis of Asis, Peter, Paul, James, and John, John the Baptist, Michael, Raphael, and Bartholomew.

I pray for my daughter, Heather, and I love her and miss her and pray to be united with her. I pray for my sister, Sherri, and I love her and miss her and pray to be reunited with her. I pray for my mother, Virginia Parker, and I love her and miss her and pray to be reunited with her.

Father, please watch over them and give them prayers.

I pray for Aunt Mildred and Uncle Cecil. I pray for grandmother Nannie (Myrtle Arthur) and Grandaddy Arthur. I pray for Uncle Shirley Arthur, Aunt Darlene Arthur, and cousin Beth Arthur. I pray for my mother's sister, Fannie, whom she never knew. I pray for Uncle Richard and Lila, Uncle Jim and Mary Lee, Marion and Ruth Arthur, Bill and Haze Alexander, Grace and Arthur Lankford, George and Emily, and Wayne Lankford.

I pray for Grandmother Adie "Bye Bye" Parker, Grandaddy John Parker, Uncle Vernon Mayberry, Cousin Debbie Parker, Aunt Edith Parker, Uncle Owen Irwin, Caroline, J.T. Savage, Legar Wilroy and Mary Bell, Lowry and Margaret Daniels, Charles and Hobday (Ed) Payne, Uncle Harold, Uncle Melvin, Aunt Doris, Owen's son Joey Irwin, and Carol Daniels.

Father, may the dearly departed know I send my love. I pray for so many friends, Father Matthew Hargrave, Lee Carr, Skip Holland, Bob and Mae Murray, Paul Tilson, Charlie Munson, Ray Gurnsey, Charlie Wilkens, Mrs. Rhodes, Mr. Bell, Doug Sadler, Mary Hudgins, Tommy Bond, Greg Lane, Herbie Munford, Carl Dunn, and Pete Shields, Jimmy Cooper, Phil Harper, Henry Wallmeyer, and R. G. Ward, Tommy Tise, Mr. Ohler, and Tod Falls, Herbert Elner and his wife, Gracie Mills and Percy Mills, Carrie Jackson, Ernest Sheppard, Mary Sheppard,

Bertha Wood, Easter Vaughan, Adie Griggs, Pearl Bailey, Martha Bailey, and Pearl Broadaxe, Woody Jones, William Jones, J.C. Strickland, Stanly Clark, "Shorty", "Stretch", Joe Sandige, Bill Lauver, Danny Lauver, Joel Howell, Reverend Bennett and Frank Nelms, Ed Jones, Ed Williams, and Ed Lewis, George (B.D.) Fenner, Joe Louis, Floyd Newby, Bill Elner, Mckinley Morrison, Jimmy Anderson, Morris Goodman, and Al LaSaunde' St. Hillaire, Randolph Preddy, C.R. Smith, Walter McRae, Lennie Hampton, Sarge, Louis Kidd, Jr., John Spain, Tank Harrison, Larry Cordell, Mike Collins, and John Coffey, Keith, George Corey, Blackie and Mary, Charlie West and his wife, Bud and Paul Yost, Howard Satterfield, Hard Rock, Buck Harris, and Hop, Jimmy and Myrtle Rust, Jake Gutelius, and Peggy Hurf

Father, I pray for my four legged friends:
Rusty and Rocky, Blackie (Beuregard), Black Jack, Shaggy and Her puppies, Beagie, Damion, Hobo, Tiger, Sinbad, Mickey, P.G., Candy, Teddy, Brandy, and Bear, Rex, King, and Brutus, Tiny and Missy, TeQuila, Trixie Jean, Candy Box Delight, Lady Bug, Mr. Smith, George, Lucky, and Spot, Ruppert, China Cat, Cookie, Lion, Sock, Oliver, Stripe, Little Man, Fig Bar Black Black, Dinky, and Minerva.

Hail Mary Full of Grace the Lord is with thee. Blessed Art Thou Amongst Women and Blessed is the fruit of thy Womb, Jesus.

 Holy Mary, Mother of God pray for us sinners now and at the time of our death.
Amen

May the perpetual light shine on them
May God have mercy on them and all souls
May souls of the faithful departed through
the mercy of God Rest in Peace Amen
Our Father Who Art in Heaven, Hallowed Be Thy Name
Thy Kingdom Come Thy Will Be Done
ON EARTH AS IT IS IN HEAVEN
GIVE US THIS DAY OUR DAILY BREAD
AND FORGIVE US OUR TRESPASSES AS WE FORGIVE
THOSE WHO TRESPASS AGAINST US
LEAD US NOT INTO TEMPTATION BUT DELIVER US FROM EVIL
FOR THINE IS THE KINGDOM
POWER, AND Glory For Ever

"You Gotta Believe"

Special Thanks to

Dr. Mylie Walker, Dr. Victor Archie, Dr. Vivian Mopanoa, and Dr. John Howard.

Thanks also to

Dr. Archie's staff including Gayle, Vallerie, Beth, Lisa, Sheryll, and C.J.

I call the girls "Archies Angels" and they deserve a lot of credit.

The people I have listed have been very instrumental in my battles with cancer

and I am indebted and grateful to them.

My cancer has returned, but I am in great hands.

I can't lose because I have many friends on both sides.

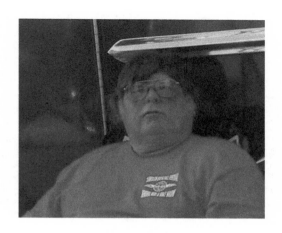

(1949-2015)

As a young boy, Craig Parker grew up
in Driver, Virginia where his family has
lived for five generations. Mr. Parker
would later accept the torch to carry
on the Driver Variety Store. Lifelong
friendships would be rekindled and
grow while new friendships would
be formed. The tornado that hit
Driver in April 2008 would inspire
Craig Parker even more to pen
"Some are Dead & Some are Living."